PHYLLIS TICKLE
⟫⟫⟫⟫ *A Life* ⟪⟪⟪⟪

JON M. SWEENEY

Church Publishing
NEW YORK

For Lillian and Carol

Church Publishing
19 East 34th Street
New York, NY 10016
www.churchpublishing.org

Cover photo by photojournalist Karen Pulfer Focht, Memphis, Tennessee

Cover design by Jennifer Kopec, 2Pug Design

Typeset by Rose Design

Library of Congress Cataloging-in-Publication Data

A record of this book is available from the Library of Congress.

ISBN-13: 978-0-8192-3299-1 (hardcover)
ISBN-13: 978-1-64065-131-9 (paperback)
ISBN-13: 978-0-8192-3300-4 (ebook)

Printed in the United States of America

Contents

Chronology

1934   Phyllis Alexander (middle name "Natalie" added by the family later) born March 12 to Philip Wade Alexander and Katherine Ann Porter Alexander. Spends childhood in Johnson City, Tennessee.

1951   Enrolls at Shorter College, Rome, Georgia, at seventeen on full academic scholarship.

1955   Graduates East Tennessee State. On June 17, marries Samuel Milton Tickle, whom she met "when he was exactly thirteen months old and I exactly six weeks . . . in the newborn nursery at First Presbyterian Church."[1] In September, begins teaching Latin and English in the Memphis public schools.

1957   After several miscarriages, gives birth to daughter Nora on June 8.

1958   Moves with Sam and Nora to Pelzer, South Carolina, where Sam works as a country doctor. Gives birth to Mary in October the following year.

1960   Appointed a graduate fellow at Furman University, Greenville, South Carolina.

1961-62 Earns Master of Arts, Furman. Family moves to 210 N. Waldran, Memphis. Third daughter, Laura, is born.

1962-65 Lecturer, Rhodes College; instructor, Memphis Academy of Arts.

1965-71 Dean of humanities, Memphis Academy. Publishes first book, *An Introduction to the Patterns of Indo-European Speech*, August 1968. First son, John Crockett, born July 10, 1970.

1971   In late May, gives birth to second son, Philip Wade, who tragically and violently dies of pneumonia two weeks later.

1972   Begins to plan St. Luke's Press with friends from the Memphis Academy. Teaches poetry for the Tennessee Arts Commission.

Begins publishing poems in magazines and journals. Sam Jr. born in July.

1974   Second book, a chancel drama about the Hebrew prophet Jeremiah, *Figs and Fury*, privately published; then produced by Grace-St. Luke's Episcopal Church in Memphis and published in a second edition by St. Luke's two years later.

1975   More St. Luke's volumes published, authored by Phyllis. Rebecca, seventh and last child, born February 10. Eldest daughter Nora marries (at eighteen) in May the following year.

1977   The family, sans Nora, moves to the Farm in Lucy, the subject of much of Phyllis's subsequent oeuvre.

1977-87   Poet-in-Residence, Memphis Brooks Museum of Art.

1983   *Selections*, first volume of poems, published.

1985   First volume of what became a trilogy of books of personal, spiritual essays, published by The Upper Room.

1989   St. Luke's Press purchased by Peachtree Publishers in Atlanta; Phyllis retained as senior editor. Two years later, she retires from publishing.

1992   Recruited by *Publishers Weekly* to be founding religion editor. Begins to track enormous growth in the publishing of, and demand for, religious and spiritual books in the U.S.

1995   *Re-Discovering the Sacred*, her first book-length work on religion trends. *God-Talk in America* follows in 1998.

1999   First lucrative book contract, for *The Divine Hours*.

2000   First *Divine Hours* volume (*Prayers for Summertime*) published in March, marking the beginning of a decade exploring the ancient roots of Christian faith.

2001   *The Shaping of a Life*, autobiography, published April 17.

2004   Retires from *Publishers Weekly*. Receives honorary Doctor of Humane Letters from Berkeley School of Divinity at Yale.

2006-7   Receives Award of Honor from East Tennessee State. Various spin-offs of *The Divine Hours* published.

2008   *The Great Emergence* published and becomes rapid success. Phyllis recognized as the historian of Emergence Christianity.

2009   Honorary Doctor of Humane Letters from North Park University. Continues to lecture, traveling thirty weeks a year.

2014   Celebrates eightieth birthday in Denver at Christianity21 Conference, and at Fuller Seminary in Anaheim during public events for a *festschrift* published in her honor. Retires from active traveling and public speaking.

2015   Buries husband, Sam, in January. Stage four lung cancer diagnosed in April. Spends summer at home in Lucy, gathering poems in preparation for a final volume: an "autobiography of sorts." Dies in her sleep the morning of September 22.

Author's Note

On Friday, May 22, 2015, a press release was sent to the media by Kelly Hughes of DeChant Hughes Public Relations:

> The Farm in Lucy, Tennessee—As was reported by David Gibson of Religion News Service on May 22, 2015, Phyllis Tickle, the retired founding editor of the Religion department of *Publishers Weekly*, authority on religion in America, and author of nearly forty books including *The Divine Hours* series and *The Great Emergence*, has been diagnosed with inoperable stage four lung cancer. She remains in reasonably good health, but has cancelled all travel and speaking commitments.
>
> A literary trust is being formed for the purposes of guiding the use of Phyllis's work in the years to come. This trust will be comprised of Joseph Durepos, Phyllis's longtime friend and literary agent, Jon M. Sweeney, another of Phyllis's longtime friends in the publishing industry and a sometime collaborator, and Sam Tickle Jr., her son. Sweeney has also been named "official biographer" by the Trust.
>
> Phyllis is contemplating a last book of reflection at the end of a fruitful, grace-filled life on the meaning of death, home, and soul. She is discussing this now with friends.

Hughes had been retained to help with the frenzy that would ensue after word got out about the cancer. That last book never appeared. Phyllis soon began radiation treatments aimed at stabilizing her condition. I was involved in the planning that led to the Gibson interview and the release. I'd found out about Phyllis's cancer diagnosis a few weeks earlier, one week after her children were told. "The dying is my next career," Phyllis said to Gibson on May 19, the day he spent with her at the farm, and we will eventually get to that, but first, my aim is to tell the story of her life.

Biographies are usually built upon dated correspondence, journals, and appointment books. Phyllis wrote legions of letters and emails, often dozens a day, but because these are rarely kept by those who receive them only a fraction still exist. They have been like gold to me. Also, Phyllis never kept a journal; neither did Sam, her husband of six decades. She did write an autobiography (nearly three, in fact), but *The Shaping of a Life* cannot be considered an entirely reliable source; it contains deflection and indirection. It has mostly served as a reference point. Then there are the personal essays, which began to appear in the 1970s, in which Phyllis didn't hesitate to reveal details of her personal life; but again, one senses much that remains hidden in them.

Another challenge has been to blend Phyllis's life with her writings. "[T]he inner life is undramatic and unmanifestable in realistic terms," wrote W. H. Auden, describing "the conflict between a person's inner and outer biography"—and that's a good way to put it.[1] And since Phyllis is not one to be understood primarily through her "outer" biography, it became my challenge to uncover her "inner."

My next challenge was convincing people to talk. Phyllis instilled deep respect and friendship, causing some to fear a biographer's inquiries. It also became clear that social and theological conservatives were hesitant to make public associations with someone who became so identified with progressive Christianity. Then there were theologians who seemed not to want to remind people of their friendship with a woman who, according to the academy, was theologically untrained.

One final, personal note: It has become common for literary biographers, since Richard Holmes's *Shelley: The Pursuit*, to take a sort of double entendre approach. In addition to telling the story of their subject, a story of the inquiry is told. There will be none of that here, beyond this author's note. Yes, Phyllis and I were good friends, but my "I" will not appear again until chapter seventeen. And, as will soon become evident, even though she lived relentlessly in search of answers to questions, her personal life was complicated in ways that were unknown to even her closest friends.

Phyllis Tickle's Books

Not a complete bibliography, but these works are frequently cited:

It's No Fun to Be Sick. Memphis: St. Luke's Press, 1975.

The Story of Two Johns. Memphis: St. Luke's Press, 1976.

Figs and Fury. Memphis: St. Luke's Press, 1976.

The City Essays. Memphis: The Dixie Flyer Press, 1982.

Selections (*National Library of Pocket Poets*). Notre Dame, IN: Erasmus Books of Notre Dame, 1983.

What the Heart Already Knows: Stories of Advent, Christmas, and Epiphany. Nashville: The Upper Room, 1985. [Reissued as *What the Land Already Knows*, Loyola Press, 2003.]

Final Sanity: Stories of Lent, Easter, and the Great Fifty Days. Nashville: The Upper Room, 1987. [Reissued as *Wisdom in the* Waiting, Loyola Press, 2004.]

Ordinary Time: Stories of the Days between Ascensiontide and Advent. Nashville: The Upper Room, 1988. [Reissued as *The Graces We Remember*, Loyola Press, 2004.]

The Tickle Papers. Nashville: Abingdon Press, 1989.

Confessing Conscience: Churched Women on Abortion, edited by Phyllis Tickle. Nashville: Abingdon Press, 1990.

My Father's Prayer: A Remembrance. Nashville: The Upper Room, 1995.

Re-Discovering the Sacred: Spirituality in America. New York: Crossroad Publishing Company, 1995.

Homeworks: A Book of Tennessee Writers, general editor, Phyllis Tickle. Knoxville: University of Tennessee Press, 1996.

God-Talk in America. New York: Crossroad Publishing Company, 1998.

The Divine Hours: Prayers for Summertime. New York: Doubleday, 2000.

The Divine Hours: Prayers for Autumn and Wintertime. New York: Doubleday, 2000.

The Divine Hours: Prayers for Springtime. New York: Doubleday, 2001.

The Shaping of a Life: A Spiritual Landscape. New York: Doubleday, 2001.

Greed: The Seven Deadly Sins Series. New York: Oxford University Press, 2004.

Prayer Is a Place: America's Religious Landscape Observed. New York: Doubleday, 2005.

The Great Emergence: How Christianity Is Changing and Why. Grand Rapids, MI: Baker Books, 2008.

The Words of Jesus: A Gospel of the Sayings of Our Lord with Reflections by Phyllis Tickle. San Francisco: Wiley/Jossey-Bass, 2008.

Emergence Christianity: What It Is, Where It Is Going, and Why It Matters. Grand Rapids, MI: Baker Books, 2012.

The Age of the Spirit: How the Ghost of an Ancient Controversy Is Shaping the Church, with Jon M. Sweeney. Grand Rapids, MI: Baker Books, 2014.

Hungry Spring and Ordinary Song: Collected Poems (An Autobiography of Sorts). Brewster, MA: Paraclete Press, 2015. [Published two months after her death.]

Prologue

On a beautiful fall evening in mid-November 2007, Phyllis Tickle was standing at a podium. She wouldn't remain behind it for long, but moved freely around a dais, taking it as her sacred responsibility to make the most of the moment that she had been given—something she learned from her father. She was dressed in a worn wool skirt, a nondescript blouse, and a gray floppy jacket. Her boss at *Publishers Weekly* said to her once in their downtown Manhattan offices, "This is the fourth time I've seen you wear that. Please get some new clothes." Phyllis did; but she was from East Tennessee, where clothes were worn to go unnoticed.

She was giving "the talk," as it was known to her and others, in the first decade of the new millennium. It was usually sixty to seventy minutes long. This was before the punctuality, polish, and fussiness of TED talks. People weren't coming to hear precision from Phyllis; almost the opposite: they came to hear her wide-ranging analysis, her global take on what was going on in the religious world, including the digressions, which were often just as entertaining as the lecture itself.

She was the retired founding editor in religion at *Publishers Weekly*, the trade journal of the publishing and bookselling industries. She was also a retired poet and regional book publisher. She was the author of about forty books, most notably *The Divine Hours*, which introduced fixed-hour liturgical prayer to hundreds of thousands of people. And she was working, just then, on her influential opus, *The Great Emergence*.

She was the Sunday afternoon general session speaker at the National Youth Workers Convention, sponsored by evangelical publishers Youth Specialties, at the Atlanta Convention Center. The roster was strong, with Shane Claiborne and Rob Bell on the docket, as well. After a lengthy introduction, which she deflected with self-deprecation, Phyllis ranged from new science to ancient philosophy to the latest fads in social media, to elaborate and exemplify the speed with which First World Christians were experiencing what she was calling "Emergence."

"Anyone who has been born since the late 1960s has grown up with an 'Emergence sensibility'; they can't help it," she said. And she made it clear that any religious professional within earshot should not only realize the sea-changes they were trying to stand in, but the responsibility they had to help others navigate the changes. The Holy Spirit was surrounding them, she explained, in the midst of what often felt only disruptive and chaotic. The future was awaiting creative, inspired responses to essential change.

When Christians have experienced these every-five-hundred-year overhauls, Phyllis explained, it has usually been bloody. Let's not make it bloody this time, she said. Religion reporter Terry Mattingly wrote: "Back up 500 years to 1054 and you have the Great Schism that separated Rome and from Eastern Orthodoxy. Back up another 500 years or so and you find the Fall of the Roman Empire. The transformative events of the first century A.D. speak for themselves. Church leaders who can do the math should be looking over their shoulders about now, argued Tickle . . . at the recent National Youth Workers Convention in Atlanta."[1]

For the decade after her retirement from *Publishers Weekly*, where she helped to transform the understanding of, and market for, religious and spiritual books in America, Phyllis lectured live to more people than any other woman, with the exception of Sisters Helen Prejean and Joan Chittister. On this occasion, her audience was mostly youth pastors and others who work in churches with young people. Many, as evidenced on blogs in the days following, experienced "ah-ha" moments. To some, her explanations and vision-sharing were like a puzzle being put together from their lives, explaining what had already happened in their churches. Others used words like "awestruck" and "beautiful" to express what this septuagenarian had to say about what was on the cutting edge of the faith.

But she also upset some people. Two years earlier, when she was keynoting at the National Pastors Convention, the feedback ranged from "Challenging/thought-provoking/insightful" to "Where is Christ in all of this? Where is the Gospel?"[2] On this occasion, two years later, before leaving the stage, Phyllis explained that the days of appealing to scriptural inerrancy were behind us. The faith was more complicated than ever before. Martin Luther's principle of *sola scriptura* had resulted in thirty thousand Christian denominations and the "every man and his Bible" principle, dear to Christian evangelicalism for so long, simply no longer worked. The present and future were seeking new foundations. To some, Phyllis seemed to be suggesting that "fringe Christianity," which is what many thought of what was then called the emerging church, ought to replace orthodox faith. To an audience of mostly evangelicals and recent post-evangelicals this wasn't easy to assimilate.

She so enraged one man sitting in the front rows that as she left the dais to applause and a standing ovation, he jumped from his seat and got in her face. In itself, this wasn't unusual. Many in the room, especially the organizers, had seen Phyllis speak before and she was often engaged with audience members immediately following a talk. Phyllis had many fans and no one was better at Q&A; she was the author of many books and people often wanted to have them signed. This night was different. As she left the dais, and people were standing and cheering, loud Christian rock music was throbbing. (There was "praise music" before and after each general session. David Crowder, Desperation Band, and Chris Tomlin were all there that year.) In the midst of this, few actually heard the exchange between Phyllis and the unidentified man.

"Shame on you for denying the authority of scripture!" he yelled at her. This was neither the first, nor the last, time that she'd be called a heretic. (A popular blogger of the Christian Right was soon referring to her as "the Empress of this Emergence apostasy.")[3] On this occasion, Phyllis could hardly hear the shouting man. He had a finger in her face and it looked, for a moment, as if he might pick her up and throw her. He was also intentionally blocking her exit.

She responded with conciliatory gentleness, "Oh, no sir. If you didn't hear me support the authority of the Bible in all of this, then I'm afraid I miscommunicated." But he grabbed her arm, and shouted again.

Phyllis had two designated "handlers" that day, Mark Oestreicher of Youth Specialties and Tony Myles, a youth pastor from Ohio. It was their job to ensure that people didn't impede her too much in making it from one event to another, and they would eventually get her back to the airport for her flight out of Hartsfield International. They jumped from their seats. Myles pulled the man away from Phyllis, in as gentle a way one could hope for—so gently that, again, the audience had no idea what was happening. Oestreicher then body-shielded Phyllis down the aisle and toward a rapid exit, all the while engaging the man in counter-argument. "I told him how completely out of line he was," Oestreicher wrote that night on his blog. "He pushed back (angrily) with a question about scripture, and I told him his questions were fine, ask away, but that yelling at a seventy-four-year-old woman after she's just finished speaking to us from her heart is what was so inappropriate. I think I said, 'didn't your mom ever teach you anything?'"[4] Myles added on his own blog a lengthy account of debating the man on what it means that the Bible is the ultimate authority. "His problem," Myles said, "was that in all that she said she shared insights that weren't directly out of the Bible. Although (in my opinion) they were biblical in nature," demonstrating, as it were, the evangelical underpinnings of both the audience and organizers.[5]

Phyllis would remember this moment in Atlanta, at the pinnacle of her career, as the only occasion when she was accosted physically.

2

Phyllis was always more sympathetic than her critics imagined to the pain and discomfort Christians felt in the face of change rocking the churches, traditional doctrine, and ways of being faithful. The changes were painful, even to her. But her life's work was then given to explaining history and giving context to what felt (and feels, still, to many) like upheaval and loss.

On other occasions, she would imagine for her audience what Christians must have felt five hundred years earlier, during the last major upheaval in the church. What to some might be just another history lesson was, to her, expressed with empathy:

> Nobody actually thought the earth was flat by 1492; it just didn't make any sense. What mattered was that the church still taught it was a flat earth and it was a stacked earth: hell—earth—heaven—and the universe beyond. Columbus sails west and doesn't fall off! At that point there's no

way to accept what the church has said. . . . If I were a devout Christian in 1494 in London and I die and ascend as the faith teaches me in a round universe knowing that my Lord ascended 1,500 years ago over here in the Holy Land in a flat universe, I'll never see my Lord again. It's a heartbreak! It may seem foolish to us, but we should never say that something a fellow Christian is going through is foolish. . . .[6]

3

Phyllis shared the Youth Specialties stage with evangelical leaders like megachurch pastor Andy Stanley in Atlanta, and evangelist Francis Chan the following year in Pittsburgh. These audiences were not prepared to hear that Christendom was falling, or had fallen, and did not want to see that they were trying still to speak with authority from the rubble.

There are a lot of things that the man in Atlanta would have disliked about Phyllis had he known her better. For one, she was a committed Episcopalian, a lay eucharistic minister and lector in her church, and a vocal supporter of full acceptance and equal rights for LGBTQ people. If he was an evangelical who voted with the Religious Right, he would have wanted to scream in her face again if he read the interview she gave to *The Wittenberg Door* just a few days before the Atlanta lecture. When asked if she thought the United States was a Christian nation, she'd replied:

We're a Judeo-Christianized nation. . . . But no nation is "Christian." "Christian nation" is such an offensive term that I can hardly speak it, even. One of the biggest blows to Christianity's vitality and legitimacy occurred on the day that Constantine made it the official religion of the Empire. Nobody in his or her right mind would want to be a member of a socially acceptable religion. It's very dangerous for the soul. A nation is in the business of doing Caesar's work, not God's. There's a distinction we get from the New Testament between religion and politics. That's not to say, however, that one shouldn't vote according to one's personal beliefs. All of us do that. But it is to say that one should never expect the state to function in accord with passionate faith. It won't. It can't. It shouldn't.[7]

Her impact on ideologically persuaded people was usually predictable.

But she was no one's guru. Disdaining any over-reverent response to a religious figure, she was physically disgusted while witnessing devotion in others toward H. H. the Dalai Lama at the 1993 Parliament of World Religions in Chicago. She also was never someone whose presence "filled a room," as people sometimes say of great intellects or otherwise dominant characters. Her effect on people was lasting, however. She seemed to be a best friend to several hundred people all at once. She was respected, but also quickly engendered feelings of filial intimacy in others. One evangelical Christian leader explained this, saying, "In that way she mirrored the heart of God to all of us, I believe."

4

At Youth Specialties Pittsburgh, one year after the incident with the unknown man in Atlanta, Phyllis was giving the talk again. It was common, during those years, for people to hear it over and over. "I wasn't as blown away by it this time," people would say, "but that's only because I heard it last year and I've already read her book." They still wanted to hear her. They may have missed something the last time.

In that blog posting of his from November 2007, Mark Oestreicher also wrote, "phyllis turned the whole thing in the last few minutes to a point that had me in tears . . . as she talked about the role that we all (in the room) play in this; the precious gift we're being given, the responsibility we have to the next 500 years. wow." That was how it felt to some people in the audience. Indeed, that is the Phyllis Tickle that the world knows the best.

But there were many others, as well.

CHAPTER 1

Her Father's Daughter

Some women have the bearing of their mothers, some, more of their fathers. Phyllis was always the latter. This was partly owing to fate, as birthing Phyllis nearly killed her mother, Katherine. The baby was born by Cesarean section on Monday, March 12, 1934. All nine and a half pounds of her emerged at 4:50 p.m. She let out her first cry two minutes later. It was fifteen days later, March 27, also her parents' sixth wedding anniversary, before mother sat up again. By then Phyllis was drinking formula. Katherine first held her, with assistance, a day later, and the attending physicians made it clear that there could never ever be another pregnancy. The two went home on March 31. To add insult to injury, Phyllis cried non-stop that night from six o'clock to ten o'clock.

Her father, Philip, was the youngest of fifteen children and could not fathom a house without many of his own. He was an Alexander, a family that traced its origins in the United States back to Cecil County, Maryland, in the late seventeenth century. They came "from Scotland by way of Northern Ireland, where they probably lived at Raphoe, Donegal, and Sligo. Church records of Ulster prove that members of the Alexander family were Presbyterians there quite early," as an extensive genealogy prepared by two of Phyllis's cousins in 1964, reads.

Philip's father, Washington Lafayette Alexander, fought at twenty-nine on the side of the Confederacy in the Battle of Shiloh, in southwest Tennessee, April 1862, one of the bloodiest conflicts of the American Civil War. This was before he found his love, Jennie, and married her four years later. Their marriage was a happy one, resulting in five sons and three daughters, but then Jennie died in 1884. Soon, Lafayette married Jennie's sister, Virginia, who had also lost a spouse and had six children of her own. They made an enormous blended family even before

Philip became the child of their old age. Philip was born April 17, 1892 in Lake County, West Tennessee, when his father was fifty-nine.

2

Both relieved and a bit heartbroken by the time Katherine and baby Phyllis came home from the hospital, knowing that he would only have one child, Philip knew one thing for certain. He would pour everything he could into the daughter that he'd held all alone for her first fifteen days of life.

He doted on her, making notes of her earliest days in a small brown leather diary.

Thursday, April 5, 1934
Slept most of the day. Appeared tired—profile grows more beautiful each day—cried "tears" to-day.

Friday, April 6, 1934
Cried from 7–9 p.m.—hungry we thought. Mother went for a ride.

Saturday, April 7, 1934
Smiled several times during day. Lovely features.

Nurses were coming and going, helping out, in those first weeks. Phyllis was growing and developing fine. At one month, she'd gained more than a pound. Philip continued to dote, writing on April 23, "Cried all morning. Angelic in afternoon. Six weeks old." By two months, Phyllis was weighing more than twelve pounds and sucking her thumb. Both mother and daughter were doing well. Philip continued to chronicle the events: as she turned over for the first time, rode in a buggy, had eczema problems, babbled, showed an interest in dolls, slept (and not) through the night, cut her first teeth, and visited family in West Tennessee where "Daddy played nurse most all day. Did not leave hotel," on the first day. Phyllis's first words were "Da-da," at eight months.

Katherine was a devout Southern Baptist before she wed the Presbyterian Philip Alexander. Philip was also a Christian humanist, well-read in classic novels, the Romantic poets, and Latin classics. As was common for a broadly educated man at that time, he also showed an interest in the histories and literatures of the East, including India, Persia, and the Arabs. Books filled every room, and were piled neatly on the table beside Philip's green leather recliner in the study. One area outside the boundaries of what he took in, however, was Catholicism; a quiet anti-popery ruled in their house.

Educated at Peabody College in Nashville (now part of Vanderbilt University), he then earned a PhD at Columbia University in New York, with a year at the University of Edinburgh along the way, writing his dissertation on the relationship between Appalachian speech and Elizabethan English. Philip and Katherine married before the PhD was finished and she helped support him through the final years of graduate school. Philip also earned money playing jazz piano in speakeasies and other clubs in New York in the 1920s. (His grandchildren remember him playing these tunes for them as children—and being shocked by the lyrics.) As an adult, Phyllis kept and treasured Philip's dissertation in a fireproof metal box, and she was deeply unhappy when her mother buried him wearing his Phi Beta Kappa pin. She wanted it.

3

Philip and Katherine were transplants from West Tennessee. Their house on Southwest Avenue near East Tennessee State in Johnson City was noteworthy for its immaculate English gardens in place of a lawn, and the built-ins stuffed with books in the living room, bedrooms, and study. Dark wood flooring and Navajo rugs set the feel when visitors walked in the front door, as did a console piano in the living room and sheep's head clock. Groceries were delivered. Philip's shirts were dry cleaned and starched.

One of Johnson City's highlights at Christmastime was Katherine Alexander's open house, or high tea, each year on December 20 and 21 at three o'clock in the afternoon. Hundreds of people came through their home, from the university community, the local bridge club, and the Alexander's church, to enjoy Katherine's *raffinement* and pecan fudge cake. Phyllis would later remember these occasions as being more about satisfying her father's career and her mother's desire to be domestically efficient, than about celebrating the religious season.[1]

Every Christmas, and more than once each season, Philip would read aloud his favorite Christmas tale, Henry Van Dyke's short novel *The Story of the Other Wise Man*, originally published in 1895. A prominent Presbyterian minister and professor of English literature at Princeton for a quarter century, Van Dyke was a man after Philip's own heart. *The Story of the Other Wise Man* expands on the biblical story of the magi coming to see the Christ child, as told in the Gospel of Matthew, and creates a "fourth magi," a Mede from Persia, who does a variety of good deeds on the long journey to Palestine—helping a dying man, selling some of his possessions to assist the needy—so that he is late in arriving after the holy birth. He is thirty-three years late, so occupied has he been helping others. He arrives only in time for the crucifixion; but then he misses this, as well, selling his last pearl ("of great price," as in the parable) to help yet another. As he's about to die, as Christ dies on the cross, the fourth magi hears a voice say the words of Jesus as recorded in Matthew 25:40: "Truly I tell you, just as you did it to one of the least of these who are members of my family, you did it to me."

With a sonorous voice, Dr. Alexander—who was tall, slender, and handsome—wouldn't simply read the story; it was an aural performance. Using a copy he'd owned since childhood, and in which he'd penciled dozens of notes and instructions to himself for these occasions, Philip would entertain and instruct family and guests. The notes included reminders as to which lines to emphasize, paragraphs to omit altogether, and certain things he wanted to remember to say, such as, "translated into 37 languages," and "something that will turn my thoughts back to the real purpose of Christmas," and, near the story's end, "true significance—service to others."[2] Through these performances, Philip taught his daughter the love of a stage and ingrained in her a respect for the gift of public speaking: One is always responsible before God for how carefully and prayerfully it is used.

4

Phyllis first learned poetry through the voice and performance of her father. She loved to listen and he loved to read to her. Throughout her life, poetry lived in her head in his voice and cadences. She didn't cut her teeth on Palgrave's *Golden Treasury*, but on hearing verse read aloud. When Phyllis was four and five years old, Professor Alexander would draw her bath, then sit on the clothes hamper, reading and reciting verses while she soaked in the tub for an hour. He started with his favorites, such as Leigh Hunt's "Abou Ben Adhem (may his tribe increase!) / Awoke one night from a deep dream of peace . . ." With crescendos in all the right places, he would briefly pause and then continue with one that begins . . .

> It was many and many a year ago,
>   In a kingdom by the sea,
> That a maiden there lived whom you may know
>   By the name of Annabel Lee;
> And this maiden she lived with no other thought
>   Than to love and be loved by me.

Of course, "Annabel Lee," by Edgar Allen Poe. But none would remain with Phyllis more than her dad reciting Rudyard Kipling's "Mandalay." A poem of the Victorian age, by its most famous author, "Mandalay" was essential to childhood for Philip's generation, known line-by-line by as many then as those who know not a word of it today. Its theme is also as politically incorrect by today's standards as can be: a British soldier yearns to experience the "exoticism" of the Far East, a world away from dreary old England. It begins:

> By the old Moulmein Pagoda, lookin' lazy at the sea,
> There's a Burma girl a-settin', and I know she thinks o' me;
> For the wind is in the palm-trees, and the Temple-bells they say:
> "Come you back, you British soldier; come you back to Mandalay!"

5

Despite the Great Depression, the Alexander household was a loving and secure one, occupied only by the three of them.

Phyllis's parents were passionate and overtly affectionate. In her innocence, Phyllis imagined that all marriages were consistently engaged and sensual. It was a shock, later, when she discovered that not all couples worked on the same principles. Most didn't. One of her warmest memories was of her five-foot-three-inch mother hopping onto the bottom step of the hall landing so she could be tall enough to reach her six-foot-three-inch father for a dead-on, daytime kiss, to their obvious and mutual delight. She also remembered him chasing her around the kitchen, flipping a tea towel at her back side, while they giggled. In Phyllis's house, when the bedroom door was closed, you didn't knock unless blood was coming from your ears. These memories gave her a sense of stability.[3]

They lived in a place immortalized with a few sentences at the opening of Flannery O'Connor's "A Good Man Is Hard to Find." In that story, the grandmother is unhappy that the family is about to set off on vacation to Florida, for she'd rather visit cousins in East Tennessee. Looking around at her grandkids and their various disobediences, the grandmother pridefully remarks, "The children have been to Florida before. . . . You all ought to take them somewhere else for a change so they would see different parts of the world and be broad. They never have been to east Tennessee." When O'Connor was at Vanderbilt in April 1959 and read that story aloud, the audience erupted with laughter as she finished that line. Phyllis herself once told the people of Memphis (in *West Tennessee*), "I'm from the mountains of East Tennessee. . . . and ultimately every decision, every choice, every judgement gets back to that central fact."[4]

In Johnson City, they raised chickens and kept hens. Phyllis remembered "cleaning up the flagstones after my father had wrung the neck of Sunday dinner and let it flop around the backyard until it died."[5]

In her fourth year, banks were failing and stocks lost half their value on the New York Stock Exchange. Unemployment hovered at 20 percent. Around her birthday, German troops invaded Austria, forfeiting the Treaty of Versailles. Pessimism prevailed. But the Alexander home communicated none of this to their daughter, except for what she may have picked up from the nightly radio broadcasts.

The summer she turned five, 1939, would be memorable for many reasons. The first took place when Philip spent a week of mornings in July damming up a nearby creek so that Phyllis could swim in it. Once the work was done, the five-year-old spent gleeful hours enjoying the cool of the water on hot, summer days. But something went wrong. Phyllis complained one afternoon of pain in her right ear. Neither mother nor father could see any obstruction, but the pain increased to a point that Phyllis was in tears. Something microscopic from the creek had gotten into the eardrum and within forty-eight hours it burst, causing "cracker jack pain," as she would call it. As a permanent result, Phyllis's tonal perception was impaired from the age of five, so that if two notes or frequencies were proximate she couldn't tell which was higher than the other. As a result, she could not sing, nor participate in church when others were singing. Her parents, wanting to aid her in recovering from this handicap, sent Phyllis to nine years of piano lessons. The result was angst in the girl toward music. She was turned off to the whole enterprise. When others were joyfully in song, Phyllis was, rather sullenly at times, silent. As an adult, she would come to listen appreciatively to music, but never with real pleasure.

Also at five, Phyllis was occasionally left in the care of her uncle, the owner of Pantaze Drug Store on Beale Street at the corner with Hernando, in downtown Memphis, when her parents had appointments in town. She would stay with her parents in the Peabody Hotel, but would walk with her father the few blocks to the drug store, where little Phyllis would remain in the company of Uncle Murph Alexander. He was a loving soul. He sold leeches and cocaine and dope when it was legal in Tennessee, and told stories about the same to Phyllis when she visited the drugstore, or at his home past Graceland on Alden in White Haven. He served as the druggist in his shop, and the neighborhood called him "Doc." Above the drugstore was a small whorehouse and Phyllis was introduced, by what she saw and heard, to the underbelly of Memphis life. She enjoyed how the ladies smelled, from their perfume, when they would come downstairs for a Coca-Cola. And they would play with her.

Another pivotal moment that summer came when the family was at a house they co-owned with two of Philip's brothers in Lake County, near Reelfoot Lake, in north West Tennessee. A place of ancient cypress and walnut trees, Reelfoot was plagued by territory battles over land and fishing rights throughout the early twentieth century. In 1908, an attorney representing landowners was murdered, and another attorney traveling with him narrowly escaped by swimming to safety on a moonless night while being shot at. By 1939, those battles hadn't been so much solved—by Tennessee governors calling out the state militia or a frequent police presence—but had been handed down to the next generation.

The Alexanders were in their house down the road from the lake when those old battles resurfaced and shots were fired. "Night Riders," as landowners seeking to safeguard their property rights were called, were taking the law into their hands. Once they even bombed a spillway and sluice that the state of Tennessee had attempted to put in place. Young Phyllis was kept far from this action, but she knew what was happening. It was the talk each night. She would remember encounters with local rebels, and even retain some of the spit and fire of those who were doing the fighting, including, like a true Southerner, what it means to protect one's land.

Tennessee has long been a place where citizens feel fiercely independent. The state's counties, for instance, were not in lock-step rebellion with the Union when the Emancipation Proclamation of 1863 was issued by President Lincoln; a few counties in the east sided with the northern states. Tennessee, thus, was unlike South Carolina, Mississippi, and Georgia, but it also was unlike Illinois or Massachusetts. Phyllis was thus raised, not exactly a Southerner, but a Tennessean. She would return to Reelfoot in middle age, in the mid-1980s, for times of writing in solitude. She would rent a cabin at Boyette's in Tiptonville and essentially lock herself in, enjoying quiet catfish dinners alone in Boyette's Dining Room next door, and an occasional walk on familiar, fought-over, ground. This area of West Tennessee, the place of her father's childhood, was precious to her, and a true contrast to the mountains of East Tennessee in which she was raised. She would write of all of this in one, rather compact, poem:

Tiptonville, Tennessee

I've come home again,
  Back to the earth that bore me,
  To the silent land and the cypress lake,

Back to the family dead
Who always knew I'd come;
To the town my father owned.
I've come to buy it back
With my poetry and my pen—
O hungry land that holds my family dead.[6]

6

Phyllis's mother was a superb domestic manager, wife, and professional home economist in the fullest, mid-century understanding. She ran the house with élan and attention to detail that amazed all who visited. She was a consummate hostess and could entertain twenty easily for dinner, or two hundred for tea—with equanimity and skill. But she had a mostly habitual, societal understanding of the maternal role; it did not include much real tenderness for her daughter.

Phyllis learned from her mother deep respect for order and clean management. This included an absolute devotion to daily prayer, since Katherine would quit her work at three o'clock each afternoon, take up her Bible and sometimes a prayer manual, and go to the front room alone for a half hour. Phyllis used to watch her through a crack in the dining room door, fascinated by the devotion she exhibited and the calm that surrounded her. Years later, Phyllis would write a poem from her twenty-acre Farm in Lucy, remembering her mother's sense of order, then in spiritual tones:

Lucy at Dusk

Our pasture tonight
is the warm teacups
my mother lifted from the water
and set to drain,
their soapy bubbles blinking
on her hands
like fireflies
across our meadow.

But just about everything else that mattered to Phyllis, as a girl and an adult, she learned from her father. "First and foremost," she said, "he taught me how to love and how to be loved. He taught me how to value the life of the mind and pursue it with trepidation as well as great excitement."[7] Her mother's domestic precision seemed artificial after a while. In another poem written in the years of establishing her own domestic and family life, Phyllis would turn the image of "teacups" to something less lovely and more trifling:

Summer Social at a Village Church
In the orchard
Where a herd of shadows
Is pasturing
Under the apple trees,
Women
As thin as empty houses
Are having tea.[8]

7

Her father was the principal of East Tennessee State College's Training School, a K–6 preparatory school, from 1927 to 1946. He taught classes and oversaw instruction and curriculum development. He even cleaned the building on Saturdays while Phyllis was permitted to roller skate up and down the marble halls. Dr. Alexander was known as hands-on. Each year at Advent he tended a large display box in the hallway, making green crepe paper palm trees to set behind the manger scene and next to the wise men. A large wooden sign hung above the entrance to the first floor lobby: "Password: I Love Children," summarizing what he and the Training School (later renamed "University School") were about.

He taught Phyllis to read Latin, which she would put to good use, professionally and personally, for the rest of her life. And he explained to her why Spanish mattered to Americans in mid-century, and why it would matter much more in the later twentieth century. Learn languages now while you can do it easily, he told her, and she did.

Her childhood reading wasn't systematic. She moved in and out of the large family library, discovering classics, secreting books to her room. She also reveled in books for kids that were popular: *The Bobbsey Twins* and *The Hardy Boys*, Louisa May Alcott, *Nancy Drew* mysteries (the first, *The Secret of the Old Clock*, appeared in 1930, and before Phyllis turned ten there were a dozen Nancy Drew books with millions sold), and the *Campfire Girls* novels. Phyllis's bedroom bookcase was filled with dark blue hardcovers. She read Bunyan's *Pilgrim's Progress*, but she was rereading constantly *The Arabian Nights*. "What's not to like about Scheherazade or Ali Baba or Aladdin?" she remembered later. "I must have read every collection and translation there was, until I knew them better than their authors did."

No books were forbidden, except for two. At ten, she discovered Ibsen, whom her father did not regard as appropriate for an adolescent. Yet, he couldn't bear to give away volumes from his own library—so he attempted to sequester them in an upstairs hall bookcase. It took Phyllis only a short time to figure that out and reread *Hedda Gabler*. The other verboten category she treasured with intensity: Gustave Dore's illustrated *Inferno*. "I am reasonably certain now that Dad was right about its inappropriateness, but Lord, did I love that book!" she said.[9] He hid it, too, but because it was oversized and padded leather-bound, it would not disappear easily into the landscape. She found it on a shelf in his office closet and took it whenever she wanted, carefully returning it when she was done. To her dying day, Phyllis swore that her father knew nothing of this, but one wonders.

CHAPTER 2

Southern University Town

When summer was over in 1939, a new world war was begun on the European continent. Britain and France declared war on Germany on September 3, two days after the German invasion of Poland and two weeks after Germany and the Soviet Union had signed a pact of non-aggression. Two weeks after that, on September 17, the Soviet Red Army invaded Poland from the east, joining the Nazis as allies. The Alexander family listened to all of this with rapt attention, as did most of the country, on the radio.

By September 7, 1940, German planes were beginning to bomb London and worry of war became even more intense throughout the United States. Soon, Edward R. Murrow was broadcasting live from Trafalgar Square, recording the sound of air sirens, describing mandatory blackouts, and talking of people streaming into air-raid shelters, for Americans to hear at home. The London Blitz felt closer to home than three thousand miles away. The Alexanders were listening to the wireless every evening.

Philip would come home, go to his easy chair, and turn on the radio as the family gathered. He had fought in the First World War, studied at Edinburgh, and trained and lived for a while in Europe. He knew that many friends were being destroyed event by event, city by city. Phyllis's most poignant memory of that time would be listening to the account of the fall of the Rock of Gibraltar, the British fortress at the confluence of the Atlantic Ocean and the Mediterranean Sea. She watched her father hug his sides and weep as he listened.[1]

Precisely fifteen months after those first raids upon London, on December 7, 1941, Japan attacked the U.S. Pacific fleet in Hawaii at Pearl Harbor and President Roosevelt declared war on Japan, Germany, and Italy, bringing the U.S. officially and dramatically into the war. Phyllis was seven years old, and well aware of what was happening. In the second volume of her autobiography, she remembered that night, watching with her parents as men of the town broke into the back door of Kress's Five and Dime department store on East Main Street in order to destroy dishes that were made in Japan.[2] This is an example, though, of how memory can trick and change when memoir is written. In an earlier essay for a Memphis paper, Phyllis didn't actually witness the breaking of the dishes. The account then was that her family saw photographs of what had happened in the newspaper the following morning. They drove downtown to investigate and saw the wreckage on a cordoned-off Market Street. Phyllis remembered, then, "it was those recognized shards that pierced me with the enormity of what was happening to us." But later, "it was the sound of dishes breaking that I heard first," is how she remembered it.

Soon, Philip was the air-raid marshal in Johnson City. And since they lived within an easy afternoon's drive from Oak Ridge, Tennessee—where, in 1942, part of the Manhattan Project was begun, with the intent of building an atomic weapon—this was a serious responsibility and appointment. It was probably a combination of her own childhood imagination, and a response to what she heard on the radio, that prompted Phyllis during these months to spend many afternoons and evenings under the dining room table in a somewhat permanent playhouse built by her out of blankets, cartons, and pillows. The siren would start, the lights would go out, and she would feel ready for what might happen next.

2

At the age of six, before the U.S. entered the war, Phyllis wrote her first play. It was designed as a production for herself and the kids in her neighborhood. Parts were assigned and scenes rehearsed. "We were all so cute and it occupied us for days," she remembered decades later, but not its subject matter.[3] She went on to script many classroom and holiday dramas throughout her elementary school years.

She was now old enough to learn about the city to which she belonged. Johnson City began in 1856 when Henry Johnson followed

the trail that Daniel Boone had blazed through the Alleghenies a century earlier and settled in the part of Tennessee that the nascent state of
North Carolina had ceded to the Union in the previous century. Johnson City began as Henry's stop along the stagecoach road from Knoxville to Washington, DC, a store and hotel—a spot that is still marked
today on West Market Street. When the railroad replaced the stagecoach, Henry's stop became an essential point of commerce for those
traveling west, known as "Johnson's Depot."[4]

A half century later, during Prohibition, Johnson City was a midway
transit point running south–north, connecting the cities of Chicago and
Detroit with what Al Capone and his cronies were smuggling through
secret ports in Miami. An apartment complex at Montrose Court in
Johnson City is where Capone himself was reputed to occasionally
hang out, checking on his operations, but the complex burned down
before Phyllis was born. Rumors persisted, however, and the memories
were fresh of "[m]en who frequently enter church with a brown taste
in their mouths from the effects of the night before," as one op-ed from
the *Johnson City Staff News* accused in 1926.[5] Young Phyllis heard all
of these stories.

And she continued to spend time in her father's library. John
Ruskin once said, "To the mean person the myth always means little;
to the noble person, much." Philip Alexander taught Phyllis that one
can't know Dante, Shakespeare, Milton, or Keats without first understanding the stories, characters, and spirit of mythology. In that library,
she read about Greek and Roman gods, Gaia and Uranus, the wander-
ings of Ulysses and Aeneas, Ovid and the Celts, Jason in search of the
Golden Fleece, and King Arthur and his Knights of the Round Table.
Combined with the lessons she learned in Sunday school, this was a
well-rounded religious education. Despite a strong Calvinist strain,
her father taught her an appreciation for other religions, and ancient
mythologies, as stories that built civilizations. He wasn't a Jungian by
any stretch, and yet from an early age Phyllis grew up with an understanding of what Jung said: "Should it happen that all traditions in the
world were cut off with a single blow, the whole mythology and history
of religion would start over again with the succeeding generation."

In the late 1970s, she would write of the "childhood gods" that molded her in an essay that made its way two decades later (she was always exceptional at reusing content) into *God-Talk in America*. By that time, the account was meant to demonstrate the broadminded approach she would bring to the coverage of religion in her capacity at *Publishers Weekly*:

> My earliest experiencing of spiritual intimacy . . . was in the closet that opened off of my first bedroom. . . . The upper shelf's walls sang with awesome pictures of Shiva, Astarte, Hecate, Medusa, all torn from the pages of my grandmother's discarded *Chamber's Illustrated Encyclopedia*. . . . And the arms of the goddess Kali . . . waxed over the whole of the shelf in constant incantation.
>
> Somewhere just near the attic crawl-through was God the Father. His beard was frequently no more than a cobweb; but still He was there, or passage to Him was. Even as a child I knew that there was no God the Mother and was glad. I did not want one. Gentleness, nurture, support, stroking were sexless in my understanding, belonging to neither gender exclusively and to both identically. It was Kali with her many-handed sexuality whom I wanted as the Queen of Forever. . . . Kali was, in fact, the only one of the closet's treasures to escape its destruction. She alone still sits on my bedroom dressing table.[6]

The sense of loss in this description suggests that one grows up and away from one's childhood influences, and so Phyllis did; however, in other respects, she carried the mythmaking power of religion with her most earnestly as each decade wore on.

3

The extended Alexander family also offered the adolescent Phyllis opportunities to expand her world. At thirteen, she was permitted to travel without her parents to stay with her mother's first cousin, Ada, in Virginia. Ada Miller lived with her husband, Haskell, and their children, including their eldest daughter, Jo, with whom Phyllis had much in common.

Haskell, or "Hack," was a Cumberland Presbyterian pastor who'd served churches in Knoxville, Tennessee, and Joinerville, Texas. But Hack felt called to leave the pulpit in favor of more study, and then teaching. Resigning his church, he earned a doctorate and moved the family to the Appalachian highlands of Southwest Virginia. There, Dr. Haskell M. Miller became a professor of sociology at Emory and Henry, a private college affiliated with the Methodist Church.

Phyllis spent much of the summer there in 1947. It was not far, as the crow flies, from East Tennessee, but it felt a world apart to her young imagination. She was able to soak in Uncle Hack's library for several weeks, having already absorbed much of her father's. There she discovered the social sciences, including Durkheim, Weber, and DuBois. She also spent time talking with her uncle, who would go on to write books, beginning with *Understanding and Preventing Juvenile Delinquency*, for Abingdon Press, in 1958. Hack was one of the denominational publisher's authors three decades before his wife's cousin would write for them. He would eventually teach ethics at Wesley Theological Seminary in Washington, DC, and transfer his ordination to the United Methodist Church. He was still teaching in the 1980s and even published on the subject of membership decline in the mainline churches—a topic that Phyllis would take up in the following decade.[7] Most importantly to her, Uncle Hack was a poet and liturgist, and Phyllis proudly snuck one of his spiritual verses into *The Divine Hours* as a vesper hymn. (She also, in early 2007, would be asked to lead the General Assembly Council of Haskell's old denomination, Cumberland Presbyterian, in a discussion titled, "Is the Institutional Church still relevant? If so, what must be done?")

4

The Presbyterian Church was central to the family's life in Phyllis's formative years in Johnson City, even though personal faith was not much talked about. But when she was thirteen, her pastor handed her a book by Presbyterian college professor and lay mystic Glenn Clark: the 1924 classic, *A Soul's Sincere Desire*, about prayer and answers to prayer.

Strangely for a Calvinist, Clark advocates "warming up" for prayer, just as an athlete warms up for a race—with devotional reading, breathing exercises, and quiet meditation. With the kind of certainty that often marks bestselling books in religion, the author almost guaranteed divine answers to prayer if his steps were followed. Chapter one boldly included the promise, "Let me stand in the market place with the physical culturists and demand, as they demand, fifteen minutes of your time every day for two months. And while I hesitate to promise, as they promise, that at the end of that time you will find yourself a new man, this I can say: at the end of that time you will find yourself in a new world."

Phyllis once wrote about Clark's influence on her:

> Within three pages, I knew! I had a soul, something that I had previously been unaware of; and what was happening to me was the borning of what I had come into life to live out. It was a consolation beyond all saying, but it also was instruction. . . . I read that book six times that year, but also and always surreptitiously. I hid in the bathroom, sitting in the bathtub night after night until the water was freezing around me. But I knew . . . I knew . . . and for better or worse, my life of prayer was born and first instructed there in that bathtub and within the pages of that book.[8]

Her spiritual life sparked by Glenn Clark, also at thirteen Phyllis was confirmed in the Presbyterian Church, an experience that she never wrote about. Her year of learning the confessions, studying the Westminster Confession of Faith, apparently did not move her.

Meanwhile, in 1946, Dr. Alexander had been promoted from director of the K–6 Training School to dean of East Tennessee State College (now University) across the street. What had been a teachers' college had expanded three years earlier, adding liberal arts faculty, courses, and majors. He would serve happily as dean for twelve years until his retirement at the end of the 1958 school year. Then he watched with satisfaction three years later when the college celebrated its fiftieth anniversary. Two years after that, the college became a university.

5

Phyllis just missed being a part of the "Greatest Generation." As a ten-year-old in 1944, she watched as boys twice her age went off to war, and later when they occasionally returned from the Pacific or Europe to a triumphant nation that had saved the world. She was, instead, more a part of the nervous generation that inherited what the war had brought: uncertainty. The young playwright Tennessee Williams wrote in a letter in 1941: "I think there is going to be a vast hunger for life after all this death—and for light after all this eclipse. People will want to read, see, feel the living truth and they will revolt against the sing-song Mother Goose book of lies that are being fed to them."[9]

Phyllis needed very little gravitas to add to the education she had received at home in order to stand out as one of the outstanding students as a Science Hill High School freshman in 1947. That first year, even before she turned fourteen, it was clear she was a young scholar and natural leader. Of these gifts, she was keenly conscious.

She did not, however, realize how beautiful she had become. The focus at home was so much on her mind that physical appearance went without comment. As a result, she was able to avoid most of the adolescent uncertainty that centers on self-image. By her senior year, an attractive, six-foot brunette, one might have expected her to be on the homecoming court; instead, she was focused on what her father taught her: not to waste time on such things. Nor was she to consider herself made for cooking, laundering, and housekeeping. If you must marry, Philip told her, that is fine so long as you are doing the overseeing of housework and not the work itself. You have a mind to tend. "Take what you have been given and spend it out for more," she was told, for "you will be held accountable in the end for what you received and didn't take farther."[10]

She continued to be a devouring reader. She learned from her father how to make best use of a book, which often involved writing in it, beginning on the half-title page, with underlining, margin notes, exclamation points—even the occasional "Holy Cats!" or "The Question!" Throughout her life she consumed books this way, particularly ones she carried with her in a school bag, or later on airplanes. Black felt pens would write on the pages and pages would be folded over at the upper corners, to make half-pages, and in triangular diagonals, all in order to make flipping back through to find one's notes a simpler task.

She excelled in every subject in high school, but most memorable for her was physics, because her instructor was arrested for un-American activities halfway through the term. Senator Joe McCarthy of Wisconsin was actively recruiting soldiers in the Cold War and rooting out suspected subversives and Communist sympathizers all over America in the spring of 1950, Phyllis's junior year, and her physics teacher was one of them, not to return to school. The class carried on and finished without him but Phyllis treasured that textbook until her dying day, always wishing that her grounding in the sciences was greater.

6

Tobacco brought employment to many in those days in the Tri-Cities of Kingsport, Johnson City, and Bristol, and throughout northeast Tennessee and southwest Virginia. To celebrate the beginning of the market season each year, starting just after World War II, Johnson City celebrated the Burley Bowl Festival on Thanksgiving Day. "Burley" was one of the primary tobacco crops, and Tennessee was second only to Kentucky in burley production. The festival included a downtown parade, with corporate and store floats, marching school bands, police vehicles, and city officials. Then everyone went home for Thanksgiving dinner—followed in the afternoon by a football game at Memorial Stadium (completed in 1935 as part of President Roosevelt's Civilian Conservation Corps) on campus at East Tennessee. This was a post-season bowl game for two small college teams and a Tennessee school was often pitted against a team from out-of-state. The 1947 Burley Bowl saw Carson-Newman, the Baptist liberal arts college in Jefferson City, take on West Chester State Teachers College of Pennsylvania. Phyllis was there with her parents.

She was also active in her high school Beta Club, an honor for exceptional grades and commitment to service in the community. National Beta Club was important in Southern schools of that era. It was then, and still is, headquartered in Spartanburg, South Carolina, and clubs were a most prominent feature in (whites only) Southern schools. For example, Bill Clinton was the president of Beta at his high school in Arkansas. The greatest honor in being a Beta for Phyllis came in the form of her first published essay, which also was the first occasion on which she was paid for her writing. She was a junior in high school when she won $25 for "I, Jerusalem." It was published in the December 1949 issue of *The Beta Club Journal*.

The nearly three-thousand-word essay is told in the first person— by the city itself. "I exist—for one could not say that I *live*—in a land far over the sea from where you are." The Arab-Israeli War had just ended the previous March; Phyllis makes no mention of it, but she has Jerusalem telling the story of the land. "Many things have I seen and heard—strange and ancient things. David's psalms were sung before my gates, Christ walked my streets, Peter visited my wall-dwellers, pilgrims have worn my streets and many foreign dusts have mingled with my own." Then, she weaves a tale of two pilgrims. Richard and Sabrine, she calls them, still from the perspective of the city: "For years he roamed my lanes and slums until at last even I lost him," she writes of one of them. With a neat Christian moral at the end, and a typo in the final sentence that must have frustrated the fifteen-year-old when she saw it in print, it is evident that Henry Van Dyke's *Out-of-Doors in the Holy Land* (Scribner's, 1908) must have made a lasting impression on her.

Phyllis was also one of the upperclassmen who traveled a few months later, in March 1950, to Nashville for a two-day state convention of all Tennessee Beta Clubs. There they did sight-seeing: visiting museums, the Parthenon, and the Hermitage, but more importantly to Phyllis, they talked about politics, international affairs, the future, marriage and family, and where they wanted to attend college. Phyllis ran for president of her club that year, and was candidating while in Nashville. She was one of a handful of students who were quoted in an article published in the Sunday edition of *The Nashville Tennessean*.

"Phyllis Alexander of Johnson City confided just before the election that she didn't believe she'd win," the reporter wrote. "'A girl doesn't have much chance,' she said. Then her dark eyes danced when she said: 'God made Eve for Adam because man was lonely.'" There she was, theologizing at sixteen. Also, what was then her Southern, Presbyterian, post-war conservatism, came through clearly. She was asked what she thought of the new United Nations (founded in 1945 at the conclusion of the War). Would it be able to stop the next conflict? Tensions were unusually high on the Korean Peninsula. No, she said. "It has no power and it will fail as the League of Nations failed." What, then, for our future? she was asked. "Christianity is the solution and the responsibility is on the United States."[11]

7

In the final semester of her senior year, Phyllis published her first magazine article, "What Science Means to Me," in the official publication of the Tennessee Education Association, *The Tennessee Teacher*.[12] The opening and closing sentences, which spread across two pages of the magazine, reveal both the burgeoning mind and the parochial mindset that filled her.

"The days when man could idly speculate on the natural phenomena that lie around him are gone," she begins. Then she goes on to preach to Southern educators, who were still recovering from and debating the conclusion of the State of Tennessee vs. John Thomas Scopes, of 1925. "We who are privileged with the opportunity to acquaint ourselves with science have a duty to understand through it the mysteries that lie around us," she wrote. "Superstition is a damning vice which only science can conquer . . ." The confidence is impressive, and she was presuming to lecture to educators, some of whom disagreed with her. Her own prejudices—also borne by her education—come through, as when she adds to conclude that last sentence, "—it is a vice that can bring about a period in history like the Middle Ages." "An educated people is one of the greatest assets a nation can have," she goes on, with youthful presumption, then to conclude: "In short science means to me—duty, obligation, challenge—Duty to My God, My People, and My Work."

She also won a playwriting contest put on by Oklahoma State College for Women in the spring of 1951. The prize was a full scholarship for the first year at OSCW, which she politely declined, although she was grateful to have won. America was still in the glow of victory after the war and her entry was a patriotic affair in which the Statue of Liberty played a leading role. Sixty-five years later and that is all she could remember of the work.[13] This experience confirmed for her a talent for imaginative literature, and for the rest of her life she would write for the stage whenever invited to do so. She never sought a career in playwriting, but enjoyed it as much, or more, than any other genre. "I have never liked acting, as in, being part of a cast, but I love an audience and love playing with, toying with, seducing them," she once said.[14]

8

Phyllis wasn't particularly proud of her high school alma mater, after graduation. Her author biography in the early 1970s usually read, "She was educated first at the University School and later at Shorter College for Women and East Tennessee State University"—skipping right past those high school years.

Just before graduation, Phyllis was recruited by a school counselor to reflect on the question, "If I Could Change My High School Training," and her three hundred words were published in the *Peabody Journal of Education*, in Nashville. "Had I known in the ninth grade what I do now," she wrote, "my course of study and my requests of my teachers would have been different in at least five major ways." What she goes on to lament reveals that the seventeen-year-old was still provincial in her outlook. She had grown up in the fertile and troubling era of the Great Depression, the Second World War, the invention and use of the atomic bomb, the beginning of the Cold War and the McCarthy era, and yet, she was lamenting her inadequate training in vocabulary, spelling, reading, Greek mythology, and the history of England. However, she graciously concluded, "The very fact that my teachers instilled in me a love of knowledge, an appreciation for quality in all things, and a realization of the smallness of my scope of appreciation is, I believe, a compliment, not only to their ability, but also to public school education in Tennessee."[15] The world-at-large was still mostly unknown to her.

CHAPTER 3

College and the Classics

I n the decade after World War II, Shorter College was one of the top undergraduate schools in the South. In northwestern Georgia, Shorter was a stately place and Rome a town with broad streets like boulevards. The college had high academic standards. Some faculty still remembered when Leo Tolstoy and Carl Sandburg had read their works on campus. The administration was intent on building the school into one of the most prominent academic institutions in the United States.

Phyllis had to plead with her father for permission to go away for school. There was a sense of embarrassment if the dean's daughter did not attend East Tennessee State. So a deal was struck. She may attend Shorter, but she must finally matriculate in Johnson City. Shorter gave her a full scholarship and the stately six-foot Phyllis enrolled in the fall of 1951 at the age of seventeen. She was a year younger than most of her classmates.

Many of her professors were pioneering women in academia and leaders in their fields. Most important to Phyllis were Dr. Clara Louise Thompson, head of the classical and comparative languages department, and Dr. Clara Louise Kellogg, professor of ancient and medieval history. (Characteristic of the times, the latter, for instance, was always referred to as "Miss Clara Louise Kellogg.")

A University of Pennsylvania PhD in 1911, Thompson was sixty-seven (Phyllis mistakenly refers to her as "seventy-plus" in *Shaping*) and had earned a legacy of Latin scholarship and trailblazing feminism.[1] She'd been a suffragist, and during World War I had been seen by some of her students as "out" as a lesbian while teaching Latin at Rockford College in Illinois.[2] There, she'd met Jeannette Howard Foster, one of her students, who would later follow Thompson to Georgia when Thompson lost her job in Illinois. Foster became a lesbian activist and early scholar of homosexuality while she, too, taught at Shorter in the 1920s and 1930s, writing a groundbreaking book, *Sex Variant Women in Literature*, during Phyllis's time in Rome.

Trysts between female students were commonplace at women's colleges, even in Georgia in the 1950s, and Shorter, during Phyllis's time, remained a predominantly women's school. They'd begun admitting men on a part-time basis in the 1948–49 academic year, but men remained a minor influence on campus for another decade. Shorter made it easy for relationships between women to develop, with mock proms and women-only parties that were a mainstay of college life. And many women, when homosexuality was still highly taboo, attended or taught at women's colleges as a way of being in relationships with the same sex without attracting undue attention.

Phyllis knew Dr. Thompson as a demanding person and an exceptional scholar. Others knew her, also, as elegantly feminine with an almost hypnotic appeal.[3] Her impact on the teenage Alexander was profound: She was her tutor in classical and romance languages, as well as a spur to the development of her fine study habits. It was also Thompson who first bolstered Phyllis's confidence as a woman in a man's field. In the foreword to her first book, Phyllis refers to the late Thompson as "the perfection, in human flesh, of the art of teaching."

2

Phyllis writes in her autobiography about the first time she visited an Episcopal church in her first weeks as a student at Shorter. She mistakenly refers to that church as St. Paul's, rather than St. Peter's, the only Episcopal congregation in Rome, Georgia, in 1951.[4] Visiting an Episcopal church was, in fact, a silent intention before she ever got in the car with her mother to drive to campus that September. "To become a true sophisticate-at-large, I would . . . have to turn myself into an Episcopalian," is how she put it in her autobiography. But she wouldn't actually go that far for another fifteen years. Not that she knew what it meant at seventeen, anyway, being from East Tennessee. "I had not the vaguest concept," she admits. "But the ones I did know were very attractive to me. In fact, based on my limited census, all Episcopalians were very wealthy, handsomely turned out, delightfully witty, socially able . . . in short, very sophisticated."[5]

On Sunday, September 16, 1951, she experienced that first Anglican worship, sitting and kneeling with the congregation, briefly exchanging the Westminster Confession of Faith for the Book of Common Prayer, fascinated by the drama of the Eucharistic liturgy. It was in keeping with her desire for sophistication that she took a taxi to and from the church that day, rather than walk or bicycle the one and a half miles. This is also indicative of how her parents were caring for her every need. She ended up taxiing to and from St. Peter's every Sunday for most of that year—until social life and peer pressure pulled her away from a weekly commitment to church early as a sophomore. Matters of faith and religion were low on her list of priorities.

(Today at Shorter University, the administration is more focused on its Baptist roots and identity than it was in Phyllis's era. The school is radically more conservative theologically than it once was. Chapel speakers are evangelists and Baptist preachers. One result: It's unlikely a student would visit St. Peter's, in town. Even the Canterbury Club, a school organization for Episcopalian students, long ago folded.)

3

She pledged Rho Delta her freshman year—which means, she was accepted, from among many applicants, based on literary merit. Rho Delta was the "honorary literary society" at Shorter, and members were elected on the basis of original work, both poetry and prose. Members were also responsible for two annual publications: *The Chimes* magazine, which was published in December, and a May issue of the school paper.

She also joined the International Relations Club, where the faculty advisor was Dr. Kellogg. The following year, Phyllis ran for one of the four elected positions in leadership of the sophomore class, and won: secretary; and she was named the editor of that December's *Chimes*. Junior year, she was elected treasurer of the class, and also served as editor of *Chimes*. She was also the president of the Spanish Club.

Although Shorter had started admitting men, Phyllis's editor's column in the December '52 *Chimes* demonstrated that it was still a women's school. It also shows Phyllis's fresh involvement in world affairs:

> There is war in our age, and it is reaching out from Korea to touch the lives of those around us. It is taking into its ugly maw the bodies and spiritual beings of those boys, now men, who ten years ago were sharing our childhood. It is for us, their women, to again share their shattered manhood. It is for us to find, here in America, the spiritual meaning to our lives, the faith that leads to sanity in a world of madmen, a peace within when fury whirls without. . . .

In her editor's column the following year, she struck a theme that sounds familiar to anyone who knows the books she wrote a half-century later: "I . . . wish for each of us a bit of doubting and a bit of wondering about the issues of life. There is no faith worthy of our support if it is not a faith which allows thinking and questioning. Beware the faith that brands doubt and ponderance as sin."

4

She started to be a poet while at college: writing verse, feeling and reciting with passion to others, beginning to put on the airs of the *femme poète*. This is how it usually begins. For example, the aspiring poet Stephen Spender once lunched in London with the already-famous T. S. Eliot. As editor of *Criterion*, Eliot had recently accepted a few of the twenty-year-old's poems for publication. Eliot asked him what he wanted to do now, after leaving Oxford without taking a degree, and traveling in Germany. Spender replied that he wanted to be a poet. Eliot rejoined, "I can understand you wanting to write poems, but I don't quite know what you mean by 'being a poet.'"[6] Of course Eliot knew what that meant. Fifteen years earlier, before "The Love Song of J. Alfred Prufrock" was published, he'd been doing the same. But as he was now established in the literary world, he was able to challenge young Spender's pretense.

What attends "being a poet" beyond the writing of poems? Every poet struggles with this in the beginning. Writing is the necessary solitary work, but then there is the business of making oneself known, and, for some at more tender ages, trying to *feel* like a maker of verse. This was when Phyllis took up smoking, her long, elegant fingers wrapping around the cigarettes. She went for walks all over the hilltop campus, and along the nearby Coosa River, feeling powerful emotions, pausing to write them down in notebooks. Of course, she also studied literature—Romantics, Victorians, Moderns—in her classes. She was carefully reading Eliot and Auden. And she began to review the work of other poets in print. For example, in the literary yearbook at Shorter (*Chimes*) in 1952, she reviewed *North of Boston* by Robert Frost. She hadn't yet learned to speak of poetry on its own terms, as one can see in the review. She analyzes it as one would prose, focusing on "description" and "character." But she concludes with this surprising insight (about poems so closely tied to New England custom): "Frost sings of a new land and of a new people, strong and vibrating, cut off from past convention. As the land and the people sing, so does he sing."

The dominant critical perspective for interpreting poetry at that time came from the work of two Southern writer-professor-critics: Cleanth Brooks Jr. and Robert Penn Warren, colleagues at Louisiana State University when the first edition of their *Understanding Poetry: An Anthology for College Students* was published in 1938. This textbook was a huge and enduring success. The authors' pedagogy was laid out in a twelve-page "Letter to the Teacher," in which they insisted poems be treated as poems and not as biographical or historical documents. They wanted to separate literary criticism from literary biography. However, their approach did not result in discovering poems as lyrical, sensuous explorations of meaning. This would become Phyllis's passion. But her generation was raised on Brooks and Warren to seek to "grasp the poem as a literary construct," rather than to experience its language and the effect that language may have on its readers/hearers.

5

The local newspaper ran a photograph of Phyllis Alexander on November 24, 1952, standing beside her friend Bert Felty. They were delivering "Thanksgiving baskets to needy families in the Rome area before leaving for their own homes for the holidays," the caption read. Phyllis looks as serious as ever, but beautiful, and immaculately made up. She was then a member of the cabinet of the Shorter Christian Association, sponsors of the benevolent effort.

She had begun at Shorter declaring pre-med as her major, but quickly switched to comparative philology (known as linguistics today), with minors in Greek and Latin. Comparative philology was a field of languages, classics, great books, and philosophy. In Britain, it was often called "practical criticism." A century earlier in Basel, Friedrich Nietzsche was a noted professor of philology.

She made friends easily; but her circle of friends tended to be the students who were serious about themselves and their work. By the end of the third year, her friends were calling her "Phyl," rather than Phyllis.

When, in the spring of 1954, it came time to transfer her credits to East Tennessee State, the process wasn't easy. East Tennessee offered no Greek or Latin, so she lost her Greek credits. And her ninety credit hours in Latin were used to apply toward a bachelor's degree in English Literature—to which she finally added a Spanish language minor. ETS had, just a year earlier, added religion faculty and courses to the arts and sciences curriculum, but that didn't matter to Phyllis— not then, not yet. ETS also, in Phyllis's first and only year on campus as a student, began to fully comply with the U.S. Supreme Court ruling, Brown vs. Board of Education (May 17, 1954), against racial segregation in schools.

6

Young Sam Tickle was coming and going from Rome to see Phyllis every month for the three years she was in school there. Friends since childhood, they had dated others as teenagers, while both attending Science Hill, but there was an implicit understanding between them that they were intended for each other. Phyllis writes painfully of the event in her family's kitchen, back in Johnson City during Easter break, when she decided to tell her father that she and Sam wanted to get married.

"But I don't want you to marry!" she remembers Dr. Alexander pleading. How did she feel? "I was livid for the first time in my life, and most certainly for the first time in my life at my father."[7] It is tempting to psychoanalyze the event, as the strong young woman molded in her father's image is suddenly face to face with that father as a nemesis. A month and a half later, in May 1954, Phyllis and Sam were engaged, with Dr. Alexander's blessing, and arrangements were made for a wedding in June of the following year.

CHAPTER 4

Wife of a Country Doctor

W est Tennessee was life in the Wild West in the early twentieth century, facing the great Mississippi, near its confluence
with the Ohio, and rolling, open plains. East Tennessee was,
then as now, dominated by the rocky hills and small towns of Appalachia. Phyllis's mother and father were in the east primarily so that Dr.
Alexander could run a school, while Sam's Mamaw and Papaw were
natives going back generations.

Mamaw was a seventh-generation Appalachian mountain woman.
Her Grandfather Witcher's land, at the time of his death, was still reg-
istered at the county courthouse under a grant signed by King George
III of England. She had a cache of stories to tell, each with a point to
make about the meaning of life or how life ought to be lived. One of
her favorites told of an immigrant Anglo-Saxon farmer who'd come
to the Appalachians and settled near her family's place. He had seven
acres and struggled for years to feed his ten children on the cultivation
of that land. When the fourth spring came around, he remembered the
wisdom of his people. "He sold off five acres," said Mamaw, "farmed
the remaining two with attention and focus, and never again had difficulty feeding his family."[1]

Mamaw was married to John Crockett Tickle. John had been married once before, to a woman who bore him many children (no one
seems to know exactly how many) before dying in her thirties of complications from surgery. After that, John grew wealthy, beginning in
1919 when Tennessee ratified the Eighteenth Amendment to the U.S.
Constitution outlawing the production, transport, and sale of alcoholic
beverages: Prohibition. He made his money ridge running: delivering
alcohol to communities deep in the mountains where law enforcement
was hesitant to go. He was also a plumber and engineer, and knew how

to modify a car with melted fiberglass to lower its center of gravity, preventing rollovers on winding roads.

So Sam came from clever people. However, from early in school, he wasn't much of a reader. His was a mind for science, for solving problems. Dyslexic, he grew up at a time when the cognitive disorder usually went undiagnosed. Sam was painfully afflicted by dyslexia and his inability to read brought with it problems of confidence. Later his partner and defender, Phyllis was always keen to explain how smart Sam was—and he was, but language processing was difficult, and led to emotional disturbances and frustrations. By high school, she was often listening to him read aloud; it was only by reading aloud that he could comprehend written words.

2

Phyllis and Sam married on June 17, 1955, in Johnson City on the campus of East Tennessee State. It was an event of the entire town: a large, Friday afternoon wedding, drawing people from the university, the church families of both the Alexanders and the Tickles, and family and friends from Tennessee to North Carolina. The Rev. Ferguson Wood, D.D., minister of The First Presbyterian Church, presided. The bride "wore a gown of white chantilly lace over satin. It was fashioned with high V neck, long sleeves and close-fitted waist," noted the *Johnson City Press-Chronicle*. "The flowing skirt was appliqued with sequins and fastened to a tulle flounce, ending in a cathedral train. . . . The bride's only ornament was a string of pearls, a gift of the groom." Southern newspapers once covered big local weddings like society pages. The matron of honor was Sam's sister, and the best man was her husband, Sam's brother-in-law. Several hundred people packed into the amphitheater for the 4:00 p.m. ceremony, which included the traditional wedding march, but also a sung rendition of Perry Como's recent hit, "Because." The final stanza of that song goes "Because God made thee mine, / I'll cherish thee, / through light and darkness through all time to be, / and pray His love may make our love divine, / because God made thee mine!"

Life was full in the first half of 1955. That March, Elvis Presley had made his television debut on a Shreveport, Louisiana, station, and

Claudette Colvin, a fifteen-year-old African American girl in Montgomery, Alabama, was arrested when she refused to give up her seat on a bus to a white woman. (Nine months later, Rosa Parks would do the same. They were both plaintiffs in the court case that ruled racial segregation on buses unconstitutional.) In April, Winston Churchill, at eighty, resigned as prime minister of England. Richard J. Daley was elected major of Chicago for the first time. Jonas Salk's polio vaccine received its full and final approval from the Food and Drug Administration. In May, the Cold War reached its highest point to date when West Germany joined NATO, and five days later eight Communist-bloc countries signed the Warsaw Pact with the Soviet Union. On June 7, *The $64,000 Question* premiered on CBS-TV, and throughout the summer, Mickey Mantle and Willie Mays were having banner years with the Yankees and the Giants. The large photograph of Phyllis in her gown that accompanied the account in the newspaper included the caption: "Mrs. Samuel Milton Tickle."

After a short honeymoon in the Smoky Mountains, Phyllis and Sam drove in a Bel Air gifted to them by Papaw and Mamaw to Memphis, where Sam was enrolled in medical school at the University of Tennessee College of Medicine. They moved into the house where Sam had already been living, 1094 Poplar Avenue, sharing the large, three-story plus basement residence with two other families and two single medical students. Next door sat a fraternity.

Phyllis had received and accepted an offer from the Memphis public school system to teach Latin and English. She would earn $225 a month for ten months, starting that fall at Messick High School.

3

Mamaw Tickle had advice when it came to marriage. She and Phyllis were about as close as any mother-in-law and daughter-in-law could be, and before Phyllis married her son, Mamaw told Phyllis that she didn't believe Sam *should* marry. He wasn't the marrying type, she said, which meant that she didn't think he would be reliable. Mamaw's own husband, John, was known to be a lustful man. Mamaw said that, had she realized how easily she would become pregnant, she might never have married him; what had motivated her was a Christian desire to care for the brood of children that John's first wife left behind at her death. Mamaw decided it was her duty to save "those poor, motherless children" from being raised by a godless, ridge running father. Then, she ended up giving birth to nine of her own.

Phyllis's mother, on the other hand, possessed an odd, but still country-bred, list of criteria for a successful match, and Phyllis and Sam seemed to measure up. First and foremost, she said, a woman should understand that her union is going to resemble that of her husband's parents. "If you like their marriage," she explained to Phyllis, "you will like yours, too." Second, she recommended "out-breeding," or marrying one who is genetically distant, to become a father for your children. And third, Mother Alexander counseled looking for an absence of hereditable disorders. By all three practical standards, Phyllis had no reason to imagine that her marriage to Sam would be anything other than a success.

4

Both Phyllis and Sam wanted children. Despite her father's expectations that she become a woman with an important career, Phyllis entered womanhood knowing that she also wanted a brood. Sam—whose mother had given birth to nine, six of whom (all boys) died within days of birth, and one (a daughter) who died at age five—felt the same. The sex life of the new couple was typical enough, but a few years into the marriage, Phyllis would learn something unusual. When Sam's sister Katherine had died, Mamaw had insisted that young Sam and his remaining sister, Lee, move into the same bedroom and bed. This arrangement had lasted until the two of them left the house as adults. And the next person with whom Sam shared a bed was Phyllis.

They began trying to conceive right away and struggled initially. Then, Phyllis got pregnant, only to soon miscarry. This happened not once but twice, which then prompted visits to the obstetrician, who, when Phyllis became pregnant for a third time, prescribed an experimental anti-miscarriage drug. She was still just twenty-one. Several weeks later, one night while asleep, Phyllis suddenly stopped breathing.

Sam, whose arms were around her at the time, felt it. He rushed her, unconscious, to the emergency room. What would happen then, in the next hour, would change her life forever.

The couple was quickly ushered past the waiting room to a bed in a private room. Phyllis remained non-responsive, and her vital signs were not good. Sam was dashing in and out of the room, speaking furiously with the doctors and nurses, who were just as furiously trying to revive her. Then, Phyllis experienced death. She would later say that she knew she died. "Without a care for anything that had ever been or ever was or ever might be, I lifted toward the light. . . . and it said, 'Come,'" is how she put it in her autobiography—but this was after decades of allowing the experience to go mostly unspoken. Sam was embarrassed by it, and so Phyllis remained quiet. A decade after that account was written, a theologian friend who'd read it asked Phyllis: "I've been reading about near death experiences, and scholarship about them . . . and am writing a book about heaven. . . . Off the record, how do you see your experience now?" She replied:

> You can show me medical datum after datum and you will never persuade me that I was not dead in the complete definition of that state, that I did not enter or was not within the world outside and beyond this physical one, and that I was not in verbal communication with God or some Agency of goodness. The result? Well, for one thing I just cannot for the life of me ever be scared of death again. If this that is my now were going to be over in the next five minutes and I knew it, then I'd be somewhere between delighted and ecstatic. For another, a whole lot of theology just becomes the noise of old men farting in the wind, an attitude that does not engender collegial relationships and that one has to constantly guard against expressing. Thirdly, Christian? You bet your sweet tush I am, and irreparably so.[2]

The miscarriages would continue and would amount to the loss of "more infants before birth than I can even name." "Even the most loving partner cannot enter into the nature of such pain," she wrote in the last weeks of her life, remembering how a plank was set between her and Sam each time it happened.[3]

5

Child number one was finally born in the late spring of 1957, and named after her paternal grandmother. In one of his regular "The Dean Says" letters to faculty, staff, and students at the college, Philip Alexander wrote nine days later:

> The proudest grandfather in Tennessee announces with much pleasure the arrival of his granddaughter, Nora Katherine Tickle, Saturday, June 8. The mother, Phyllis Alexander Tickle, is doing nicely.

This was the lead news in that week's missive, preceded by a quote from Robert Louis Stevenson and followed by news of a faculty member's illness, including "We are happy to report that Miss Brumit continues to improve satisfactorily."

Sam graduated from the University of Tennessee College of Medicine, completing his residency in internal medicine and a fellowship in pulmonary medicine. His doctor of medicine degree was conferred upon him in September 1957.

He probably couldn't have done it without Phyllis. She regularly endured hours each day listening to Sam read aloud his textbooks. He could glance at lines of numbers and understand them effortlessly, but struggled mightily to comprehend an abstract from the *New England Journal of Medicine*. And not only did she listen to him read, but if she didn't type his correspondence or check his written work, there was no telling if it would come out right.

6

In the fall of 1958, Sam, Phyllis, and baby Nora moved to the rural South Carolina Piedmont because Sam specifically wanted to learn how to be a country doctor. He was already recognized by professors and clinicians as a pulmonologist with potential. Now, he wanted to gain practical experience. "I know how to do it with bells and whistles [in the city]. Now I want to know how to do it without them," he told Phyllis.[4]

Sam and Harold Maxell West, a friend from medical school, pur-chased a practice in Pelzer, South Carolina. Max had gotten himself ordained a Baptist minister five years earlier, and then decided to become a doctor in order to serve the needy. His wife, June, whom Max met and married during medical school, would become "Aunt June" to Max's "Uncle Max" for young Nora.

Sam's motivations for becoming a physician were more scientific and clinical. In addition to wanting hands-on experience, he was also interested in why Yankees seemed to be falling sick in large numbers when they moved south to work on the Eisenhower interstate construc-tion projects that were then common—something he'd been reading about in case studies in school. Histoplasmosis, a fungal disease caused by bird and bat droppings, borne in the air, would turn out to be the answer, and Sam would play a role in diagnosing it. Pelzer also turned out to be a good place to study epidemiology, another interest of his.

Sam and Max's wasn't simply a practice, but a small hospital. It was not uncommon to purchase such a for-profit medical treatment enterprise of this sort, in those days, and they quickly set out to pro-vide physician house calls as well as half a dozen hospital beds. June acted as nurse, and Phyllis, for a short time, as hospital receptionist and administrator.

Phyllis and Sam took out a mortgage on a house on Lebby Street with the help of the mill that ran the town. Pelzer was founded in the late nineteenth century on the banks of the Saluda River, but had roots going back to the late sixteenth century Roanoke Colony founded by Sir Walter Raleigh. Today, the town has fewer than one hundred inhab-itants, but in the 1950s it was forty times that size. It was the largest cotton mill town in the South and one of the largest in the world. Life centered around four active mills of the Pelzer Manufacturing Com-pany until the company was sold in 1923. By 1958, the cotton business was smaller than it had been, but still central to the town. The Tickle house was a two-story white clapboard, only four blocks down the street from the hospital. Retired missionaries from the Belgian Congo lived on one side, and would become close friends. The Pelzer Presbyte-rian Church, also white clapboard, was just a block away.

7

After the move, Sam was back in Memphis for nine days in October, selling furniture from their old apartment, while Phyllis was setting up home and medical office. "It will be wonderful to get to Pelzer and be together," reads one of Sam's letters from Memphis, in his nearly illegible handwriting. He wrote four letters to Phyllis over nine days, each time telling her how much he missed his young family.

They were happy in Pelzer. A full-time housekeeper—which wasn't considered an extravagance for a middle income couple—came and went at twenty dollars a week. The family lived well, eating tinned beef, a small luxury, as well as Phyllis's good cooking. Nora was enrolled in kindergarten church school. Sam was highly regarded in town in his role as physician. Phyllis became a regular smoker. Many people smoked in the South in those days (one in three women, one in two men), and most of the young couple's friends were smoking at dinner, and at parties, including weekly bridge games with friends and while walking with their children in the neighborhood. Phyllis went through a pack and a half a day. She smoked for twelve years and then quit at the age of thirty-two, overwhelmed by the evidence against it from her pulmonologist husband.

The work was both difficult and colorful for Sam. His children would remember stories he told about the characters he treated. He told of drawing blood and putting a test tube down to settle, then watching as the saturated fats floated to the top, leaving a quarter inch of thick, greasy skin on top. He told of treating large women whose breasts had been pinched in laundry wringers. Pelzer was a town built by a growing middle class, but Sam also treated many in the backwoods. He made house calls, a practice he would continue for forty years, and he used whatever supplies were available to treat his patients. His bedside manner was friendly, and he was always up to the task of finding uncommon solutions to common problems his patients faced. Often, he accepted payment in the form of rabbits, venison roast, and chocolate pies. He had some patients who never paid a bill—but they kept things even with barters.

When the Berlin Wall went up in Germany, Tennessee Local Board No. 97 sent Sam a letter instructing him to come and discuss selective service in the armed forces as a medic. In August 1959, Sam drafted a response requesting an "occupational deferment" based on the fact that there were only two men practicing general medicine in Pelzer. Phyllis edited the carbon and then retyped a final draft. "Since October, 1958, we have added about 4,000 different patients to our medical files," it reads. "It would be impossible for one man to give medical care to this large area." But, the correspondence continued, so Sam made application to be a reserve officer in the Air Force Medical Corps. The Air Force asked for a variety of paperwork, including a fingerprint. When the one Sam sent was "found too indistinct," Sam failed to respond to repeated requests for another, and eventually the whole thing went away, much to everyone's relief.

With the hospital up and running, Phyllis applied to the master's program at Furman University. Its new campus was only a half hour from Pelzer, just north of Greenville, South Carolina. There, she began studies in the summer of 1960, and it wasn't long before her literary and scholarly aspirations began to conflict with the surroundings at home. She was often gone in the evenings for lectures and library time. And Nora remembers one night "watching Mother taking an Ortega y Gasset (thin, with a light gray cloth binding) book off an end table before some party, because folks would be scandalized. But that is the only time I ever remember not thinking Pelzer was our happy home."[5]

By the fall of 1960, Phyllis was appointed a graduate fellow at Furman, where she also taught classes in literature. The "leftist" books that she often brought home were best kept away from friends in their neighborhood. These books included *The Dead Sea Scrolls* (1955) by Yale professor Millar Burrows, an author with whom Phyllis briefly then corresponded, and theologian Paul Tillich's *The Courage to Be* (1952), which Philip Alexander had recommended to his daughter, and she subsequently asked the bookstore in Greenville to order for her.

8

Phyllis and Sam were born and bred Republicans. They liked Ike, wore "Like Ike" buttons, and voted for him in 1952 and again in 1956. They were a natural part of the anti-slavery, pro-civil rights mindset that was the old Republication party and ruled East Tennessee for a century. It was the assassination of President Kennedy—a 9/11 experience for every adult American at that time—that was the crack in the foundation of their allegiance to the party of Lincoln. A decade later, Watergate broke the dam, and after Watergate, Sam, in particular, took the position of advocating anything to the left of the current administration. Phyllis, too, became issue-driven and eschewed all party allegiance.

They were successful in Pelzer. Sam and Phyllis were a two-car family with Phyllis in 1960 driving a small yellow Lloyd that they bought used for $500. She loved that car for its gas efficiency and compactness: she would easily fit two kids plus the groceries, and could even park it in many places in those days on the sidewalk. When they moved back to Memphis a few years later they would sell it for $300, since Sam believed that those same good qualities in a car would prove to be dangerous in a more urban environment.

When they did return to Memphis, it was because Sam wanted to learn internal medicine, and needed three more years of training. This would be followed by three more years of pulmonology. For her part, after earning a Master of Arts in Education from Furman in June 1961, and even though she loved the "nesting" with Nora ("I began to like fussy things . . . ruffles and swooshy pillows and anything with little teddy bears on it . . ."),[6] Phyllis, too, wanted more professional challenge. So in April 1962 they packed up their things and returned to West Tennessee.

By now, they had two children: Nora (June '57) and Mary (October '59), and Phyllis was in her final trimester with a third. Her due date was so close to the planned move that Sam and Phyllis worried about the possible strain on the pregnancy. So, while Sam stayed in Pelzer attending to final details, Phyllis dropped the girls with their grandparents in Johnson City, and then went on, giving birth to Laura Lee on May 29, 1962, in Memphis, alone.

9

They bought a cute house inside the I-40/240 corridor, at 210 N. Waldran, in the heart of midtown. There, the Tickle home became a thoroughly Christian one. With three daughters, soon to add sons, Phyllis and Sam (mostly Phyllis) began to raise everyone in the faith. Each child was baptized and eventually confirmed, and each was parochial-school educated. They were exposed to scripture reading via an illustrated book of Bible stories given to Phyllis by her Presbyterian pastor when she was a girl. Later, not yet, would they begin a daily use of the Book of Common Prayer.

The family observed the liturgical year with close attention, and charity work was expected of all, including preparing and delivering meals to shut-ins, setting aside cans for the local food pantry, and taking offerings to church on Sunday. The one exception to a thorough Christian family routine was the absence of family prayer time, other than grace before meals. Sam's work schedule was too unpredictable for that (which is also why the family often ate dinner at the John Gaston Hospital cafeteria), and Phyllis hadn't yet begun her own intensive prayer practice.

It was in the late 1960s that Phyllis finally convinced Sam that they should join the Episcopal Church. In an early essay, Phyllis recounts an occasion when her eldest son, John (b. 1970), at twenty-two months old, "brought me my Book of Common Prayer and demanded that I watch while he pointed out and read aloud all the 'the's' in the Psalter."[7]

CHAPTER 5

A Woman among Men

Throughout her life, Phyllis trail blazed as a woman in what were believed to be men's endeavors. Whether in the academy (as one of only two full-time female faculty), in publishing (heading her own house), or in journalism (a woman leading a department), she would be ahead of other women, working more often beside men. At the same time, she quickly grew tired of feminism and feminists.

She was caught between second- and third-wave feminism, having already married and begun raising children before Betty Friedan wrote *The Feminine Mystique* and Gloria Steinem came to national prominence. As a result, she often wearied of feminist preoccupations. Fighting for the Equal Rights Amendment in the 1970s didn't interest her much. It seemed largely unnecessary. On the other hand, neither did she have interest in the family ethos promoted by conservative Phyllis Schlafly. Phyllis Tickle knew well that Job's wife suffers just as much as Job does in the ancient story, and that it's worse for her because she doesn't even have a name. She also knew that de facto inequalities existed, yet she didn't feel subject to them. Nor did she complain. She believed in getting to work and changing one's situation. That was the Calvinist in her.

"Any woman who bears seven children to the same man doesn't get to call herself a feminist," she often quipped, after all of her kids were grown. For the first decade of marriage she was often known as Mrs. Samuel M. Tickle. (At her death, she still owned books, including a 1962 paperback of James Joyce, bearing such a stamp.) There was always a deep sense within her that she was a woman and a wife before she was whoever Phyllis Tickle later became, and acknowledging this didn't seem to diminish her.

In the second volume of her autobiography, she begins by recounting an unpleasant conversation with a male friend who criticized her for not acknowledging the privilege of security that marriage had afforded her over the course of frequent career changes. She, after all, was teacher, then dean, then poet, then essayist, then publisher, then journalist, then lecturer-at-large. For the first forty years of marriage, she was not remotely the chief breadwinner. But even the recounting of this episode shows her pre-dilection to accept a prior reality. "I was, and for fifty years have been, married to Sam Tickle. We have had seven children together. . . . Over those years I have indeed moved from the domestic to the professional and back again as the need arose and, in my later years, from one occu-pation to another with the book industry, as the opportunity arose."[1] She was criticized as a feminist early in her career, and condemned by pro-gressives later in her career for betraying the feminist cause.

The Presbyterian ethos and moral code would remain ingrained in her throughout her life. She lived always attentive to matters of sin. She was never, for instance, someone that would consider experimental drugs in the 1960s, as did many of her colleagues in poetry and aca-demia. And she was always faithful in a marriage that was sometimes unsatisfying and unfaithful to her.

2

Despite his busy work schedule, visiting patients at all hours of the day and night, Sam managed to be an active presence in the girls' lives. Thanksgiving was the holiday when the family was most likely to travel across the state to Johnson City to see grandparents, but Christ-mas was the holiday of record at home, and Sam reveled in it. The girls were allowed to begin opening presents on Christmas Eve and then Santa would come with more gifts overnight, to be opened on Christ-mas morning.

Phyllis and Sam didn't agree on everything when it came to the holi-day, and quarreled occasionally about its priorities, its food, and accou-trements. They came from different backgrounds, and this showed clearly in the form of the Christmas "tree" that Sam had inherited from his father: made from toilet paper roll sections, covered in foil, with a push pin in each segment to hold a tiny ball. Phyllis hated it, and didn't conceal her feelings. Perhaps as a result, the kids loved it.

The kids looked to their father more than their mother for the spirit of the holiday. Phyllis's approach was a bit too "heady" for their young spirits. She wanted to read the stories of Advent and talk about what they meant. In contrast, Nora remembers, "Daddy was the motive force for Christmas celebrations." By the Friday after Thanksgiving, he was singing Christmas carols in the car, insisting that everyone join in. He also crafted confectionary art, and made fudge (the real, calibrate-your-thermometer kind) at least twice each season. He would make enough to give away to friends and neighbors. "I remember being up past midnight many times in the various Decembers to finish a batch of mints or to perfectly decorate cut out cookies," says Nora. "Baked goods were *sous chef* responsibilities, but he insisted that we all become perfect at them."[2]

When Easter rolled around each year, the girls would not only dye eggs, but—this was, after all, Tennessee in the early 1960s—their parents bought them each a new hat and gloves for the festivities on Easter Sunday.

3

When they arrived back in Memphis in 1962, Laura Lee was Phyllis's primary concern for several weeks, and then of course there were the other two girls. It wasn't long, however, before she wanted to teach again. After earning her M.A. she had briefly taught languages at Furman and loved it. But with three children now, how could she return to the classroom? Housemaids were the answer, and the Tickles hired a series of them. First there was Pearl, then Corinne, who Phyllis met because her husband was the maintenance engineer (janitor) at the Memphis Academy. Corinne would become a steady point in the lives of the three girls, and her daily presence allowed Phyllis to teach once again.

She was hired to teach Latin, Greek, and English literature at Southwestern at Memphis—which was the name of the college, in order to distinguish it from other Southwesterns in the South—for 1962–63. (The school would be renamed Rhodes College in 1984 to honor former college president Peyton Nalle Rhodes.) Phyllis wasn't even a decade older than most of her students.

Part of the pedagogical inheritance brought over by the Pilgrims from England, the study of Latin was once intimately associated with gaining proficiency in English grammar and education generally. But Latin's place in the curriculum of elementary and secondary schools in the United States began to cease at precisely the time that Phyllis began teaching. As a result, she saw many of her students coming to college without an adequate understanding of any language, and within a year she was teaching a course in what became *An Introduction to the Patterns of Indo-European Speech*, her first published book. But the course was more successful than the book. Its title portends its inaccessibility. The foreword reads "The love of language is a blessed illness which this text attempts to make both contagious and pandemic." But this is followed mostly by elaborations of grammatical structures and syntactical devices, and comparative philology. She soon earned a promotion to instructor at Southwestern, and her reputation was growing as a serious scholar.

4

One morning, the head of the English department walked into Phyllis's new office and there sat Phyllis, reclining in her chair, both feet propped up on the big oak desk in front of her. "Mrs. Tickle," he scolded, "that desk you are sitting at was once occupied by Mr. Penn Warren!" (Robert Penn Warren had taught at Southwestern for one year as an Instructor in English three decades earlier, in 1930, before they called him back to Vanderbilt.) Phyllis uncrossed her long legs and responded with a meek, "Thank you."

She was a female pioneer in academia, one of only two faculty women teaching at Southwestern at that time. The other was the dean of women. "I remember the first time I walked into the faculty lounge, all men, and the conversation coming to a complete halt," she later remembered. She was also young, which didn't help her stature with older colleagues. But her gifts in the classroom were immediately evident, and her Freshman Composition and Western Civilization students praised the way that she nurtured them and taught them to think.

She had her own imposing physical qualities, not entirely unlike Mr. Penn Warren. One student remembered Phyllis years later in the Rhodes alumni magazine:

> She was tall and looked stern and usually the highest grades she gave were A- or B+, and she only awarded two or three of those. However, we soon became mesmerized by her. I've often said that she reminded me of the Ancient Mariner—she "held you with her glittering eye!" Her lectures were fascinating, and we knew she cared about us—we were lined up each day outside her office for conferences with her.[3]

"I was very lucky . . . that Rhodes [*sic*] extended me an invitation to come as lecturer to the college," she told an interviewer in 1988.[4] But she was soon restive at Southwestern, a school known for preparing its students to go on to medical school, law school, or graduate school in engineering. Phyllis was the resident classicist, which also means that she was the only one. She grew lonely there.

Two years later, Edwin "Ted" Rust, the director of the Memphis Academy (now College) of Art, called to ask Phyllis to come and teach verbal arts to students majoring in visual arts: pottery, painting, jewelry, metalsmith, sculpture, silkscreen, and printmaking. She accepted the job over the phone and that fall moved across town to teach great books and composition (the humanities) to students she found to be fascinating. Just a year later, in 1965, she was promoted to dean of humanities. She was only thirty-one years old. She would remain at the Memphis Academy for six more years, continuing to teach while taking on various administrative duties.

There were sometimes tensions with other faculty, when Phyllis's rigor in the classroom put too much pressure on their students' art: "Occasionally, [they] would get hysterical, ream me out for having done in one of their kids, have a screaming fit, and then laugh about it. I always got the message. And we usually fixed it . . . because we weren't about to lose somebody that was gifted in fabric over a dadgum Dante test."[5] But she loved her students studying for their BFA degrees and relished the role that she played in their educations.

5

Nora, Mary, and Laura spent many days with Phyllis on campus in these years before anyone knew what to do with the children of a fast-paced working mother. As Phyllis puts it in her autobiography, "Many of my colleagues became avuncular playmates to the lot of them; and those connections have held as emotional anchors ever since," and that is true. Nora, for instance, was introduced to marijuana in the fourth grade by a small group of pottery students; and Ted Rust, sculptor and director of the Memphis Academy, taught the girls to play "Go Fish" on the front steps. He also later did the flowers for Nora's wedding.[6]

One of the programs under Phyllis's responsibility, once she was promoted to academic dean, was the organization each year of student trips abroad. One fall while planning a two-week trip to Mexico for the following spring, one of her colleagues, an instructor in watercolor painting, insisted on personally and anonymously paying for one of the students who couldn't otherwise afford to go. Phyllis asked her why she wanted to do it. "Someone helped me to get to where I am," the colleague replied, "and so I need to help others." That stuck with Phyllis for the rest of her life.

The following summer, during *Julio* 1967, Phyllis herself went on the Mexico trip. They took a Greyhound to San Antonio, then on to Saltillo, Mexico, where they stayed in private homes and studied at the Universidad Internacional, an intensive Spanish-language school. The students each attended classes and worked on their respective arts (weaving, pottery, glass blowing, and painting). Phyllis had time to roam, attending the theater, a piano concert, even a bullfight. In a black notebook she jotted poems. "Make love to me with words, / With the wanton thinness of regard. / Rub my front with kind affection, / My ambitious parts with pride"—reads one. After two weeks in Saltillo, the entire party moved on to Mexico City where Sam and Nora flew down to join them. Phyllis wrote a postcard home to Memphis, addressed to "Misses Mary Gammon and Laura Lee Tickle," who were with their grandparents:

> Mexico continues to be a marvelous experience but much more fun with Daddy and Nora being here. . . . The pyramids were the best of all. They climbed Teotihuacan but I couldn't make it. . . . Mama

6

It was in the mid-1960s when Phyllis's commitment to fixed-hour prayer first began to take root—a spiritual practice that would take her, daily in discipline, throughout the remaining half century of her life. She remembered her mother's daily practice and, now with the resources of the Book of Common Prayer, began her own.

One cannot truly pray the hours unless one appreciates the Psalms, so central are they to the practice, and it wasn't until she was about thirty years old that Phyllis believed she came to understand the Psalms and how they express the range of human emotions. "The Psalms are an older person's cathedral," she said to Bob Scott of Trinity Church Wall Street in an interview when she was almost seventy. She was probably thinking of what had happened to her over the decades of praying those words, and she was conscious that she was then growing old. She also explained to Scott:

> "It took me years to understand what the Psalms were about. As a young woman of twenty and twenty-five, I was essentially clueless: I was aware of their *poetry* . . . but to understand how they are the most primordial, if you will, of *gratos*, almost the last vestige of Eden. Space not only built by words, but hallowed by all of the hands that have touched them and smoothed their surfaces. . . . The Psalms are the whole treasure house of man's experience of God. It's all there."[7]

Other spiritual practices began for her then, as well. She was always conscious of the fact that she had one Jewish grandparent, her paternal grandmother. She never knew Grandma Wahl, who married the Alexander who fought in the Battle of Shiloh, but she carried with her the knowledge of the Jewishness that her father was born with. Partly from this came Phyllis's commitment to keeping the weekly Sabbath, albeit on Sundays rather than Saturdays. But there was a Jewish spirit to how she practiced it: as a time for recreation, joy, even sex with her husband. Later, when personal computers became essential to daily life, she adopted as part of her Shabbat practice not to turn them on that day. (Not until the final two months of her life would this change, as she realized that her time of rest would soon be ultimate, and would come soon enough.)

Over the years, she would occasionally remark to a Jewish friend, or to a friend considering marrying a Jewish man or woman, "I could easily be Jewish." By this she meant not that she had a Jewish grandparent, but that the prayer practice, ethical priorities, and serious attitude toward this life were essential to her spiritual outlook, even as a Christian. In *The Shaping of a Life* she briefly remarked, "I have visited many of the places in doctrine, ethos, and practice where Judaism shares common ground with Christianity."[8]

7

Raising a family went on as usual for Phyllis and Sam, as it did for most couples in America, despite Cold War scares, bus boycotts, and McCarthyism. Then there were Freedom Riders, enforced school integration, the shooting of President Kennedy, the Vietnam War, and the fight for civil rights for non-white Americans. These world events, during which the United States was on the world stage, were occasionally experienced by Phyllis in the lives of her students. As a dean, she was often behind closed doors with those who were puzzled or in trouble. On at least one occasion, she even counseled with a male student just before he left Memphis for Canada in order to avoid the draft.

The events of the times impacted the family directly, as well. The day that JFK was assassinated, the kids in the Memphis schools were sent home early without knowing why. Nora was half way up the second turning of the back stairs, headed to her parents' room, when Phyllis came to the head of the stairs and told her that the president had been shot. She wasn't a particular supporter of Kennedy at that time, but she was visibly shaken by his death. Nora remembers that together they went back to Nora's bedroom and Phyllis talked to her as if she were an adult. That was the first time that Phyllis's eldest child felt like a confidant of her mother's.[9]

In 1964, the house they were renting in Memphis was identified as one of nearly a hundred homes in central Memphis that needed to be torn down to make room for an expansion of Interstate 40. That expansion never ended up happening, but it gave the landlord an excuse to terminate their lease, which he did, and the Tickles prepared to move.

Their new home, 1474 Harbert, in the Central Gardens neighborhood of Memphis, was condemned when Phyllis and Sam purchased it, but the ranch-style house only needed a few things fixed to bring it up to code. Danny Thomas lived on the block briefly while founding St. Jude's Children's Hospital, but the best part about 1474 Harbert, for the kids, was that the house had four bedrooms.

It was in the summer of 1964 that the Civil Rights Act was finally passed in Congress and signed into law by President Lyndon Johnson. A little more than a year later, Nora's Uncle Abe confessed one day to her that he had taken part in harassing blacks in Tipton County, Tennessee, during the Jim Crow era of the 1920s. Although she loved Abe, Nora was a judgmental pre-teen at the time and all the way home in the car that day she tried to condemn her uncle. "Don't be too harsh on him," Phyllis finally said. "He was a creature of his times." She explained the pressures and taboos that he had faced. "He was also young," she said to Nora, explaining that men and women usually do not yet have fully formed consciences at the age of twenty. Full culpability comes with adulthood.

The years 1967 and 1968 were another time of turmoil in the world, some of which affected the Tickles keenly. During the Six-Day War in Israel and Palestine in June 1967, for instance, even the recovering Presbyterian Phyllis turned, like millions of American evangelicals at the time (and anyone who looked at the cover of *Time* magazine), to ponder what the Bible had to say about the end of the world. She spent that anxious week reading the book of Revelation. What was happening in the land of Jesus's birth and an anticipated Second Coming filled the air with portents of Apocalypse as Phyllis pulled out her Bible to look up what she hadn't considered for decades. She actually paced the floor on Harbert Avenue for days with Bible in hand, consumed with millennialist ideas.

8

In April 1968, the Tickle home in Memphis was still full of girls. Nora Katherine was about to turn eleven; Mary Gammon was eight and a half; and Laura, nearly six. This was when Phyllis began to truly enjoy parenting. Infants and toddlers were a necessary part of raising a family, but not an enjoyable one, for her. It was when the kids could begin to read and talk in paragraphs that their mother began to feel most comfortable in her mothering role.

Still, she needed her time alone. Sometimes this took the form of reading and study, asking the children to play on their own, and other times, inspired by her mother's devotion to prayer, Phyllis would be all alone with a book on her lap praying the Divine Office. She kept the mid-afternoon office of None so faithfully at 3:00 p.m. that it left her kids often feeling without a parent at what was probably the most important hour of a school-age child's day.

One Thursday evening, April 4, as the dinner dishes were being put away, Phyllis received a call from Sam, who was not at home but on a consultation at St. Joseph's Hospital in downtown Memphis. It turned out to be the very night that Martin Luther King Jr. was shot while standing on a hotel balcony and rushed to that hospital. Sam was at St. Joseph's and saw what happened from just outside the emergency room before 7 p.m. He found a phone and called Phyllis at home. Speaking in a low voice, he told her that Dr. King was dead, the news would soon be announced to the press, and to get the girls out of town. She hung up the phone and told each girl to grab one doll and hurry to the car. They drove out of midtown to a friend's house in East Memphis. There they stayed for the night, and once the girls were asleep, Phyllis sat up listening to the radio and heard about Memphis burning. The next afternoon they all returned home, having received assurances that the rioting wasn't in their neighborhood and with the knowledge that their neighbor across the street had a fallout shelter, a product of the Cold War, available to them if things got bad on night two.

CHAPTER 6

Anesthetizing Grief

t was just after the turn of the decade, in early 1970, when Americans felt little hope for the future, after the pain and disappointment of a few more miscarriages, when Phyllis realized she was pregnant again. Her first son would be born on July 10. His father named him for his own father: John Crockett.

Many homes would be full with four children, but Phyllis and Sam weren't done yet, and they eschewed the modern convention of birth control. As a result, only six weeks after John was born, Phyllis was expecting once again, and on May 29 (the same birthday as Laura Lee), 1971, she gave birth to a second son, their fifth child. This time, the boy was named for Phyllis's father. They baptized him, while still in the hospital, Philip Wade. He would actually never leave the Pediatric Intensive Care Unit.

From birth, Philip Wade's lungs were not well. Sam, one of the South's premiere pulmonologists at that time, was helpless to watch the infant die with obviously violent pain only thirteen days after he was born. Watching his tiny chest gasp for air, Phyllis wanted to expire right along with him.

That afternoon, ravaged and exhausted, she was weeping alone in the living room at home and teenage Nora didn't know what to do. She had watched a similar scene every evening for nearly two weeks. When Phyllis and Sam were not at the hospital PICU, Phyllis was in tears and Sam was sitting in silence. "Normal" life had all but stopped. The whole family had been living on edge. But Nora needed something—a supply for school. Most of all, she probably wanted her mother to be her mother, rather than the ravaged creature that she had become. So she asked for whatever it was that she needed, and Phyllis exploded, shrieking, telling Nora to go away. "How could you ask anything on the day that my son has died?!" she screamed.[1]

2

Phyllis left her position as dean at the Memphis Academy largely because Wade died. (Her second son would come to be called, simply, "Wade.") Her life changed irrevocably at that moment. Nothing would be the same again.

Such experiences can end many, even strong, marriages, and Phyllis later described the year after Philip's death as a time of "almost anesthetizing grief."[2] Sam was often angry at her for dwelling on what happened for what he felt was too long a time. When she would cry, and she cried for weeks and months, Sam would become frustrated. Then he became fearful about having more children. The couple had the intention of raising almost as many as they could, but Wade's death scared Sam. Phyllis later remembered that her son's death was the first time that any real split was felt between the two of them. "My unfilled hours settle into days, / And grief wearies into sadness. / Even love cannot survive / The violence of such passing," she wrote in those weeks of lament.[3] It was the first event in their already long lives together that they could not talk about.

Sam's frustration came from the East Tennessee ethos that they shared, and which Phyllis praised several years later in an essay: "There is one thing about mountain living, and very peculiar to it alone. Survival there doesn't mean continuing life until it can propagate itself; it means maintaining life in harmony with all other life, whether violent or benign. . . . God made and God ordered. Blessed be the name of the Lord."[4] It is almost Stoic, but that was later.

Now, her heart was broken. Causing even more friction between them, Sam's impatience with her grief then began to include hints that a car accident was to blame for bringing on the birth prematurely. Several days before Wade's birth, and more than a week before her due date, Phyllis had been rear-ended at a traffic light by a car that was itself rear-ended. It wasn't a bad accident, but her body was thrust into the steering wheel. At the time, it seemed that everything was fine, but several days later, she went into labor. Searching for answers in his own way, Sam began to wonder if the accident might have been preventable. It was cruel, but he felt helpless. His son had just died of pulmonary failure brought on by pneumonia, and Sam could do nothing to stop it. He didn't know how to work through his grief without denying it.

Phyllis's grief did not ever come to an end. For the better part of a year she couldn't control or explain her emotions. Even good friends were worried, but feared stopping by. The children were often walking on eggshells, too, not sure whether to fear for themselves or for their mother and father. On one occasion—the only time this ever happened—Phyllis slapped one of her children for a smart remark when the girl was sitting at the piano practicing the difficult measures of "Raindrops Keep Fallin' On My Head." When Nora began to cry, Phyllis too broke into tears and spent the next hour alone in her bedroom.

She would later refer beautifully to what such pain can do in a life: "a pain so immense, so unbearable, so omnipresent that we are burned by it beyond pain . . . and brought instead, whimpering and infantile, into the presence for a while of the substance of things hoped for and the evidence of things not seen."[5] At a certain point, her grief was simply exhausted, and she had to pretend to be "normal" again. She was keenly conscious of this, and wrote: "When the redness of my pain / Has died away to brown, / I arrange myself like foliage / To feign a full bouquet."[6]

3

Wade's death wasn't the first occasion when the couple was frightened with health scares related to their children. Phyllis had of course experienced multiple miscarriages before Nora was born, and then again in-between her various successful pregnancies. "Over and over and over again I miscarried, until it seemed that for every child we brought to term, three had been lost," she said.[7]

There were other scares, too. A couple of months before the death of baby Wade, his brother John almost died from a thyroglossal cyst. Then, Sam got cat scratch fever and became seriously ill himself. And after the baby died, Sam contracted a particularly difficult strand of mononucleosis, with fevers and long-term weakness. Phyllis also began to develop migraines in the year after Wade's death, but they remained, most often, manageable with medication.

Eventually the couple repaired their relationship and were able to move forward, even becoming pregnant again six months after the tragedy. It was another boy. They named him Sam Jr. and were relieved by his immediate, obvious, and vigorous health. Still, Phyllis continued to grieve, and Sam seemed to be constantly down with one ailment after another. By the time that Rebecca, the last child, was born, she was carried around by Grandmother Alexander much of the time because Phyllis had her hands full with the others, and those older kids were busy being afraid—with active imaginations, as kids often have—that their father was going to die from the complications surrounding mono and his other recurring fevers.

As for Sam's emotional pain, it remained mostly silent, which didn't serve him or the others well. Occasionally, it would burst out in the most unhelpful sorts of ways. There were moments, for instance, during the middle-seventies, after Wade's death, when Sam would announce laconically that he might kill himself one day. On one occasion, he did this while the family was sitting at the dinner table and Nora, a ripe sixteen years of age, replied, "Just do it, then. Stop promising!"[8]

4

One of the oddities in Phyllis's late 1980s essay collection, *The Tickle Papers*—which celebrated the soul, humor, and heart ("parables and pandemonium," as the subtitle put it) of a large American family—came on two baffling occasions when the children were mentioned by name and a certain "Philip" was among them. "While the babies fell asleep on the floor and the sofa respectively . . . Mary and Philip and Laura watched television," one chapter relays. Only a careful reader who also knew something of the tragedy visited on the Tickle household would have caught it. But . . . Philip who? Was this somehow Philip Wade, who had died years earlier?

The second occasion was especially troubling. Writing of her son, John Crockett, going off to college, Phyllis reflected with some wistful sadness: "[T]he conversations of his coming back will be, as they have been with Nora and Mary and Philip and Laura, active exercises in trying to reconnect when most of the pieces are missing."[9] Was she still grieving the death of Philip Wade to the point of total denial—even in print?

Not quite, although that second instance in *The Tickle Papers* will always carry an emotional tone of regret, and not simply regarding son John's going off to college. On top of this, one year later in the preface to another book, Phyllis wrote, "I was born to make babies and knew it from the beginning. I make them easily, bear them lightly, and love them dearly. There are seven of them now. . . ."[10] This is odd, as seven were born, but only six lived in the present.

The partial answer to these quandaries is that the Philip who is mentioned in *The Tickle Papers* passages was in fact Philip Cox, the son of a Memphis neurosurgeon and one of Sam's closest friends. Dr. Cox was driving his wife and son to a Florida vacation when the car got a flat tire on the interstate. While changing the tire, a tractor trailer on the other side of the highway lost a tire of its own and it bounced across the road and hit Cox in the shoulder, breaking his neck. He ended up back in Memphis under Sam's care but never fully recovered. Eventually there was a blood clot and a pulmonary embolism.[11]

Dr. Cox's widow was a needy woman with disability, so their son Philip moved in with the Tickles for the better part of four years, beginning in early 1972. He had a bed and a chest of drawers, sharing a room with one of the boys even though Philip was several years their elder. It was de facto foster care. *That* is the Philip mentioned on those stray occasions in Phyllis's essays. After high school graduation, he left their house and was mostly gone from their lives; but in the first years after Phyllis's son, Philip Wade's, tragic death, mothering Philip Cox seems to have been some comfort.

5

Her large family and its pandemonium were a combination of comfort (*The Tickle Papers'* working title was, at one point, *Growing Up Tickled*) and caustic to Phyllis. As with Philip Cox, she knew how difficult the teenage years could be. Struggles with her own children were common, and their home, despite the generosity of taking in a child in need, was not known to be an easy place. Each of the daughters left quickly, to get away, and marry—but then they also were often coming back home to visit and even stay at times.

Phyllis always subscribed to the theory that families are complicated, necessary, and painful, but also instruments of grace. She often counseled other women in these ways, including when she wrote in a devotional book specifically for women in the church: "[F]amily is our greatest burden in life. . . . God gives us as our nearest associates those who are most like us and, therefore, most repugnant to us."[12]

6

With all of these boys around, Phyllis was increasingly intrigued by the effects of testosterone. She became a fascinated observer of the male drive and its energy. Long before she became involved in, or even knew about, discussions of breaking down the binary of the sexes, she could relate to ways of being both "male" and "female" herself, and she often admired the first over the second.

She was always more aggressively minded than other girls while in school. She could never understand why a girl would pretend not to know the answer to a question or act shy and submissive in the presence of boys. Phyllis wanted to meet any male straight on, as an equal.

It was soon after the death of Wade and the birth of Sam Jr. that she wrote this poem about a real character who was a neighbor of theirs, a somewhat disreputable man, who nevertheless intrigued her:

The Bull Shooter

Above the smell of sweat
and the sound of god-damn,
he savors most the bellow of the calf
when, castrator in his hand,
he grabs the balls
and bands them off.

His stoop-shouldered sons
(who both call him Daddy)
steer wide of him when he's in the lot,
cowed as they are
by the bull and the god-damns.

And she watched as her own two boys followed their daddy around, doing the things that boys do, things, many of them, that her own professor father would have found distasteful.

CHAPTER 7

Making It in Verse

Family, circumstances, and education all prepared Phyllis to become, not just a writer, but a Southern one. In *Absalom, Absalom!* Faulkner writes about being from the South: "What is it? . . . Something you live and breathe in like air? . . . You can't understand it. You would have to be born there." Phyllis possessed that pride.

One experiences throughout her writing a perspective that stands alien to the cheeriness, progress, and gesturing to enlightenment that characterized most spiritual writing of the late twentieth century. Even in sermons, which she preached with reluctance and infrequency, she never set out to inspire. Instead, she pointed to virtue and placed value on risk-taking. Instead of optimism, she articulated a Christian hope. In her essays, she often concluded with the kind of mystery that, by definition, eschews simplicity. The same might be said of a Eudora Welty story. Phyllis also stood apart from the over-simplifying "life as pilgrimage" mode of diagnosing the human condition. She was more interested in the human heart and history than the ultimate destiny of human beings and souls. This also seems somehow Southern—for instance, in drama, this is characteristic of Tennessee Williams, over against Eugene O'Neill.

Even when she was later writing from the Farm in Lucy, Phyllis was never sentimental. Her youthful experiences in the mountains of East Tennessee and near the powerful Mississippi in West Tennessee taught her never to simply commune with nature. She comes to understand natural things, as best that one is able to do, enough to respect them. The characters in a Faulkner novel do the same, fighting with the land as with themselves. Finally, there is the way in which family can unite, divide, and challenge, as it so palpably does in a good Faulkner novel, and in Phyllis's poems and essays.

2

Her father, Philip, died on September 26, 1969, in Johnson City. While in Hot Springs, Arkansas, two weeks earlier he had taken ill with a gastro-intestinal problem and was sent to Methodist Hospital in Memphis where he remained under close supervision. When his condition worsened after multiple treatments, he was then sent to the Intensive Care Unit. Officially, the cause of death was diverticulitis, but it was probably a rupture. His last day was twenty-four hours of intractable pain that had him in tears, at times, unconsciously weeping and calling out for his mother—something that Phyllis would remember, and fear for herself, for the rest of her life. She was holding his hand when he died.

She was immersing herself in verse at that time, in addition to teaching. Catullus, Cavafy, and Eliot were her steady diet. She would read and recite them—Catullus in Latin, Cavafy in English translation, and Eliot, all the time—while walking alone, or while peeling carrots and browning ground beef on the stovetop. All three, despite the nineteen hundred years that separates them, wrote with intensity about the predicaments of life. Then, when Wade died and she quit the classroom, Phyllis turned intently to the tasks of a poet. She jotted lines, as they occurred to her, in pocket notebooks. She was seeking juxtapositions, writing down stray lines that included "Anxiety has an odor," "The noise keeps me warm," and "The hope of Advent lay shattered in Epiphany." She composed entire poems, as all poets do, that never came close to seeing print or an editor's desk. As fall turned to winter in 1973, one of the unpublished ones was "A Sonnet for Advent." It began "So long that year, so long / Before the winter came." And it read like an elegy. Other poems—dozens of them—were published in journals and magazines.

Drama and theater were also her consolations, and her outlets. The year 1974 saw the first production of her chancel drama about the Hebrew prophet Jeremiah and his faithful scribe, Baruch: *Figs and Fury*. She didn't for a moment think about trying to make Jeremiah relevant to contemporary culture even though this liturgical play was first performed during the summer of the Watergate scandal when Americans experienced the end of trust they once held for those in authority.

Richard Nixon resigned on August 9, 1974. Gerald Ford pardoned him a month later. And in Phyllis's play, Yahweh says to Jeremiah:

> [G]o stand at the gate of the Temple and there proclaim this message. Say to all the men of Judah who come in by those gates to worship Yahweh. Yahweh Sabaoth, the God of Israel, says this: Amend your behavior and your actions and I will stay with you here in this place, but put no trust in delusive words which say that this is the sanctuary of Yahweh.[1]

3

Chancel dramas are written to be performed in a sanctuary with minimal stage effects and lighting. They are written and staged with a particular chancel in mind. The worship atmosphere is preserved throughout the production, since the purpose of liturgical plays is to enhance worship, not replace it.

In some respects, Phyllis grew up in the golden age of chancel drama, if one can use that expression to describe interest in an art form that remains basically unknown. But Phyllis grew up in the age of the great Dorothy Sayers, writer of mystery novels and later translator of Dante, who wrote *The Man Born to Be King*, a series of twelve liturgical dramas that were performed during World War II on BBC Radio from London. Her series—about the life, death, and resurrection of Jesus—was a sensation. It began on December 21, 1941, two weeks after the bombing of Pearl Harbor, when America entered the war and ordinary Americans were particularly tuned to what was happening in London. Phyllis was seven years old.

The Alexander home was always attentive to all things English, and had been keeping close eyes and ears on news from Britain. They were also fans of Sayers's work. *The Man Born to Be King* made headlines in England. There were even charges of heresy, since English law forbade any depiction of one of the members of the Holy Trinity on stage, and Sayers had an actor (Robert Speaight) playing Jesus. There were also charges of propaganda (particularly keen during wartime), with atheist groups arguing that such programming was inappropriate on the BBC. The series was hugely popular, and caused people in every segment of the population, from dock workers to bishops, to reconsider Jesus Christ. A new drama was broadcast every fourth Sunday evening from December until October. Then the London publisher Victor Gollancz, published the full cycle in a handsome jacketed hardback the following May (1943). That book sold through seventeen printings over the next decade.[2]

But Phyllis never took chances, the way that Sayers did. Although she paid careful attention to who might, and who shouldn't, produce her plays, the writing itself was always conservative. One can see this in the excerpt from *Figs and Fury*, above. Sayers, by contrast, in a lengthy introduction to *The Man Born to Be King*, described her intent to shock audiences; her characters were designed to bear a striking resemblance to the living:

> Caiaphas was the ecclesiastical politician, appointed, like one of Hitler's bishops, by a heathen government, expressly that he might collaborate with the New Order and see that the Church toed the line drawn by the state; we have seen something of Caiaphas lately. As for the Elders of the Synagogue, they are to be found on every Parish Council—always highly respectable, often quarrelsome, and sometimes in a crucifying mood.[3]

Phyllis's plays did not attempt that sort of contemporary relevancy. They tended, instead, toward eternal verities.

Drama was a teaching tool. As she explained to the members of a Catholic parish in Memphis for whom she later wrote on the book of Tobit: "For the first twelve hundred years of her life the Church depended almost entirely upon dramas, pageants and oral readings for teaching the books and history of the Bible. With increased urbanization and technology, however, the Church began to depend instead upon the printed word for the instruction of believers." More recently, she goes on to say, the sensibility has swung back. We are beginning to "once more appreciate the greater power and effectiveness of . . . the enacted presentation . . . that some matters of both faith and fact are more accessible and more effectual in dramatic form."[4]

4

In 1977, Phyllis was hired as the poet-in-residence for the Memphis Brooks Memorial Art Gallery. She began to organize poetry readings in public schools throughout Memphis and West Tennessee, convinced that kids needed the imaginative arts and opportunities to express themselves outside the boundaries of traditional curriculum. Artists-in-Schools, the program was called, or Poets-in-Residence. It began in January 1978 with help from the Tennessee Arts Commission, the Memphis Board of Education, and private funding. It involved residencies at the art gallery—a poet teaching every Saturday for a month to adults, teenagers, and elementary school children. Kids would also visit the art gallery for classes, and Phyllis would visit their schools.

She was a working poet, now, in more ways than one. One of the journals in which her work appeared was *Front Street Trolley*, based in Nashville, which also often received Tennessee Arts Commission grants. The *Trolley* was edited by Molly McIntosh, a permanent faculty member of the Cumberland Valley Writers' Conference. In the Winter 1981 number appeared Phyllis's poem, "To the Company of Poets (After the manner of Catullus)," which perhaps shows more wit than grace:

> Like Aleph, the sacred cow,
> festooned with garlands of blooms,
> Poetry has carried us all our life
> on her warm back
> toward Xanadu,
> leaving behind us there
> a waft of strong air
> and even an exquisite turd or two.

Whether composing poems or reading them aloud to schoolchildren, Phyllis was focused on the musicality of language—the sounds that words make and how those sounds and words may be enjoyed. She demonstrated this principle before gymnasiums, libraries, and classrooms of kids on hot afternoons at Campus School, Georgia Avenue School, Oakshire School, Snowden School, Springdale Magnet School, and Grahamwood Elementary on Summer Avenue, all in the Memphis City Schools system.

Typically, she would open by reading Shel Silverstein's "Sarah Cynthia Sylvia Stout," a silly poem about a girl who refused to take out the garbage. "Coffee grounds, potato peelings, / Brown bananas, rotten peas, / Chunks of sour cottage cheese . . ." it goes.[5] The images in the poem, and the music of it, made kids laugh, breaking down barriers that lead kids (and adults) to say that poems are uninteresting. What a change this was from the obligatory Keats, Blake, and Shakespeare of the typical curriculum! Not that Phyllis didn't appreciate those, but she viewed her work in schools to move kids beyond them. It wasn't simply the words she used; it was the way that she read and performed them. "Phyllis Tickle seemed radical," recalled one student. "She gave herself over fully to the language, gesturing her arms and looking us directly in the eyes, abandoning her self-image—that thing so important to a high school teenager."[6]

The readings would wander into some of the newer twentieth-century classics: Dylan Thomas's "Fern Hill," for instance, and Robert Frost's "The Road Not Taken." She would always read Edgar Allen Poe's "Annabel Lee," just as her father had once read it to her. "A good elementary school poetry program should begin . . . not with writing poetry but with having it read aloud by an adult and with games and exercises for exploring human sounds," she explained.[7]

She was part of a movement in the 1970s aimed at teaching poetry to children. Poet Kenneth Koch first published his book on the subject, *Rose, Where Did You Get That Red?* in 1973, and it received wide acclaim. He'd tested his anthology and his methods for conveying the wonder and splendor of poetic language on the kids at PS 61 in New York City. Kids ages six to fifth grade are quoted in his introduction, and teachers across the country, including Phyllis, used *Rose, Where Did You Get That Red?* as an instructor's guide.[8]

5

Phyllis was known to go into schools with local actors, and a mime, in order to bring verse alive for kids. Groans, giggles, and shouts would fill the room as the audience responded. She took to describing the act of listening to great poems, "the art of letting dead men play with your bones."[9]

Sometimes during a reading, her voice would change suddenly. Her tone would go from energetic to deeply elegiac, even somber. This would happen throughout her life. Decades later, audiences heard something similar happen quite suddenly in the middle of a lecture, often when she was quoting scripture. Such moments were a sign that she was filling with reverence. To some, it came across as a kind of awkwardness, but it was actually the opposite. She explained once that this came from her father: "[H]e taught me how poetry could give body to the soul and how the voice speaking words aloud could give life to the printed page."[10] So, those times when her voice changed while reading aloud—she was attempting, often unconsciously, to give body to the soul.

This was a rich time for her creatively. By the end of the decade, she and Margaret (Peggy) Ingraham, a friend and fellow poet, began to meet and discuss each other's verse. They shared many things, including an education in the classics and languages. "I have never been able to resolve the limitations of too much intellectuality and too little depth," Phyllis wrote to her. "Yet damnit, I know that training and academic background should be an aid not a limitation" in the writing of good poems.[11]

Peggy was teaching English in the schools, and Phyllis was then poet-in-residence at the Brooks Museum in Memphis. Her educational programs were drawing poets of many backgrounds—including Etheridge Knight, Gordon Osing (who would become known as the "Zen blues poet of the Delta"), and Ingraham—to school readings around the state. Phyllis and Peggy met frequently, and corresponded regularly by letter when one was traveling. Their friendship and their communications were unique in Phyllis's life.

At one point, Phyllis proposed a most unusual collaboration. She had taken the presumptuous step of attempting to improve upon a poem of Peggy's. The poem was, and is, titled "Hope, Arkansas." Phyllis wrote to Peggy: "I awoke during the night . . . just enough to confirm my original judgment that it was superb in its opening lines." But, she went on to explain, it "failed as a poem, despite its strong beginning." Phyllis then offered that she thought she could improve it, explaining how the idea "came" to her: "[After] breakfast, a hasty good-bye to the people who were once my family and passingly still are, bless 'em, and [I was] on the road again—to Arkansas, of course. And driving along somehow the magic of what you had said about the Arkansas landscape . . . the whole thing focused in my mind. I got off the road and did this to your poem. Never before have I ever presumed on someone else's beauty, but having done it, I can't resist any longer sending it to you."[12]

In that explanation, Phyllis was speaking from an experience common to every Memphis resident: entering Arkansas by driving across the Memphis-Arkansas bridge. Suddenly, one has left the gritty and the dangerous for something quite different. The experience has been imagined by some writers as a liberation, as in the final sentence of Shelby Foote's novel about Memphis, *September September*: "Reeny laughed, again on a rising note, then looked over at Podjo, who was smiling under his broad mustache, and drove on into Arkansas and October."[13]

Ingraham was not put off by Phyllis's presumption; she welcomed it, and soon they began to ponder a name under which to publish collaborative poems, bringing together each of their middle names to form Natalie Bartlum. Within two months, they had started several others together and discussed the matter of the pseudonym with Phyllis's lawyer son-in-law. He concluded that it still carried the legal protections of copyright. Then, with the pretension of ones who had created a work of art rather than poems, Phyllis explained to the editor of a literary journal:

> Natalie Bartlum is a collaborative effort between me and Margaret Ingraham. It would certainly be incorrect to say that Natalie is a pseudonym; rather she is a person—or on her way to becoming one, at the very least. While Peggy and I each have voices of our own, Ms. Bartlum seems determined to have a distinct one also, a very insistent gal, in fact.[14]

6

It was also during this decade that Phyllis began building her reputation as an essayist. Again, her instinct was to establish a regional reputation. She began to write thousand-word pieces for Memphis's alternative newspaper, the *Dixie Flyer*. (It was later bought out and became the *Memphis Flyer*.) The paper was advertising-driven for its revenue with copies free for the taking at bookstores, coffee shops, hotels (including the venerable Peabody), and in *Dixie Flyer* sidewalk boxes throughout Memphis. Like the *Chicago Reader* and the *Boston Phoenix*, the *Flyer* was a combination of alt-journalism, opinion pieces, coverage of the local music scene, advertisements, and sometimes salacious classifieds. Circulation was high, but true readership, much less. Phyllis's essays took the form of a regular column. She referred to them as a "series of urban essays." Many were later collected into a book of forty-eight pages published by the short-lived Dixie Flyer Press, *The City Essays*.

She wrote and edited two other books of regional interest at this time. The first was obliquely titled *On Beyond Koch*, published by one of her employers, the Brooks Memorial Art Gallery, in 1981. It's a work aimed at elementary school teachers, explaining how to teach poetry and inspiring them to do the same. The title is a reference and honor to the aforementioned Kenneth Koch. The book includes several black and white photographs of teachers with kids in classrooms, including some that show Phyllis with full cheeks, cropped hair, and large, round glasses indicative of the time.

The other local work came out in 1982 from Raccoon Books, a non-profit imprint that Phyllis was then running jointly with fellow poet David Spicer. It too had an obscure title: *On Beyond AIS*, using the initials for the Artists-in-the-Schools program, and aimed at extending this work beyond what Phyllis herself could do in person. She co-wrote *AIS* with Vangie Piper, who was the director of the folk arts programs at the Tennessee Arts Commission. In it, Phyllis pleads: "We train, not for art, but for wholeness."

7

The collaboration with Peggy Ingraham was filled with an uncommon intimacy. (Only thirty years later would she collaborate with another friend, Emergence leader Tony Jones, with the same warmth of feeling. "Ours is really a love affair," she said of their relationship.) At times, Phyllis seemed to write as one in love: "Dearest Peg, My cup runneth over—and that's a serious statement. I would have written last night when I got your letter, but I was too swept up in my own confusion of sensations to make sense either to myself or to you. . . . I can't leave without writing and I can't write until I can really write. I have so much to say—this feels so good, so right."[15]

A year after their collaborations began, Peggy was called in by Phyllis to mediate between her and another poet, Robert Mitchie, with whom they both often shared a stage at readings. Mitchie had been unpleasant toward Phyllis on several occasions, including publicly. Peggy knew him better than Phyllis did, and Peggy asked him for the source of what seemed like real animosity. Ingraham's report back to Phyllis demonstrates how close the two women had become. In Peggy's words, Mitchie told her, "I was a bit surprised you gave 'Hope, Arkansas' away to the new persona shared with Phyllis. I understand the soul mate need for you two and applaud it. But hold on to your self in the poems." "On he went," Peggy added as commentary, and then she added, "What I see there is a frustrated man."[16]

A bit of context is perhaps necessary. When Ingraham and Phyllis began submitting their Natalie Bartlum poems to literary journals they met with rules that usually forbade submissions of multi-authored work or work authored by pen names. These rules were inviolate and the editors of the journals were then lordly. This was before the days of writing programs (Iowa was the only one), writer's groups, and online options for publishing new or experimental work. By the time Peggy and Phyllis got their big break from Donald Davie, which wouldn't have happened had Phyllis not known him personally, only three Natalie Bartlum poems had been accepted for publication. And each time it took six to eight months of waiting for a response in the mail. The British-born, Cambridge-educated Davie was a poet of international renown and had taught at the University of Essex and Stanford before coming to Vanderbilt in Nashville in 1978. He included the Natalie Bartlum poem "Aubade" in volume 1, number 1 of his journal *The Cumberland Poetry Review*. Poets William Stafford, Donald Hall, Diane Wakowski, Louis Simpson, Mark Jarman, and John Hollander (quite a list!) also appeared in that inaugural issue. Davie chose well. "Aubade" is surely the best that the pair ever produced. An aubade is a morning love song—the counter to a serenade, for the evening.

> Every morning early
> before the wrens,
> the elderly rise and go
> places no one knows of.
> Cheekbones red with rouge,
> sensing if they walked
> too plainly into life,
> out and in,
> their boldness would offend.
> And so they go,
> frail fingers, fragile skin
> warmed in the secret wind
> they follow,
> rising on a breath
> thin enough to flit and bend
> and turn, victorious
> in the end,
> to light
> beyond the places
> of the wren.

But before this literary break, in the midst of the experimental process and after long months of rejections and waiting for rejections, Phyllis decided to "take the poems to the people."[17]

With Ingraham's permission, she began reading them aloud at places like Union University in Jackson, and soliciting audience discussion and feedback about them. After one reading, she wrote to Peggy this account: "[T]he audience stopped me to hear the ringnecks read again—really, really enthusiastic reaction and interest from five or six vocal folks in the crowd. So it's sound on its first trial run. After the evening was over I wished I had time to try the mountains one—it's still bothersome in those two places—can hardly wait to see what you will do, if you will be bothered in the same places. I think it probably needs an audience reaction and last night is my last reading until after the holidays."[18] This was when the somewhat flamboyant Mitchie, who was then the poetry editor of a mimeographed literary journal, first confronted Phyllis during Q&A. He was, by certain accounts, almost beside himself—a reaction with no reasonable explanation other than professional jealousy.

Despite that unpleasantness, Phyllis worked her poems as one struggles against any raw material to make art, like a blacksmith with his iron, or a sculptor and her clay. She was often re-writing, culling, testing the strength of an emotion in place of another, dissatisfied with what she saw before her on the paper in the typewriter. And her love for this work led to positive feelings in other aspects of her life. As she said to Peggy on January 3, 1980: "The holidays have been really good this year—first good Christmas I can remember in years, as a matter of fact."[19] It had been seven years since she and Sam had buried Wade.

8

The Natalie Bartlum poems began a long hiatus in 1980, when Peggy moved away from Memphis to Washington, DC, and were not discussed between the collaborators for nearly twenty years, when they once again turned to the work.[20] There were no new poems published after the first flurry of activity; but several find their final form in *Hungry Spring and Ordinary Song: The Collected Poems of Phyllis Tickle*, compiled by Phyllis in the summer before her death. One of the title poems, "Ordinary Song," was in fact the first Natalie Bartlum poem ever composed by the two women. It was honored by the state of Tennessee in 1996, which inscribed a portion of one stanza in black granite on a wall of the "Pathway of History" at Bicentennial Capitol Mall State Park in downtown Nashville. "I sing of the mountains that sing in me / the cadences of plaintive earth / and only give you back the land / that framed the valley of my birth . . ." it begins. Then "I sing of the mountains that sing in me / soft harmonies I've known from birth. / I only give you back the land again / and the plain magnificence of earth."

It was also in 1980 when Phyllis and Sam celebrated their twenty-fifth wedding anniversary. Phyllis wrote one of her most beautiful poems, "Anniversary Song," as a gift for him on that occasion. It is a paean to an earlier, easier time, when what was unquestioned was followed, and loved. There is a sadness to the singing of the stanzas, and the final one is this:

> Snow sleeps deep upon the arms
> Of ageing mountain trees,
> But soft are the boughs, and blue the light,
> In the woodland halls
> Of the cloud-wrapped yarrows.
> Warm is the air and warm the earth
> Under the spreading limbs
> Of the silvered yarrows.
> You in your knickers and I in my gown
> Are caught in the winter's wind,
> Are lulled by the pine trees' songs,
> While down below, along the rill
> And under the midnight hill,
> None can remember, none recall,
> The April day
> We slipped away,
> You in your kickers and I in my gown,
> To play at house,
> As children will in a mountain town,
> Under the blue-green boughs
> Of kindly mother yarrow.

The reference to the "April day" is a bit of a puzzle, as the poem is intended to speak autobiographically, and they wed in June. It could be that they consummated their relationship, after so many years of friendship-turned-courtship, on a day in April, ". . . slipped away, / . . . Under the blue-green boughs."

9

One day, Phyllis did a reading at Hardin County High School in Savannah, Tennessee, and met a tenth grader, Jeff Hardin. Jeff was an aspiring poet and Phyllis gave him some general advice. The following year, when she once again visited his high school, Jeff presented her with a folder of his work, asking if she would critique it.

"She met with me the next day and told me I was 'the one,' the one she'd been looking for," Hardin, now a professor of literature, remembers. "She made me feel like I had great potential and was a 'born' poet." Hardin went on to apply and be accepted at Austin Peay University, following one of Phyllis's recommendations. This was followed by an MFA at the University of Alabama. "I like to think that her visit to my school was a miracle," said Hardin. He is the author of several collections and his poems have appeared in places like *The New Republic*, *The Hudson Review*, and on Garrison Keillor's "Writer's Almanac." "I wrote a poem this morning, just as I attempt to do every day. The whole process of thinking and writing seems both mysterious and holy. Phyllis will always be a part of that process for me."[21]

Erasmus Books of Notre Dame published the first volume of Phyllis's verse in 1983. Erasmus Books was one of a few entrepreneurial efforts of the Rev. John H. Morgan, PhD, a postdoc at the University of Notre Dame, who also taught sociology at St. Mary's College and was rector of the Episcopal Church of St. John of the Cross in Bristol, Indiana. He was the author of many of the books, or booklets, he published, including a study of the diaconate in the Episcopal Church (*The Diaconate Today*), and a study of clergy wives (*Wives of Priests*, co-authored with his wife, Linda). In the year in which Phyllis's book appeared, Morgan advertised in the classifieds of *The Living Church* magazine: "POETRY WANTED for a memorial anthology to Samuel Seabury (first Episcopal bishop) marking his consecration bicentennial," for a volume to be published the following year.

It is difficult to imagine Phyllis having titled that volume, *Selections*. She enjoyed metaphor and the lush sounds of language. She admired most "a strong, muscular, quotidian poetry."[22] So, *Selections*?

Perhaps Morgan had a hand in it. One thing is certain: Phyllis was delighted for the book to come from a publisher other than the one she then owned, and so she probably looked past the cheap design and side-stapled binding. It was really a chapbook. And Erasmus Books, by marketing only to Anglo-Catholic Episcopalians, added little to her reputation as a Southern poet.

CHAPTER 8

The Mid-South Phenom

The publishing house that Phyllis owned when *Selections* appeared was St. Luke's Press. "I was driven to found St. Luke's because I wanted to write and couldn't bear the frustration of writing without being published," she once explained to an audience at the Society for the Study of Southern Literature.[1] Started with a few friends from the Memphis Academy of Art in 1975, in addition to providing an outlet for her writing, St. Luke's was also her salvation, a way to return to life and work after Wade's death. Witness the power of "For Wade" (which was re-titled "Medusa Quietly Screaming" in her final *Collected Poems*), written at this time:

For Wade
May 29–June 11, 1971
There was such an easiness in his going,
Such a freedom once they said, "He's gone,"
Such a stilling peace for us. It followed
All the days that came and left
Until our friends began to say,
   "Won't you come to dinner?
   "Attend this play?
   "See ballet?
"Take for your sorrow some cliché of
   'God will provide'
   or 'Life must go on.'"
And so it is, my son,
That your burying has begun.[2]

Her most important book to date would be one of the first books published by the fledgling St. Luke's: a story about death and life that was only slightly disguised as fiction. *The Story of Two Johns*, published in June 1976, is a poignant work, with deep and hidden meanings. It is the story of a grandfather, whose name is given as John, but who fought in the Battle of Shiloh (as Phyllis's Grandpa Alexander did). Grandpa is a presence that is almost mystical in the narrator's life—for instance, "Grandfather was never there and was always everywhere all at the same time. . . . I could feel him loving me. . . ."[3] This sense of presence is used to guide children through grief over the death of a loved one.

The narrator speaks of specific memories of Grandfather John, recalling what he said and how he looked. But eventually, she admits, "I never saw my grandfather face to face or touched his hand or felt his skin, for he had been dead a long time when I was born." Then comes the second John of the title, and Phyllis re-emerges as the narrator as she reveals, "I have a little boy of my own now . . . and his name is John." Phyllis's son John had been born in 1970. In him, she explains, she sees her grandpa.

The Story of Two Johns was presented as fiction, and the line— "now in young John I see Grandpa just as he used to be"—was not really about the two Johns of the story's title. It was about Philip Wade Alexander, Phyllis's father, and Philip Wade Tickle, her son, who shared the "fierce blue eyes" given to the two Johns in the book.

2

The second book published by St. Luke's was compiled by Phyllis. Unlike the first, her name does not appear on the copyright page. Also for children, it was titled *It's No Fun To Be Sick*, and the author was "Paula And Her Friends." In this book, Paula tells her class, through personal memory and drawings, how it can be scary and worrisome to be sick, to spend time in the hospital, to see nurses and doctors, and to undergo procedures. The book was written and test-run in the city that had recently become home to the famous St. Jude's Children's Research Hospital, in Memphis, where it was also marketed and sold. *The Story of Two Johns* was popular at St. Jude's, as well. Both books were sales successes, and then, with *Figs and Fury* also in production, Phyllis and Sam were beginning to feel like real publishers.

So with the assistance of lawyer friends, they incorporated their various enterprises in publishing under "Tickle, Inc." The original charter was dated January 5, 1975, and took a broad view. A for-profit corporation was established "To publish, purchase, own, lease, produce, exhibit, present, represent, license, sell, and otherwise deal in and with masques, pageants, community dramas, theatrical plays, dramatic compositions, musical compositions, operas, sketches, scenarios, books, scores, and moving pictures." The chief officer and president was Sam. Four days after they mailed the charter off to the state of Tennessee it was certified by the Tennessee secretary of state Joe C. Carr for a processing fee of twenty dollars.

3

Beyond authoring books, Phyllis's managing editor position at St. Luke's didn't begin to communicate how fully she was involved in every aspect of the business. She was also the administrator, most of fulfillment and warehousing, and sales and marketing. In their first year she spearheaded an effort to convince book retailers in the Germantown section of Memphis to establish "Small Press" sections in their stores, and solicited small presses around the country to send titles on consignment to St. Luke's, who then fulfilled the orders from these retailers. This would raise the profile of St. Luke's among small presses nationwide. She also imagined that other presses in other cities might do likewise: A rising sea would raise all boats. That same year, Phyllis helped a fellow poet submit a grant request to the Memphis Arts Council for teaching poetry in West Tennessee prisons, which was accepted.

Soon, St. Luke's adopted the tagline, "A National Forum for the Regional Artist." They leased office space in the Mid-Memphis Tower, Suite 401, at 1407 Union Avenue, while many author meetings, writers' gatherings, and annual board meetings of Tickle, Inc. took place at Phyllis's and Sam's home. She was regularly involved in publicity, as well, instructing her assistant in planning readings and receptions, for instance, at the annual convention of the Tennessee Library Association. She mailed personal letters to writers, media, and friends to encourage attendance and support for her authors' upcoming readings. "I would deeply appreciate any and every thing you can do to get the word out and build the audience," she wrote in one, adding "She's an old friend and I'm feeling desperate to get her a crowd enough to not be embarrassed. Thanks . . . P."

Her passion for contemporary literature didn't wane as she began to build St. Luke's into a commercially successful enterprise. When the inaugural issue of a small literary magazine called *raccoon* reached her desk, she was immediately impressed. Soon, St. Luke's acquired this creation of Memphis poet David Spicer and the second issue of *raccoon* became the *belles lettres* arm of St. Luke's. Raccoon Books was re-founded by the Tickles and Spicer as a 501(c)(3) non-profit aimed at publishing magazines and chapbook length works of literary merit. Annual sales would remain low, even by small press standards, but some years saw grants and donations from anonymous benefactors. They even innovated in how they published, creating a "raccoon monograph" series in which each issue was a single printer's signature, or sheet, printed on both sides, and folded, so as to create sixteen uncut pages. Phyllis authored the first of these, *Of Snakes and Their Skins: Poetry and Painting in Contemporary Life*; her text was followed by a book review by someone else, and a short editor's page authored by Spicer.

4

Phyllis's migraines once again became severe, and the best drug known to cure them at that time was the birth control pill. Anathema to her previously (she wanted *children*), this is the primary reason why there were no children after Rebecca, their seventh.

Phyllis loved her work. "St. Luke's was just a mid-South phenom and we were doing it all for the joy of the thing," she later remembered. Their list included *At the River I Stand*, an oral history in the aftermath of the assassination of Martin Luther King Jr.; and books by Ethridge Knight, Oliver Pitcher, and other Southern literary luminaries. "We honestly believed in the worth and worthiness of it all. Sounds young and idealistic, doesn't it? Maybe we were. I'd do it all again, and this time for the fun of it as well," she said.[4] St. Luke's published *Rankin: Enemy of the State* by John Osier, a fantasy/crime thriller about America run by a military junta. Books like his helped to pay the bills, and Phyllis used a sub-rights specialist, Mary Jane Ross, who quickly sold its paperback rights to Viking Penguin.

They would publish, woo, or simply entertain many of the interesting figures of that period. There was Marilou Awiakta, the Appalachian Eastern Band Cherokee storyteller whose *Abiding Appalachia: Where Mountain and Atom Meet* was published by St. Luke's in 1978. Its subject was reverence for life in the era of the atom bomb. Awiakta was uniquely qualified to reflect on this, having grown up on the atomic frontier in Oak Ridge, Tennessee, as well as under the influence of a Cherokee spirit-teacher. There was also Selma S. Lewis, a Memphis historian who wrote about a pioneering African American Memphis woman in *The Angel of Beale Street: A Biography of Julia Ann Hooks*. This is a book for which Phyllis was willing to risk her reputation after she discovered from their sales representative that pre-orders were sluggish. "Blacks don't read and whites don't care," was the repeated excuse they were hearing. Phyllis was furious. So she "called out" her industry for institutional racism in a June 1986 *Publishers Weekly* op-ed.

They published on topics of regional interest that also had national appeal, including the origins of blues and rock and roll. W.C. Handy, for instance, played a major role in *The Angel of Beale Street*. Another of Phyllis's favorites was Tom T. Hall, the Grand Ole Opry star. She published him, but most of all she remembered the pleasure of just hanging out. Hall had a country place, Fox Hollow, outside Nashville and a touring bus. Phyllis spent time in both, along with characters like Will Campbell and John Egerton and even Alex Haley.

Tom T., whose big hit, "That's How I Got to Memphis" was released in 1968, would give parties at Fox Hollow and everybody would come. At one of these parties, Phyllis literally ran into Johnny Cash by going around the corner into the kitchen too fast while the singer was bent over investigating the innards of the refrigerator. At the same party, she spent another rough few minutes trying to make conversation with Jimmy Carter, which, according to many in those days, was never easy. Rosalynn was the easy one to talk to. "I was so relieved when she rescued me from having to figure out what to say to Jimmy," Phyllis remembered. On another occasion, probably in 1985, Phyllis was invited to stand backstage at the Grand Ole Opry while Bill Monroe, the Father of Bluegrass, was playing his guitar and mandolin and singing. Phyllis stood just outside the range of the lights and when the set was over, as Monroe turned to leave the stage and moved from the lighted area into the dark one, he somehow caught his foot on a riser and, quite literally, fell into Phyllis's arms. "My real claim to fame, though, seemed to be not that I caught Bill Monroe, but that I somehow managed to catch the mandolin before it went crashing into smithereens!"[5]

One year earlier, Phyllis was elected chairperson of the organizing committee of a new Publishers Association of the South. She was quoted in Bob Summer's October 12 *Publishers Weekly* story about their launch and accompanying the story was a photo of Phyllis and Sam at the Southeastern Booksellers Association, in which one sees the double chin she had in those days. She would be forty pounds lighter a decade later. By October 1989, when Phyllis published Tom T.'s *Christmas and the Old House*, St. Luke's Press had moved from Memphis to Atlanta, swallowed up by Peachtree Publishing. Tom T.'s book was then a Peachtree title. "I remember it as a kind of last hurrah to days that had been great," Phyllis said.

5

An author whom Phyllis was most proud to have published was the African American poet of the Black Arts Movement (the artistic branch of Black Power) Etheridge Knight. Gwendolyn Brooks was credited with discovering Etheridge, a troubled military veteran from rural Mississippi, in one of her prison poetry workshops. He was serving ten to twenty-five years for snatching a woman's purse. The severity of the sentence surely involved race, and Etheridge knew it, which infuriated him, and fueled his artistic ambitions. He read Malcolm X and Langston

Hughes behind bars, and Brooks quickly became his friend, mentor, and promoter. Etheridge Knight once said, "I died in Korea from a shrapnel wound and narcotics resurrected me. I died in 1960 from a prison sentence and poetry brought me back to life."[6] *Poems from Prison* was published just after his release, in 1968. He would go on to receive grants from the Guggenheim Foundation and the National Endowment of the Arts, and to win the 1987 American Book Award.

With Knight came Oliver Pitcher, a Harlem Renaissance poet, and also Brooks, on a couple of occasions, to Phyllis's home. She remembered one: "We were all sitting in my living room, maybe fifteen to twenty of us, one night, and Gwendolyn was sitting in a harp-back chair that had been my father's. Somehow, she got tickled over something, reared back laughing, and broke one of the spokes in the harp-shaped chair back. We all thought the dadgummed chair should be reverenced afterward as something close to a sacred object. One of my daughters still has it, in fact, in her living room, mended, but not repaired per se. Never repaired, that would be a sacrilege!"[7] Some of these poets and others contributed to a short anthology published by St. Luke's Press in 1979, *The Good People of Gomorrah: A Memphis Miscellany*, edited by poet and teacher of poetry Gordon Osing. Many of Phyllis's own poetry readings in schools, at Union University, and elsewhere throughout the state, were done in part to promote this book.

The editor's preface to *Gomorrah* begins with this paragraph, which is the only explanation in the book for the title. It is written as prose, although it could just as easily have been verse. Authored by Osing, edited by Phyllis, it is fair to say that it approximates closely to her attitude toward organized religion at this time:

> In that Gomorrah of the mind, that lives on, poesy, spirits, privacy, and other delightful offenses of the past have long since given way to various clean, well-lighted public religions, chiefly those of the social order that surrounds us, and the air above the boudoir-and-dining room town is filled mainly with sunshine and damp weather these days. Darkness drifts out from under the cooling leaves.[8]

These were days for her when literature, art, and beauty had a purity that religion and every other aspect of the approved social order, easily explained by sociology (or corruption—this was post-Watergate), could not match for holiness.

6

Phyllis's poem "On a Sunday Morning in the Spring" first appeared in *Gomorrah*. It is deeply sexual, and hints, like St. Augustine, at the sin in sex's pleasure.

> Your father laid you into me with pain—
> I still can hear the groan he gave;
> But those low moans I made
> Before I gave you back to him? . . .
> From a joy so like his pain
> That I am ashamed
> When I remember now.[9]

Not only in poems did Phyllis write fondly of sex. Her essays from the middle 1970s show an attentiveness to the pleasures of the body. Witness this example on the subject—of all things—of harvesting okra ("the most sensual of plants"): "The stalks snap and bleed their milk as I gather the thrusting, penile pods and then yank from below the wound the leaf that has borne the pod in its upward thrust. The okra is womanlike in its need to be hurt, and only in its bleeding will it come to bear again for me."[10]

CHAPTER 9

Moving to Lucy

Eldest daughter Nora married at the age of eighteen, in May 1976, in part because she was anxious to leave home. Her father's depression and outbursts made life difficult for a teenager. That fall, Phyllis and Sam began to talk about a desire to leave Memphis, to leave city for country. They were both from the mountains and if they couldn't have that again they at least wanted a bit of open space, some land.

The despair of Vietnam and Watergate were still fresh and they talked about worries for the future. Moving to the country, and learning the rhythms of the land, would, quite literally, teach them again to feed themselves. The children needed to know, Phyllis thought, how a handful of seeds could grow to feed many people. They should understand how steaks start out on the hoof. This was the libertarian in her: wanting as little to do with the government as possible. The otherwise urbane professor, poet, and publisher rested easier in the knowledge that on a remote piece of land they would have guns and privacy and would provide as much as possible for themselves. The Tickle kids who remained at home would learn self-reliance.

This rebelliousness comes through clearly in the opening paragraphs of her essay "To My Pear Trees," about a time when the city forced those living in Lucy to accept piped-in city water:

> After my bath I stay long in the tub, listening to the soft, cotton suck of the water as it circles the drain. I lie through that instant of near bursting when my bones take up the weight of my flesh again from the retreating water. I feel the vacuum as it pulls my back hard against the porcelain bottom and as flat as if I were young again. My skin and hair release the water, droplet by droplet, to the gravity of air and drain, and I live briefly in the slow effervescence of their drying.

Even when it's finally gone, this will still be my water. It will come back again to me, to my body, to our house. It leaves now in copper pipes which run off into cool clay ones which, in turn, drain just beyond the orchard fence into the gravel overrun where, purified, it sinks slowly under the roots of grass, trees, and vines. Some spring soon it will flower or make milk for a new calf; some fall soon it will drop from the juice of our pears or fatten a steer for market. This water leaves us only for a few seasons.[1]

2

Perhaps the change of scenery would also bring some hope back into their troubled marriage. Phyllis was desperate to find ways to make Sam happy, or satisfied. Soon, they found twenty acres owned by a Memphis restaurateur that needed tending. The place didn't seem like much at first—a ranch house far from town on a narrow winding road—but they were soon able to turn it into the "Farm in Lucy."

The house on Harbert had to be staged in order to be sold. Three elementary age school kids and two teenagers had been making messes there for years and the place was a wreck. Such stressful moments were the rare occasions when the kids would witness anger, not a commonly expressed emotion, in their mother. She would either fill her large frame with air and use what they came to know as her "stage voice" to vent, or, much worse, she would become quietly furious. At those times, she could knock a kid over with her earnest whisper of dissatisfaction.

Phyllis's emotions aside, it was known to all who loved the Tickle family that Sam was not a man with deep emotional intelligence. He came to the marriage having been raised by a dominant mother, and his relationship with Phyllis was never easy. They were clearly in love in the early years, but he had never been quite the same since moving from Pelzer back to Memphis; he lost a measure of his confidence, it seemed, which Wade's death made even worse. In fact, Nora had a quiet understanding with her mother, when she married at such a young age, that one of the benefits would be getting away from Daddy. His pathos, rantings, and insecurities had worn her thin.

After closing on the Memphis house and before moving to Lucy, they had some dirty work to do: thousands of cockroaches, leftovers from the drippings of the work of the restaurateur, had to be eradicated at the farm. Always one to take a scientific approach to problems, Sam purchased spiders from a friend and let them loose in and around the house and its out-buildings. The spiders devoured the eggs of the nasty bugs in short order.

In Lucy, there was no end to what needed cleaning and fixing—but everyone joined in. The boys, John and Sam Jr., especially loved the work and the farm. They enjoyed discovering its hidden treasures, exploring its many acres, and returning to the house covered in dirt in a way that city kids can't appreciate. They were also given responsibilities and chores early on; this was part of the plan that Phyllis and Sam had for the place, to teach the kids how to tend things. Soon there was a working barn, cows, and a hen house. Rebecca was just two and a half and shy, but she too seemed to thrive on the farm, even if at first she stuck closely to her parents' legs.

To Phyllis, the farm became her grounding. It was a firm place to stand upon—a feeling that she had never had as an adult in any other place. The affinity she developed for those acres came through clearly in her writing. The farm became, not just her inspiration, but the primary subject of her oeuvre. It became for her what a farm near Port Royal, Kentucky, was becoming at the same time for a young Wendell Berry. Phyllis began to write about her land in ways similar to how Berry wrote about his, and not unlike how one of her favorite contemporary writers, George Scarbrough, was writing about his mountains in Tennessee. After a day's work in the city, Phyllis would go home to Lucy, find her folding chair under the walnut trees on the hill above the pond, and with pen in hand, write essays and poems among the cows. "I was so used to my cows coming like pets every time I clanged the pasture gate and to having them nuzzle (even the horned ones)," she told a friend.[2]

She wrote poems constantly, and carried poems around with her. The children knew their mother as a poet, first and foremost. So when the kids in Rebecca's kindergarten class were invited to dress up for career day, Rebecca put on what looked like a house dress and went as a poet herself. (Rebecca also grew up surrounded by paintings and painting supplies, at the Memphis Academy, and eventually became an accomplished oil painter.) The poems Phyllis wrote in the late 1970s emphasize fierce attention to land, and human disconnection from it. "Ordinary Song" is testimony to this: "I learned by heart the ancient sounds / of bird and pine, of stream and fawn, / waiting to hear spring waters clear / below the stones they played upon, / the litany of earth." The farm was a place that put life into perspective. Phyllis would talk about it in her writing and in interviews for the next four decades. Only by living close to the rhythms, limits, power, and verdancy of the land can one understand the powerlessness we truly have over our lives, she believed.

3

She loved to walk at twilight in her fields, while Sam liked to cultivate large gardens for vegetables to go on the dinner table. Together, they kept finding ways to teach the kids how things work.

Sometimes it was Sam demonstrating how to remove the bladder from a cow. The slaughtering of cows was a part of their annual fall ritual. Phyllis wanted the kids to know that death was a natural, essential part of life. She'd rather they connect viscerally to death and its natural processes in the face of an animal (even a cow that they had named and cared for), than the gun violence and car crashes that were part of common life in Memphis. She would write about the children playing with a steer bladder in one of her most memorable essays, "The Day of Slaughter." The scene might remind some of similar passages in Laura Ingalls Wilder:

> The next hour was punctuated by John's enthusiastic messages from the back door, messages that always began, "Mom! Mom!" until I could get to the back door to receive the latest piece of intelligence.
>
> "Mom, did you know Oscar made this big, huge cloud of steam when Dad cut him open?"
>
> "Yes, son, I knew that."[3]

And then, a sort of summary: "The boys, during those years, took turns over who got the horns and who got the hooves, but Becca always ended up with the bladder."

Both the essay, and the reality of the doing of the thing, disgusted some of her city friends. Her "urban essays" were rapidly being replaced by rural ones. Other aspects of rural living were fine for those friends, such as Sam's desire to teach the boys to take trash in the truck to the town dump rather than have a service take it away, but there were those who wanted nothing to do with the side of her life that seemed easy with death. In another essay she wrote about raising turkeys and naming them Christmas and Thanksgiving. "The children raised them as pets with a certain ferocious sadism [parentally indulged, presumably], since there was no question in anybody's mind each year about where the two were to end up."[4]

It was also during these years that Phyllis began to understand poetry differently, and began to disdain some poets for a lack of realism. The later Wordsworth, for instance, she found devoid of the grit of real life. Wordsworth was a constant reviser of his own work, and as his Christian commitments grew later in life, his poems became tame. Phyllis read this as inauthenticity. She also disdained bourgeois culture, agreeing with Ortega, whom she read avidly at Furman: "For what was the theme of poetry in the romantic century? The poet informed us prettily of his private upper-middle-class emotions."[5] Such judgments created small but significant distances between Phyllis and some of her writer friends.

She *was* easy with death—even human death. Much later, in *Prayer Is a Place*, remembering those days on the farm, she tossed off the line, "We buried the calves that didn't make it and shot the coyotes and wolves that wanted to strike those that did."[6] One had to realize that she was cavalier about death, in general; this would include, eventually, even her own. But it made people uncomfortable. For example, at a time when the debate about abortion was at its highest pitch in America, in a book published on that subject, she wrote this about her miscarriages. Many read it as callous, but to her it demonstrated true feeling: "Most of them were lost to me in a flood of waste and blood when they were half way toward safety. They were lost as children whose sex and shape I could plainly see as they floated away from me in the commode where I had to flush them or the old newspapers in which my hands had to wrap them, for in the 1960s and 70s they were children only to me."[7]

Rural, country living informed not just the poetry and the essays, but even her insights into liturgy. She wrote a decade before *The Divine Hours* was ever conceived: "[I]t is Lent once again, and for one more snow I can luxuriate in the isolation of the cold, attend laconically to who I am, what I value, and why I'm here. Religion has always kept earth time. Liturgy only gives sanction to what the heart already knows."[8] Her childhood in the mountains and her life on the farm both gave her an understanding of the liturgy and the Psalms and how they are meant to bridge earth and heaven. As St. Jerome once said: "These are the songs of the country; these, in popular phrase, its love ditties: these the shepherd whistles; these the tiller uses to aid his toil."[9]

4

Deep pleasures for her on the farm included killing snakes, planting lettuce, and singing in the yard. One of her favorite tunes from those days was Three Dog Night's "Joy to the World" with the opening line, "Jeremiah was a bullfrog!" One of her children remembers: "This was all before she settled down into being a writer instead of a poet. She still had idealistic hopes about the world and the farm life and all those things. She picked peaches and green beans."[10]

But one day while walking in the tall grass, Phyllis was bitten by a tick carrying Lyme disease. Neither she nor her physicians ever knew precisely when or even where on her body the bite occurred. It was likely in the summer of 1986, and was accompanied by symptoms that were misunderstood at the time. Not until two years later was she suddenly rushed to the intensive care unit of the local hospital with an arrhythmia—and then, they had no idea why it was happening. It would then be several more years before she came to understand that she was suffering from Lyme disease.

In the summer of 1994 she was again hospitalized for a week, after collapsing in the driveway in Lucy, sending a plea to Sam's beeper, and being rushed to the emergency room. More tests were run and it was finally determined that, for nearly a decade, she'd been suffering from the effects of the disease. Her doctors told her, then, to treat it prophylactically with twelve hours each day of rest. This became as religiously observed for her as her observing of the divine hours.

At this time, too, Phyllis was of a larger physical size, in a way that would surprise those who only knew her from her *Publishers Weekly* career and the years immediately following, when she was always lean. Toward the end of her child-bearing years she reached a size twenty. Her six feet in height and relatively ample middle combined with her always large personality to make a woman that was, to many, unforgettable. She was sometimes seen as a sort of earth mother, without the hippie trappings.

She never stopped mothering, despite joking that she had little interest in young children. And before long—just a year after they moved to the farm—Nora gave birth to a son, Phyllis and Sam's first grandchild. He was only three and a half years younger than Rebecca, their youngest child, so he was often piled into the back of the car along with his uncles and aunt (and usually his mother). His experiences of Phyllis wouldn't be so much as of a grandmother, as of a mother.

5

Phyllis and Sam were not particularly social. They were friendly and knew many people but seldom had more than one or two friends over to the house at a time. Rarely did they attend large social gatherings, but rather, stuck to the homes of intimate friends. However, throughout the 1980s Phyllis and Sam threw tremendous parties for their writer friends at the Farm in Lucy. As one of their kids remembers it, "Once a year we had the whole thinking part of Memphis suddenly show up in our backyard for smoked chicken and alcohol."[11]

Each kid would be put to work for days of preparations, beginning with one of them handwriting postcards to the invited guests a month before. One of these read:

A backyard supper at the Lucy Goosey Farm
Date: June 23, 1985
Time: 5:30 p.m.
RSVP
Sam & Phyllis Tickle

They had a large smokehouse on the farm, built by the previous owner, that Memphis restaurateur. Sam began using it to cook turkeys for Thanksgiving. Then, he smoked the occasional side of venison—usually gifted to him in exchange for a house call. He would smoke the whole thing and then pack the two sides of ribs in large garbage bags, explaining to the children that smoked meat needn't be refrigerated, tucking them instead into a bottom kitchen cabinet. There, the children would sneak and steal a rib here and there over the course of the following weeks, carefully tucking the bag back in its place, and their father would pretend not to notice.

Preparing the smokehouse for a Lucy Goosey summer party became serious business. The smoking was an eighteen-hour process. Sam would bring home waxed cardboard boxes full of chickens—as many as one hundred birds—from a local butcher. John and Sam Jr. were taught to stoke and baste. They would begin their work in the morning and then stay up all night messing with the fire and occasionally brushing the meat with oil that was mopped on with a tube sock tied to the end of a stick. (Their father was never one to purchase unnecessary tools or forego home remedies.)

For several days before the smokehouse was fired up, Phyllis and the girls were working in the house making pasta salad, and baking brownies and sugar cookies. Both refrigerators and the freezer were full of food. Ice chests were packed. The girls thought it ridiculous how small their mother asked them to cut up the brownies, since no one but Louise Collier (a beautiful, genteel, Southern author of theirs) would naturally take such small, stamp-sized bites.

The morning of the party, the boys would go with Sam to pick up tables and chairs in the pick-up truck. In the early years they borrowed these from their church, but by the mid-eighties they had to rent them because the crowd of party-goers had grown so large. Fruit was cut up and put into piles on platters, sodas were loaded into a kiddie pool full of ice, roasted nuts and cold salads were put out on serving tables. Sam put out the liquor, including plenty of Jack Daniels, jugs of Rossi wine, and Old Kentucky Colonel vodka, most of which had been purchased *en masse* at the PX of a local Navy base, thanks to the hospitality of an old veteran friend.

During the party, the kids acted as car valets, servers, gophers, and answerers of all sorts of questions, such as the perennial, *Where is there a bathroom I may use?* They cleaned up and changed their clothes quickly just before the guests began to arrive. Then they were on duty until late into the evening when they, too, could feast. This was the highlight of their summer. They would gossip about who had come, who was doing what, which writers were obviously Yankees and which ones were not. Some famous writers got drunk on the lawn. Occasionally, someone fell out of a chair. The novelist John Fergus Ryan impressed everyone one year when he pulled up in a beautifully restored Volkswagen Karmann Ghia coupe. The vibe was electric, exciting. "It was bizarre to see my parish priest chatting with this or that poet who I only knew from his name on the cover of a book and one of our country neighbors joining in," remembers Sam Jr. from when he was a boy of eleven.

6

St. Luke's Press was doing well. Phyllis's only real frustration was the lack of national (Northern) attention for Southern publishing. As she explained, "[T]here is an abiding prejudice which questions, not Southern literature, which the nation adores as bizarre if nothing else, but Southern publishing, which the nation regards as a learned profession unlikely to be well-practiced in the land of reddened necks and mud-clotted fingernails."[12] And yet, she believed that Southern writers possessed certain things that the broader culture needed, namely, "earlier American virtues of love of the land, love of family, love of the dark. . . . [W]e bring to contemporary American taste the literature which still contains naturally those elements of value-system," she explained to an audience in Mississippi at the Southern Literary Festival.[13] Her session was titled, "Deep South vs. New York—A Literary Relation."

St. Luke's and all of Tickle Publishing Group were sold in 1988 to Peachtree Publishers in Atlanta. Phyllis tells the story with characteristic élan in the second volume of her autobiography, *Prayer Is a Place*, but the way she tells it is not entirely accurate. She makes it sound as if, on a whim one day, she offered the company to Peachtree publisher Wayne Elliot in the midst of a telephone call about other business. The truth is that Phyllis and Sam had been talking about possibly selling for months. Also, Peachtree was a calculated match, and the value of the Tickle Group was at its highest point, a reality made visible in the publishing business in the final quarter of the previous year when a St. Luke's book, *The Lost First Edition of Upton Sinclair's The Jungle*, was featured in the arts section of the *New York Times*. But Phyllis has it all happening in about sixty seconds in the family kitchen, with her suggesting the sale ("I heard myself saying, 'do you want to buy a publishing house'") without any premeditation, and nothing more than a nod from Sam, cooking spatula in hand, as agreement.[14]

This says something important about how Phyllis thought and lived: She saw her life as magical. Stories such as these occur frequently in her books—again, for instance, several pages later in *Prayer Is a Place*, when she tells how she came to found the religion department at *Publishers Weekly*. What could be a careful narrative is instead a story told like the Gospel of Mark, the gospel writer who uses the word "suddenly" so often. *Suddenly*, Jesus appeared before them. *Suddenly*, Phyllis found herself on a plane to New York. And *suddenly*, she was being offered a job, accepting it, and founding a religion department at her industry's premier trade magazine. One of her closest friends offers this explanation, which is probably better than any other: "Mystics don't have measured, balanced, not-overboard experience. It's in the nature of the mystic to perceive things as *big* and expansive and *wow*."[15]

7

Just before St. Luke's was sold to Peachtree, Phyllis and Sam were approached by Shelby Foote and Cybill Shepherd, two of Memphis's most famous residents, who had an idea. Shepherd, the actress, after a start in *The Last Picture Show*, came to fame in the controversial hit *Taxi Driver* with Robert De Niro. Now she was experiencing her greatest commercial success playing the smoldering Maddie Hayes in the television hit *Moonlighting* (1985–89). She'd purchased the film rights to Foote's 1977 novel, *September September*, about Memphis in racial turmoil in September 1957, and it was being scripted for the big screen. She was to be the on-screen star. She was also its co-executive producer and was co-writing the script with Larry McMurtry and Susan Rhinehart. Shepherd sought financial backing for the film, believing that it could be raised through the sale of a tie-in book. Phyllis and Sam never understood how this could work, and of course, according to publishing logic, it couldn't: Books don't pay for movies, but movies can make hits out of books. So the deal never happened and "Memphis" ended up premiering on the TNT cable network. The much deeper pockets of Ted Turner provided the capital that the project required.

Phyllis had known Shelby Foote for years. One of his daughters was a student under Phyllis when she was dean of the Memphis Academy. They also saw each other on Memphis literary social occasions, although they were never exactly neighbors. Throughout the 1960s and '70s, Foote lived on the northern edge of town, eight miles south of Lucy on the Raleigh Millington Road. Phyllis and Sam then lived in midtown. When they moved to Lucy, Foote and his family moved into town, just off Central Avenue. She would include his humorous short story "A Marriage Portion" in her 1996 anthology, *Homeworks: A Book of Tennessee Writers*, along with short pieces by other Tennessee greats Will Campbell, John Fergus Ryan, John Egerton, Nikki Giovanni, Steve Womack, Tom T. Hall, Coleman Barks, Charles Wright, and Jerome Wilson. That book even included a piece by Lamar Alexander, the former Tennessee governor who was then running for the Republican nomination for U.S. president. New authors Ann Patchett and Abraham Varghese, both of whom would later outsell all the others, were there as well.

Then there were the annual Southern Festival of Books gatherings of publishers, writers, and booksellers. In 1989, when Phyllis was the editor-in-chief of Iris Press, by then an imprint of Peachtree, she was proud to present *Invitation to Kim*, a new book of poems by George A. Scarbrough, whose *New and Selected Poems*, published by Iris in 1977, had been the small literary press's first breakout title. St. Luke's purchased Iris in 1980 and nurtured it and its authors carefully for years, before selling it, together with all of the other Tickle, Inc. publishing assets, to Peachtree. Scarbrough's *Invitation to Kim* was nominated for a Pulitzer Prize the following year.

When the Wimmer Group of Memphis then purchased the various Tickle publishing enterprises in 1990 from Peachtree, they kept Phyllis on, almost obligatorily, as "Director Emerita, Trade Publishing." But she wouldn't stay long.

CHAPTER 10

When Daisy Called

n the spring of 1992, Phyllis woke up one night to go to the bathroom. She stepped awkwardly in the darkness and hurt her right foot. But she was tired. She got back into bed and went back to sleep. The following morning, she couldn't put pressure on it at all, and so went for an x-ray. The foot was broken and was cast in a medical fracture boot. A few days later, she was expected at one of the South's most important independent bookstores, Mary Gay Shipley's That Bookstore in Blytheville, Arkansas, for a book-signing. John Grisham had just done a signing there for *The Firm*. This was not a store to cancel on—but Phyllis couldn't drive with that boot. The job fell to Rebecca, then seventeen.

A year earlier, Phyllis had retired from publishing and was busy re-emerging as a writer. The financial management aspects of running St. Luke's had drained her, and sapped some of her creativity. Even so, when she took stock of her writing over two decades, it was impressive: projects for St. Luke's, chancel dramas, personal essays in Memphis publications, and poems in poetry journals. Most recently, even before the sale of St. Luke's to Peachtree, she had published a trilogy of books telling humorous, heart-warming stories of family and farm life, organized around seasons of the liturgical year. A long letter composed on her new word processor ("I can't type . . . literally can't . . . [so this] is a god-send") to the head of marketing at The Upper Room, her publisher, apologized: "Poets, as you know, have a very limited general or popular audience or following. As a result, I come to you bringing little cross-over between what I have done in the past and what I am now doing." But she adds, "I have written rather broadly within the Episcopal community in the essay and liturgical genres."[1] This is why the last sentence of her biography on the back flap of these three books—*What the Heart Already Knows*, *Final Sanity*, and *Ordinary Time*, from 1985 to 1988—read "Ms. Tickle is an active layperson in the Episcopal church and is a frequent contributor to church publications." By "church publications," they meant *The Episcopalian*, *The Tennessee Churchman*, and *The Church News*, a publication of the Memphis diocese; Phyllis even sat on their editorial board. Soon, she was also writing book reviews for John Mogabgab, the editor of *Weavings*, The Upper Room's new "Journal of the Christian Spiritual Life."

Then she came to the attention of the United Methodist Publishing House, the largest of the Protestant denominational publishing houses. Their editorial director, Ron Patterson, asked his young, Episcopal trade editor, Michael Lawrence, to get in touch with Phyllis. She mailed him some short pieces, some of which had appeared in her *Dixie Flyer* column, and they arranged to meet at the UMPH downtown Nashville offices a few months later.

At the meeting, Phyllis pitched the idea of a book of essays about raising a large family with a mixture of rural and Christian values. She told Lawrence about the farm, their life, the animals, and how she and Sam tried to instill neighborliness and self-sufficiency in their kids. The result was *The Tickle Papers*. The title was Lawrence's idea but Phyllis loved it immediately. She and Sam had only two children left at home by the time the book was published, but the stories she told took the reader back a decade. The book packaged its author as a religiously-inspired Erma Bombeck: "[S]ometimes hilarious, sometimes richly inspiring escapades," advertised the dust jacket. A painting was commissioned for the front cover to appeal to the same audience that had recently devoured books like Jean Kerr's *Please Don't Eat the Daisies*. It shows Phyllis with pencil and paper in the middle of a scrum of seven children, four girls and three boys, arguing, playing ball: hectic family life. Phyllis always spoke of being the mother of seven children, as if in the present tense. A family tree that's drawn inside the book then indicates each child's birth year without any indication that Philip Wade didn't make it out of infancy.[2]

One other oddity about the book is in that same cover art: Sam, the father, is missing. That was an unintentional mistake. When Lawrence received the painting back from the artist, he shared it around the office with jubilation. It had taken some cash, uncommonly spent by a smaller press. They planned on advertising the book on the cover of *Publishers Weekly*. But then a feeling of horror waved over him. There was Phyllis in the center, and seven kids, but no Sam. He phoned her to explain the oversight and to beg her forgiveness, because they also had run out of time and money to redo the art or even to go back to the artist to try and fix it. "Don't worry about it," she said.

2

There were other writing projects, as well. Phyllis loved historical mysteries all her life, often reading one before bedtime. With time on her hands, she began to imagine writing a series of mysteries herself. In appreciation of Father Brown, she dreamed up an Episcopal canon missioner who solves crimes and named her character the Reverend Adam Wahl. Her book proposal was quickly snatched up by Michelle Rapkin at Bantam for a $5,000 advance. However, by the time Phyllis wrote and submitted the first book in the series nine months later, she knew that it was no good. "It got more complicated and convoluted the more that I fiddled with it," she later recalled. "It became clear that I wasn't a writer of fiction." After about four rounds of edits and attempted rewrites, the book was going nowhere; in fact, it was getting worse. "Just keep the advance," Rapkin finally told her. "You've earned it!"[3]

The better part of two years of creative energy were taken up with the writing of the never-to-happen novels. Some in her family believed that she was floundering. Also, her need to earn real income was becoming more acute. Sam's behavior was becoming more unpredictable and he was seeing fewer patients, while spending more money. There was always a new project, or a new cause. Only a decade later, when Sam was first diagnosed with early dementia, did the family begin to look seriously at what he had spent in those years—and what Phyllis had assumed they still had, they didn't.

It was at just about that time, as the novel-writing was tossed forever into a bottom drawer, that Phyllis caught the attention of *Publishers Weekly*. Her reputation as a writer and publisher were clear. And Robin Mays, who worked with Southern publishers for the trade journal, knew of Phyllis's strong credentials in religion. "We think you might know something about God," Daisy Maryles said to her on the phone in the fall of 1992, when first calling to gauge Phyllis's interest level in starting a religion department at *PW*.

3

Long before that conversation, the market for spirituality had been growing. Phyllis liked to say during her *PW* tenure that the crossover, general market appeal religion bestseller was born in the early 1990s. But that just isn't so. The "Death of God" movement of the 1960s had shocked the institutional church to its core and produced both bestselling books and famous authors. Harvard professor Harvey Cox published his seminal, youthful work, *The Secular City*, in 1965 (more than one million sold), chronicling the ways that religion had become secularized. "Is God Dead?" became a *Time* magazine cover story the following spring. Another example of the activity in religion publishing was to be seen in the body-mind-spirit market, which heated up in the 1970s, as did the success of publishers like HarperSanFrancisco and Jeremy P. Tarcher, who branded themselves by tapping into "perennial spirituality" over against what was then the staid publishing of religion by denominational and religion-specific houses.[4]

Also notable, evangelical layman Ken Taylor's paraphrase of the Bible, published as *The Living Bible*, was the bestselling book of 1972, and not just in the religion category. Evangelist Billy Graham's *Angels* held the same honor three years later. But Phyllis was right that the 1990s quickly shaped up to become something even bigger.

Publishers Weekly had had religion reporters and contributing editors in religion before Phyllis, including William Griffin in the 1980s. A former senior editor at Macmillan and biographer of C.S. Lewis, Griffin was a talented writer and editor, but he wasn't judged to be the right person to start a new department. Maryles knew Phyllis from editing the "My Say" column for the trade magazine, to which Phyllis had contributed—and then Robin Mays, their southern sales manager, spoke up on Phyllis's behalf.[5] So, first came that phone call from Maryles to Phyllis: "We think you might know something about God."

Next, on October 5, Phyllis was writing to Daisy, "Robin Mays called this morning with the delicious news that you wanted to see some of my review work," eventually concluding, "I hope this goes somewhere, and that somewhere will turn out to be adventuresome and feisty as well as substantial, but who knows?"

4

Daisy told Phyllis that she would have the freedom to build a team, and to travel, meeting with publishers and attending conferences and meetings where religionists, booksellers, librarians, and publishers gather. Phyllis found the opportunity irresistible. She would be the founding editor of the religion department. Even so, when the announcement appeared in the December 14, 1992, issue, Phyllis was annoyed by its inaccuracy—which was probably a calculated oversight of Maryles designed to avoid bad feelings. Phyllis's new role was downplayed: "Phyllis Tickle has been named religious books editor at *Publishers Weekly*; former religious editor William Griffin will continue to write for the magazine on a freelance basis."[6]

Within weeks, Mays was promoted to religion marketing manager, charged with convincing publishers to support expanded coverage of the category with advertising dollars, and within the year, Phyllis had hired Lynn Garrett as the first religion correspondent. Another change to *PW*'s coverage that Phyllis wanted to make was of language: "It's not 'childish' publishing or 'fictional' publishing," she said. "By the same token, it is not 'religious' but 'religion' publishing."[7] But, just like the mistake in the December 14 announcement, she would lose this battle, too. Her pages in the magazine would be headlined "Religious Publishing," followed by "Editor: Phyllis Tickle" for a year. Ten months later, she had succeeded in fixing it to "Religion" on the contents page (occasionally), but then it became "Religious Books" heading her section inside. She fumed, but quietly. Not until January 10, 1994, was it corrected in both places. But this was small stuff compared to what she was accomplishing: increasing the magazine's coverage of religion ten-fold, as ad dollars kept step, which pleased everyone in New York.

Her first monthly column as religion editor appeared in January 1993. She laid out her mandate plainly: "As more Americans search in bookstores for the tools of their own consolation as well as for manuals of instruction, so more librarians and general trade book-sellers must meet this burgeoning national need with acumen and an uncommon sensitivity."[8] The magnetism and personality she brought to this task—to what was usually dry, trade journalism—went beyond anyone's expectations. Audiences loved her wit, humor, storytelling, and her intelligence and sincerity earned her respect in every quar-ter. Soon, she was giving keynotes at Catholic Publishers Association meetings, Evangelical Christian Publishers Association conferences, and leading discussions with Latter-day Saints, Christian Science, Jew-ish, Muslim, and New Age leaders. Within a year, she was asked to sit on boards of libraries, publishing companies, and websites devoted to these audiences.

5

Her coverage of religion in the magazine was wide-ranging, thought-ful, critical, and enthusiastic. For wide-ranging, she brought small press religion publishing to a national stage in a way that it never had been before. For instance, in an article on new biographies of female reli-gious leaders, she placed a small publisher like the United Church of Christ's Pilgrim Press on an even footing with big trade houses, such as Hyperion and Tarcher. A month later, while surveying important new titles about evangelical and fundamentalist Protestantism, her range included university presses, denominational publishers, evangelical houses, and a conservative think tank whose publications were never, at that time, stocked in bookstores or purchased by public libraries.[9]

She brought advocacy journalism to her reporting. She was never content to simply relay facts, sometimes frustrating her journalist bosses. Within that story about books on female religious figures, for instance, she added a sidebar to highlight an in-house women's advo-cacy group recently started by one of the large evangelical publishers. There were also times when she failed to write as a journalist, and the literary essayist shone through. This also frustrated her bosses, but it delighted her readers as unusual and fresh. In her first year she titled an article on new books coinciding with the Parliament of the World's Religions meeting in Chicago "Heralding a Book Harvest," and wrapped it up like the poet on the Farm in Lucy:

> Fall in any year, even in one far less portentous than this one, is harvest time, proof of the spring and summer that have preceded it. But in matters of religion, a good harvest can sometimes be more; it can be the substance and the vision that make a fertile season of winter. This 1993 Fall Religion Issue, like the events that are contemporary with it, is about such a harvest; it heralds such a winter.[10]

At times she could be critical, even unreasonably so. There was the book review, for instance, in which she challenged a swami's interpretation of Hinduism, saying: "[T]he idea that Hinduism has four main denominations . . . makes Hinduism appear to be parallel to the schismatic Christian tradition, a flawed analogue." And then there was the occasion when she accused a prominent evangelical author of taking too narrow a view of the issues, and of sermonizing. Those, of course, had long been hallmarks of bestselling evangelical books. Or, the time when she reviewed a Norman Vincent Peale book and concluded: "[F]ans will find a continuation of his principles and personal beliefs here. Others may feel that there is more exegesis than good scholarship, and may sense some overkill on the anecdotes."[11] One could reasonably counter: That is precisely what an avid reader of Norman Vincent Peale expects in one of his books! But there was an agenda at work in Phyllis's coverage: She was asking religion publishers to move out of their niches and reach for the wider readership she was detecting was interested. She wanted everyone to raise their game, so to speak, in order to match the special moment they had been given.

This prodding extended to areas beyond content, as well. In her first year, she praised a book but lamented its shortcomings: "[Gerald] Mann has much to offer hurting people, but sadly, his wisdom is obscured by poor editing and design contrivances, forcing the reader to dig for the riches."[12] In a talk given at the American Booksellers Association's annual conference in the summer of 1993, she emphasized a similar point, saying that religion publishing was "a holy trafficking in humanity's most honored mode of communication," and as such, "Until the product is aesthetically, intellectually, and professionally true to the standards of its format, its contents will forever be restricted." Publishers began to respond. Many would call her, asking, what would you have us do to publish better? She was soon busier than she ever imagined she could be. And she continued to write and speak to publishers, regardless of their niche orientations, as if to one large community with shared intentions.

Most interesting to those who are already familiar with the books that Phyllis would write and compile after these first few years at *PW*, it is possible, occasionally, to see how her perspective on certain matters—important to her later work—changed over time. For example, on a single page of the magazine from late 1993, one finds her referring to an Episcopal priest from Queens as an "Anglican"; the Book of Common Prayer also as "Anglican"; and she writes in a review of a prayer book, "it may be easier for readers with a Catholic background to understand what some of the terms ('divine office' etc.) mean"![13]

6

Soon, Michael Leach of Crossroad Publishing in New York was calling Phyllis to ask her to apply her critical assessment of the religion marketplace into a book. Leach realized that a book by Phyllis might bring her analysis of burgeoning faith in America beyond the audiences of publishing pros and religion journalists. *Re-Discovering the Sacred* was published by Crossroad in 1993, and *God-Talk in America* followed four years later. In both books, Phyllis looks carefully and entertainingly at how religion is being expressed in the culture, from movies to commercials to novels. Both books reminded her that she was a writer, first and foremost, and prompted her to try to quit her job at *PW*, or at least, take a step back. (In his fax, asking her to write the second one, Leach concluded, knowing her well, "Sorry to stir your adrenalin again, but that's my job. And all of us are deeply in love with your adrenalin."[14] Only five days later, Phyllis faxed him back a complete, annotated table of contents.)

She had other motivations for wanting to leave, as well: She was never entirely comfortable as a journalist. Daisy Maryles once complained, when Phyllis sent in copy, "God deliver me from ever having another writer on staff!" And Maryles was always trying to get Phyllis to simply tell readers what happened, rather than why it happened, or what it might mean for the future.[15] Phyllis felt called to speak to the church, more than to an industry. But on this particular occasion, when she suggested after her first two years on the job that perhaps her work was done, Maryles convinced her to stay. But Maryles accepted that Phyllis would become *contributing editor* in religion, allowing Garrett to take her place as editor.

7

Ever since they were married in the Presbyterian Church, and spent their first decade together somewhat out of sorts in Calvinism, Sam had become uneasy with religion entirely. Faith in the Tickle home took on a variety of expressions, but Sam was rarely comfortable in it. Phyllis remembers, "After we married, we would find a congregation whose theology and ecclesiology pleased him, join it, settle in happily, and then within a couple of years, there would be some kind of rupture or blow-up that made him want to move on to some other parish. . . . [W]e left a trail of 'former congregations' behind us, much to my discomfort."[16] This made her work at *PW* sometimes awkward.

By the late 1990s, Sam seemed to be uncomfortable to a new degree and it was not entirely clear what that was. He may have been uncomfortable with his wife's increasing fame as an expert in the field. He seemed to resent the impression that he was a successful author's helpmeet and began acting out to differentiate himself. Comments at public events and contrariness in e-mails to Phyllis's colleagues became embarrassingly common. Phyllis was often on the road, which, everyone agreed, often made many things easier. And as much as she enjoyed rural life, there was no question that she was energized also by leaving for New York. Even before *PW*, travel had become for Phyllis a creative, anticipated pleasure. Throughout the late 1980s, for instance, the only man whom she'd allow to cut her hair had his salon in Nashville.

The kids—who were then Rebecca, Sam Jr., and John—seemed to grasp that their mother needed times away, and so did Sam, who didn't necessarily fully understand, but also didn't entirely mind.

Every partner has aspects of life that are more comfortable when his spouse is not within earshot. Sam, for instance, came to think that he was the better cook, and he enjoyed having the kitchen all to himself. Phyllis's mother had been the daughter of a hotelier, raised with a French cooking influence that she passed on to her daughter. Phyllis's braised carrots and turnips didn't interest Sam, who grew up with Appalachian foodways, and when World War II took the men away and his mother went back to working in an office, it was Sam who prepped dinner for the family. He knew what he was doing in the kitchen and was proud of it, taking the opportunity when Phyllis was away to make things like extra sweet tea and food that his wife didn't always appreciate, such as catfish chowder or homemade fudge. He would occasionally bring Popeye's chicken home. The kids enjoyed these things, too, getting to know each parent on her or his own terms. They even speculated with each other that if mom were able to earn enough on her own, they might divorce or separate, although they also knew that their mother believed divorce was not an option for a Christian.

This was also when their parenting time was winding down. Only Rebecca remained to be cared for in a meaningful way. At the end of her sixth-grade year, greater Memphis stopped bussing students long distances, which required Sam and Phyllis to find a new school for her the following year. She landed in an over-crowded school at the beginning of seventh grade. When that shock sent the girl into a tailspin, they pulled her from it and decided to drive her each morning into midtown Memphis to attend a small, private school. The academic rigor of it was tough for the adolescent, but so was the fact that both parents were often unable to pick her up on time when school was over. She would wait usually until her father had a chance to come get her, sometimes not until five o'clock. Then, he'd often take her back to the hospital if he wasn't yet finished with work, before driving the twenty miles back home to Lucy. It sometimes felt as if both parents were at the height of their careers and neither particularly happy.

8

Phyllis made many new friends among authors and experts in religion while at *PW*, but none quite like the Episcopal bishop of Newark. Phyllis loved John Shelby Spong. Ever-controversial, he was at the height of his powers in 1993 when they met, a stunningly handsome, outgoing, aggressively affectionate, sweet-talking gentleman. The same Jack Spong who could "work a room" could also put the naturally glamorous Ms. Tickle in a good mood.

"Hello, Beautiful!" he would greet her, almost always, when calling on the phone. "Anyone who begins that way can be as wrong as rainwater and he'll still get my attention!" she used to tell him, and others.

Spong grew up in segregated Charlotte, North Carolina, and became an active Episcopalian as a teenager. By his own frequent admission, he started out with conservative, traditional views of most everything, and moved gradually to a more expansive, progressive understanding of the Christian life and faith. He was first galvanized toward social justice in the late 1950s just after the Supreme Court decided in favor of desegregation in Brown vs. The Board of Education of Topeka, Kansas. In the years after that landmark decision, the entire South was roiling, and Spong was the rector of Calvary Episcopal Church in Tarboro, a tobacco-growing town, in eastern North Carolina. It was then and there that he began to challenge his traditional views, prompted in part by the demand he felt to personally protect African American children attempting to enter a previously all-white school in town. It was years later that Phyllis and Jack first met—long after Spong served two other, larger churches, one in Lynchburg, the other in Richmond, Virginia, and after he was elected a bishop in Newark, New Jersey (1976), giving him a near-New York City platform for his increasingly radical ideas, and after his first marriage to college sweetheart, Joan Ketner, had ended. (She died in 1988, after a nearly two decades-long struggle with mental illness followed by cancer.)

It was in the mid-nineties that they debated theological ideas, always prompted by whatever Spong was arguing against from traditional Christianity in his latest book: the virgin birth, the authority of scripture, the bodily resurrection, or the divinity of Christ. Phyllis never understood why being progressive had to mean throwing out every traditional aspect of faith, and she never really approved of the ways progressives replaced one set of certainties with another.

They first met in November 1993, when she was in San Francisco at Grace Cathedral speaking at a conference also headlined by Spong. After the last session, they met for drinks at the famous Top of the Mark restaurant on the nineteenth floor of the Mark Hopkins Hotel (now the Intercontinental Mark Hopkins). The plan was to have a drink and chat before Spong's wife, Christine, joined them for dinner. So they had a drink, and then another, and then another. Apparently, Spong had told Christine that they would have a drink and then come find her for dinner, so at 8:30 p.m., when Jack and Phyllis still hadn't turned up, Christine came and found them at the bar, mucking it up on their third or fourth round. She said, "Jack, I'm going to dinner with or without you," and they all went off together. Years afterward, Christine would tease her husband and Phyllis about that incident, whenever they were together, saying, "Don't go off and start drinking, you two," and Phyllis would tell her, "There is nobody in this world I'd rather have a drink with than Jack because nobody is more fun and more in need of theological help."[17]

9

It was somewhere in the midst of conversations with Spong that Phyllis first moved out of a modernist theological position, into a postmodern one. Before *PW*, she didn't know "postmodern"—no one did, outside the academy. For example, in a brief essay about the theological mystery of the Transfiguration, she had reflected that most Christians don't know what to make of it because it's inexplicable, and so, "I simply walk around it and go through the motions of it because I don't know what else to do with it—how to grasp it."[18] She would never say that a decade later.

On February 4, 2000, PBS's *Religion and Ethics Newsweekly* would have Phyllis as the expert in a segment that was unlike most every other on the program. She reviewed Spong's autobiography, *Here I Stand*, which had been published a couple of weeks earlier. She positioned him as the man who wants to continue the Protestant Reformation—a project that, by then, she personally deemed unnecessary and outdated. Still, by review's end she seems to advocate for, if not his method, his conclusions:

> Whether you love him or hate him, Jack Spong has written a very important new book. . . . *Here I Stand* . . . tells you a good deal not only about why he's frequently hated by his detractors, but also about where he sees himself. He sees himself in the tradition of Martin Luther, in the tradition of the Reformation, in the tradition of a theology—Christian theology—that once more has to evolve and has to make some strides forward in order to meet the new millennium. . . . [I]n *Here I Stand*, there is a clear call. . . . [H]e takes on his fellow bishops and others in hierarchical Christianity, saying the time has now come when what you say among yourselves and what you do must be one and the same. The pew and the nave must hear the same thing that you say in the academy and in the seminary, and those things must agree with what you're doing. If you're ordaining gays under 'don't ask, don't tell,' shame on you. Let's all come out and say to the people of God in the Christian tradition, this is what we understand Christian theology to be.[19]

Others critiqued Spong from the same vantage point, but less kindly, including *Newsweek*'s Kenneth Woodward: "Some of the saddest people I've come across—I think of Bishop Spong of Newark—are people who were in full flight from a fundamentalist background . . . they become fundamentalists of the left! . . . Spong, he picked up every bad idea he could like a blotter."[20] In fact, Phyllis had written Jack a congratulatory card about his book back in November; he'd replied: "An autobiography creates a sense of vulnerability and exposure. My critics have attacked my ideas vigorously over the years, but this book will enable them to attack my being. . . . Your card made the risk worthwhile. My love, Jack"[21]

In the years to come, Phyllis would become a standard bearer for a new theological outlook that redefines truth, belief, and their roles in the life of a Christian. Spong's example—and even some of that sadness that Woodward pointed to—were what turned her around. Several years later, she would privately debate with Brian McLaren on these issues, as McLaren was another whom Phyllis believed had taken up the banner of Luther that had been so stubbornly carried by Spong. On one such occasion, Phyllis told McLaren that she could say the Nicene Creed and mean every word of it. McLaren was shocked and challenged her, suggesting that she could say the Creed because she was laying a different interpretation on the words than the original drafters had in mind. She replied,

> Perhaps. But even so, does that not mean that sacred literature and even on occasion, a holy-but-less-than-sacred piece like the Nicaean are, as the Jews say of Torah, a living thing that cannot be confined to a scroll, or set of covers, in our case?[22]

CHAPTER 11

The Boom before Amazon

Phyllis didn't believe it was an exaggeration when she wrote:

> The years from 1992 to 2004 were the closing ones of a near half century in which American religion effected a reconfiguration and cultural repositioning that history will, I wager, see as having been more comparable to the upheavals of Europe during the Christian Reformation and preliminary to Counter-Reformation than to anything else. By the grace of God or, perhaps, by appointment—who knows?—I was standing on the street corner, pad and pencil in hand. . . .[1]

Yet, she wrote those words without historical distance (in the year 2004), and that time period happens to have coincided precisely with her tenure at *Publishers Weekly*.

Overblown rhetoric aside, it could be argued that before Amazon sold its first book in June 1995, two women were transforming the market for religious and spiritual books. Those women were Phyllis and Sallye Leventhal, the religion category buyer for the superstores of Barnes & Noble, Inc. Leventhal and Phyllis never met, but they were each in the right place at the right time. They were also prescient, and possessors of enthusiasm. Most importantly, they saw, before and more completely than most everyone else, that books had the power to carry religion and spirituality where churches and synagogues, priests, pastors, rabbis, and imams, no longer could. They understood something that theologian Paul Tillich had said back in 1963 (Phyllis often quoted it in lectures during those days): "Never consider the secular realm Godless just because it does not speak of God."[2] And they knew that philosopher Karl Popper was wrong when he declared, in 1989, that the ancient Greeks, by creating the first commercial books in the centuries before Christ, did away forever with their sacredness.[3]

2

The superstore became, in the early nineties, the megachurch for spiritual books. One might credit Leonard Riggio, the chairman of Barnes & Noble, rather than Sallye Leventhal, for his visionary creation, or at least his rapid duplication of these "third places." (Independent booksellers called them other, less complimentary names.) The success of Barnes & Noble's flagship store at Fifth Avenue and 18th Street, which first opened in 1932 and was acquired by Riggio in the early 1970s, led him to believe that people in other parts of the United States—in places with far less to do than in bustling Manhattan—might be attracted to a shopping experience that involved expansive inventory, readily available coffee, magazines, and comfortable armchairs. It was after adding many lucrative acquisitions to the B&N fold in the 1980s that the chairman turned his attention to creating these larger stores. At the time, he was also spurred on by the Borders brothers in Ann Arbor, Michigan, who were doing the same thing, but never had the quality and efficiency controls of B&N.

The superstore was defined as a seriously large bookstore, between 50,000 and 150,000 square feet, offering at least a hundred thousand titles. They were distinguished from big-box stores in that "big-box" usually also meant a literal box shape, strictly rectangular, and also one, single floor of cavernous shopping space, whereas many of the superstore bookstores did not fit that mold. They also were not an exclusive creation of B&N and Borders: Independently-owned superstores also flourished in the nineties, such as The Tattered Cover in Denver, Powell's in Portland, and BookPeople in Austin, Texas.

By the end of 1989, Barnes & Noble had twenty-three superstores across the U.S. By 1992, there were more than a hundred. In the 1990s, one superstore on the Upper West Side of New York once enjoyed a year with sales of more than $16 million. Most superstores were doing $3.5 million a year. By the end of 1995, B&N owned and operated 358 superstores, and by the end of 1997 the company posted annual sales of nearly $2.5 billion. This was the high point for bricks-and-mortar selling of books in America. The good independents remained strong—stronger, in fact, due to the presence of competition between B&N and

Borders, which challenged them to do a better job of representing a wide spectrum of inventory.

Almost overnight, with the creation of all of this space, the market for books was transformed. The old knock against independent booksellers was that they were idiosyncratic in their tastes, finicky about what they stocked, and notoriously averse to handling religion. It is no secret that "average" readers—and most people, studies show, are more than willing to call themselves average—were intimidated by independent booksellers. Whereas the superstores made no distinction between books worthy of inclusion and merchandising, people often had experiences of walking into an independent bookstore, inquiring after a certain book, and being told that it was not, and would never be, stocked there. In fact, before 1992, to probably nine out of ten independent booksellers, all books dealing with God or prayer or spirituality were deemed religious, and "Religious Books" were the supposed domain of evangelical bookstores—then defined as the Christian Booksellers Association. Spiritual books without the word "prayer," and often replacing "God" with "Goddess," were to be found in so-called New Age stores. People will go to *those* stores to buy those books, the independent booksellers believed.

But, of course, they were wrong, and Phyllis (and Sallye) knew it. In this way, one might say that the superstores of B&N, Borders, and Books-a-Million (predominantly in the South) literally built the market for religious and spiritual books in this country. In England, retailers have always been called stockists, which puts a fine point on the purpose of retailers in the minds of consumers: places where one can find goods that one may want to purchase. Due to the growth of superstores throughout the U.S. booksellers became effective stockists for the first time. The superstores hurt the independents, but the independents, on the whole, were not friendly to religious and spiritual books; as with other categories (e.g., science fiction) they needed the superstores to force them to see that religion and spirituality were subjects of broad and popular appeal.

In the final analysis, Len Riggio built the stores knowing that consumers would come, but it was Sallye Leventhal who stocked them with enthusiasm. Other categories had less interested managers.

Publishers often could not get the attention of many of the other buyers, but Leventhal was sensitive, attentive, and passionate about what her books—the ones in those large Religion sections—could do in the world. A graduate of evangelical Hope College in 1978, she quickly "got it," knowing how important religion and spirituality are to Americans, and how underserved they had been for so long.

3

Consider, too, the small, vital, religion trade publishing houses that were born at that time. There were dozens that started in the late 1980s and throughout the '90s. For example, Wisdom Publications decided that they would begin publishing translations of Buddhist sutras and tantras from London, England, in 1987, and then moved to Boston in late 1988. They believed that if readers had the opportunity to find such books, they might become popular. The strategy worked, in large part because of the ripe climate and the support they could count on from Leventhal and Phyllis.

From another religious perspective, Jewish Lights Publishing started in rural Vermont in 1990, and became the first publisher dedicated to popular Jewish spirituality. Before Jewish Lights, Jewish books meant resources on ritual for rabbis or the synagogue and books on history and the Holocaust for scholars and libraries. The company began simply, bringing a few Lawrence Kushner books back into print that had been dropped by the old Harper & Row. Jewish Lights had the idea to create an inspirational literature from Jewish sources "for people of all faiths, all backgrounds." They figured that Christians might even become their largest customer segment if they were given the chance to find such books in bookstores, and to hear about them in the media. They were right, and with Phyllis's support in the pages of *PW*, and Sallye's support in the stores, they flourished.

The great old dames of religion publishing had been around for a long time. Doubleday, for example—where, if your book made it into the Image paperback imprint it meant print and distribution longevity and breadth comparable to ancient Roman Caesars—was founded in 1897 by Frank Nelson Doubleday. In 1910 the company moved

1. Washington Lafayette Alexander, Phyllis's grandfather, at about the time her father was born

2. At fifteen, from her high school yearbook

3. At eighteen, in Fort Myers, Florida

4. Wedding day, June 17, 1955, Johnson City, Tennessee

5. The Young Mother, ca. 1957

6. With her father, Philip Alexander, East Tennessee State, 1958, the year he retired.

7. *Above*: Sam, Nora, Phyllis, Mary, ca. winter 1961

8. *Right*: With baby John under the portico on Harbert Ave., Memphis, August 1970

9. With teenage Nora, 1971

10. Oscar and friends, on the Farm in Lucy, mid-1970s

11. The Poet, ca. 1980

12. The Publisher (with Mary Gay Shipley, bookseller, Blytheville, Arkansas), 1986

13. The Religion Journalist, ca. 1995

14. In Johnson City receiving the Award of Honor from ETSU, 2006

15. With Fr. Martin Poole, Denver, 2013 (the author in the background)

16. The famous photo. Swapping identities with Nadia Bolz-Weber, Denver, 2013

operations to Garden City, on Long Island, where the city of New York even built the firm its own train station. Image emerged as an imprint in 1954 and was the domain of Doubleday's mostly Catholic titles. In other words, there were books on and about religion long before Leventhal and Phyllis were on the scene, but the market for them, pre-1992, was quite different.

Even a great old publisher like Harper was a part of this demarcation in the market for religious and spiritual books, pre-1992. It was in 1977 that a dozen employees moved from the New York City offices of Harper & Row and established HarperSanFrancisco (now HarperOne). In those days, their list was dominated by body-mind-spirit titles, because the "Religion" category meant evangelical Christian, and "Spiritual" meant body-mind-spirit. Authors and books that blended these and other religious categories had not yet been discovered. Throughout his life, for instance, Fulton J. Sheen published his bestsellers with such exclusively Roman Catholic publishing houses as P. J. Kenedy & Sons and Bruce Publishing Company. These books sold in the millions, but almost exclusively to Catholics. They were reviewed only in Catholic media. They were stocked and sold only in Catholic shops, next to holy cards, holy medals, and first communion dresses.

4

Upon assuming her role at *Publishers Weekly*, Phyllis began calling books in religion and spirituality "portable pastors." She saw how they were beginning to do for people what they used to have to go to church, synagogue, or zendo to obtain or realize. For example, in her first year, reviewing a new book about Jesus, she praised it, saying, "The opportunity . . . to study in private some of today's most vexing issues of dogma under the tutelage of accessible, clear scholarship . . . will be an enormous consolation to many."[4]

Her talent was the ability to prophetically see what was coming, and then explain it in attractive detail. She was a journalist, writing weekly copy, but more importantly she became a prognosticator and encourager to professionals who cared about religion: publishers, booksellers, librarians, clergy, therapists, para-church workers, and educators in congregations of all sorts. She was often referring to herself as "a student of religion commercially applied,"[5] because she knew that she was particularly gifted to accomplish that.

She began to break down the trends, interpret recent history, and predict what was coming. For example, in a talk given to the staff of a publishing house she said:

> We are probably in a time of re-formation. Don't say reformation because that's a capital R and everyone immediately brings baggage to that. But it's re-formation. . . . It's happening for a lot of reasons. And it would be simplistic to say that you could give all those reasons at one time. But if you could, there are about four things that have happened in this century that have affected religious publishing very, very deeply. . . .[6]

She was uniquely able to distill the changes being experienced into four, simply understood, reasons. The list that day began with the founding of Alcoholics Anonymous in 1937, and immediately after she said it, there were ripples of laughter, which is why she added, "I'm being dead serious. It empowered adults to talk to each other with impunity about their interior life. It made it all right to talk about what you're like inside." She would later write in *The Great Emergence*: "Not only did AA, almost by default, begin to supplant the pastoral authority of the professional clergy and open the door to spirituality in the experiencing of a nondoctrinally specific Higher Power, but it also revived the small group dynamic that would come to characterize later twentieth-century Protestantism."[7] It would be taken for granted today that the founding of AA was centrally important to the boom of spirituality that came two generations later, and yet when Phyllis started talking about it, the idea was new.

Soon after she began talking about "portable pastors," she pointed to the synchronicity between movies like *Dancing with Wolves* and *Last of the Mohicans* and the marked increase in books of Native American-inspired spirituality. Years later, she would point to the success of *The Matrix* on the big screen, and more importantly, what it meant that the movie sold more copies on DVD than any other movie had before that time. Again, there was portability. And when she began pointing to the television series *Touched by an*

Angel, encouraging audiences to pay attention to a growing interest in angels, publishers often snickered, but soon the trickle of angel books become a stream and she was reviewing them in her monthly "Religion in Review" column.

She also noted how awash the country was in a pseudo- or quasi- or neo-medievalism that was presenting itself not only as *Star Trek*, *Star Wars*, and *Lord of the Rings*, but in Mel Gibson's *The Passion of the Christ* and *Joan of Arcadia* and the use of chanting monks to sell everything from soft drinks to photocopiers. Religion commodified was especially present, even seen in the uptick in sales of guide books to monasteries and the renewed popularity of Taizé services and liturgies.

The point is, when she talked about such things, she sparked a deeper renaissance. And there *was* a renaissance in religious books and spiritual book publishing from roughly 1990 until 2005. As she was the first to explain, industry distributor Baker & Taylor's sales of books in religion and spirituality to libraries almost doubled in 1991. And by 1993, the other big distributor, Ingram Book Company, watched its sales of religious and spiritual books jump by 246 percent in a single year. The race was on, and publishers created more books and found more readers than ever before. Phyllis did not preside over this burgeoning; she schooled it and fueled it with her passion, intelligence, and articulation.

These were also the days when *Publishers Weekly* took a thoroughly journalistic approach to its subject matter. Critical book reviews appeared frequently, investigative articles were published, and articles requiring research that went beyond interviewing publishers were commissioned. One such research article from Phyllis's era was "Stirring the Waters of Reflection" by one of her favorite freelancers, John Spalding, in 1997. Spalding researched the history of religion publishing in America for the better part of a month and distilled it into two thousand words. *PW* became an essential resource for the religion professional.

Phyllis presided over the market for books in religion as President Bill Clinton was presiding over the American economy: with confidence and enthusiasm. The comparison is apt: As a cheerleader-in-chief was in the White House boosting the Dow, a similar figure in publishing journalism was working for the religion business always somewhere between her home in Lucy and a hotel room in New York City. She once self-deprecatingly declared that her advocacy journalism was about "98 percent ham and 2 percent information," but that was misplaced modesty.[8] She even instructed booksellers in how to organize their religion sections—at one point counseling the Borders chain through a complete redesign of theirs, "opening up twenty-three different categories of which five are now specifically textual, i.e., Koran is now a section separated from Islam, the Kabbalah is separate from Jewish Sacred Writings, and the Apocrypha has a category all to itself, independent of General Biblical Studies," as she explained.[9]

5

Some of the topics that fueled the religion and spirituality burst of the 1990s are no longer burning as they once did. The bestselling nonfiction book in January 1991, a year before Phyllis's appointment at *PW*, was *Iron John* by Robert Bly. That book surprisingly sparked an interest among men to explore a distinctively male spirituality. Simultaneous with Bly's bestseller was the birth of a Christian men's movement called Promise Keepers, founded by a football coach in Colorado. July 1991 saw their first, big conference. Soon, the organization published a handbook, *What Makes a Man?* Shortly after nearly a million men gathered on the National Mall in late 1997 to hear speeches about the need for men to take faith seriously however, the movement began to wane.

Then there was Jack Miles, born in Chicago and trained as a Jesuit, who published what became an unexpected bestseller in 1995, *God: A Biography*. It won the Pulitzer Prize for biography. Miles's perspective was to characterize the Divine as a literary figure, without making claims for or against matters of faith. This trend grew throughout the decade and ultimately prepared readers to accept what would become known as atheist theology, written by the Slovenian philosopher Slavoj Žižek, as well as by a writer with evangelical Christian roots who Phyllis helped to modest prominence: Peter Rollins. She was an early champion of Rollins's breakthrough *How (Not) to Speak of God* in 2006.

Interest in the historical Jesus also reached a high pitch, sparked by a review of John Dominic Crossan's *The Historical Jesus* in the *New York Times Book Review*, not a place known for covering religion. That December 23, 1991, review was sign and signal that religion speculation was entering a new era. Crossan's book then became the centerpiece of what was called the "third quest" for the historical Jesus. Almost exactly two years later, Phyllis would give Crossan's sequel, *Jesus: A Revolutionary Biography*, her first starred review as religion editor in *PW*. She seemed to speak personally at the conclusion of that review: "Crossan emphasizes that a Christian's current relationship to Christ is enhanced through reconstruction of Jesus's past. We are fortunate to have a writer and a scholar of Crossan's abilities to lead us in that reconstruction."[10] She was, in fact, actively tracing the lines from Albert Schweitzer (*The Quest of the Historical Jesus* 1906) to The Jesus Seminar (founded in 1985 by American biblical scholar Robert Funk), referring to books like Crossan's and fueling the publishing of others. She loved to attend The Jesus Seminar's twice-annual meetings at the Flamingo Hotel in Santa Rosa, California, and throughout the '90s had the phone numbers of its famous members: Funk, Crossan, and Marcus J. Borg on her speed dial.

Borg was a major figure in the third wave before his first bestseller, *Meeting Jesus Again for the First Time*, was published in 1994. Raised in Minnesota as a Lutheran, he studied math and physics in college but always had an abiding interest in matters of faith and understanding the Bible. (For years, his email address was xegete@.) At Union Seminary in New York City he became the progressive Christian that he later became famous for. *Jesus: A New Vision* introduced the Borgian perspective in 1987, but *Meeting Jesus Again for the First Time* came out at the height of the search for the historical Jesus. His publisher, HarperSanFrancisco, was adept at making headlines, and showing their authors how to tap into culture conversations with the ideas in their books. Their publicity team developed relationships with television producers, including at *ABC World News with Peter Jennings*, where programs soon appeared on the historical Jesus. Phyllis and Borg became good friends. A decade later, he would inspire her to take her own initiative as a writer-participant in these waters with *The Words of Jesus*.

She was interested in all of the places where religion was growing, from increased enrollment of undergraduate majors in religion in universities, to the use of spiritual and religious language in the marketing of consumer products. And it wasn't just Phyllis, but the team in religion at *PW*, tracking these things. On November 2, 1994, for instance, sales manager Robin Mays circulated a memo to all their in-house sales staff, with special copies to Phyllis, Maryles, and publisher Fred Ciporen—a clipping from the front page of that day's *USA Today*. Its opening sentence read: "Hope dawns for our national soul: Pope John Paul II's book has overtaken Faye Resnick's tell-all tale about Nicole Brown Simpson."

With her energy for learning and communicating what she knew, Phyllis fueled dozens of other conversations burning in religion and spiritual life. There was chaos theory and chance, followed by domesticity and wildness as alternating images for spiritual life. The appropriation of Eastern religious practice into Western religions—assimilation, or just the latest form of imperialism? Zen Catholics. Kabbalah for everyone; for instance, Madonna—not the Mother of Jesus—and how in the late twentieth century a rock star could invigorate interest in Jewish mysticism. Ecumenism, interfaith, multi-faith, and what they all mean. Why people look for religion in spiritual books, and what does this trend mean for the future of faith, and of organized religion? Womanist theology, Mujerista theology, Green theology. The environmental revolution and what it means for God and the Earth. Changes in the language that we use for God. Changes in the language that we use to describe ourselves in relation to God. The rapprochement of East and West in Christianity. The rapprochement of Judaism and Christianity—which she first picked up from Bishop Spong, and later began to explore while a guest at one of the meetings of the think tank The Jewish Public Forum in New York City, sponsored by CLAL—The National Jewish Center for Learning and Leadership. Christian hunger to learn about the Jewishness of Jesus. The rediscovery of mysticism and meditation as native within Judaism. The impact of the Global South on Westernized or Latinized Christianity. The growth of Islam worldwide. Gnosticism and other secrets: "The pursuit of truth through the acceptance of mystery," she called that phenomenon.[11] No wonder Phyllis loved her job.

6

Once Lynn Garrett was in place as editor in religion, and Phyllis transitioned to her new role as contributing editor, she had more time to travel and to speak.

There were hundreds of lectures, interviews with authors and publishers, articles for the magazine, and even trips to European cities beyond the annual Frankfurt Book Fair, including Wiesbaden, Bruges, Paris, and Amsterdam, each with official responsibilities as well as pleasurable asides. In May 1996, for instance, the Italian Trade Commission invited Phyllis to attend Koine, the largest trade show in Italy of books and religious objects of all kinds. By fax, they invited her with the offer of complimentary round-trip airline tickets to Rome, hotel accommodations, dinners, and translation services. Phyllis called Robin Mays immediately, and by the following day Robin was faxing back to confirm that they would both gladly come. They were in Rome for four days and nights in mid-June and, two days after returning home, each of them was in suburban Chicago for the Religious Book Trade Exhibit, followed immediately by the American Bookseller's Association annual convention at McCormick Place.

CHAPTER 12

Prayer Manuals and Mysticism

From the very beginning at *Publishers Weekly*, Phyllis was reporting on bestsellers by spiritual mediums: men (they always seemed to be men) who wrote from a private revelation, sharing divine insights, opinions, and predictions with what became enormous audiences. The first of these was James Redfield's novel *The Celestine Prophecy*, in which the main character discovers a series of hidden spiritual truths that governments and churches had long kept deliberately hidden. Redfield self-published his novel in 1993, selling a hundred thousand copies of it, which was unprecedented for self-publishing in those days. It was then bought by giant Warner Books who went on to sell twenty million more. Devoted readers of *The Celestine Prophecy* did not regard it as fiction. Its success was paralleled by Marianne Williamson's *A Return to Love*, which popularized *A Course in Miracles*, a recent religious text purported to be dictated to its authors by an inner voice that they sometimes identified with Jesus Christ.

But the most enduring spiritual medium book of all was *Conversations with God: An Uncommon Dialogue* by Neale Donald Walsch. First published in 1995 in paperback by tiny Hampton Roads, it quickly became a bestseller in outlying, mostly New Age, bookshops. A year later, the rights were sold to giant Putnam who in turn made the book a fixture on the *New York Times Best Seller* list. When Walsch published further revelations (that's how they were titled/styled) in books 2 and 3 in subsequent years, an industry was created around his locutions. Authorship was always shared between Walsch and God, with Walsch posing questions and God answering them. Films were made for both *The Celestine Prophecy* and *Conversations with God* by 2006.

Next came *Talking to Heaven: A Medium's Message of Life after Death* by James Van Praagh, topping the nonfiction bestsellers lists in

February 1998. It quickly became a CBS-TV miniseries. Phyllis made reference to all of these successes in her talks during this period as examples of spirituality's impact on popular culture. Also at this time, beginning in the summer of 1997, Billy Graham's massive autobiography, *Just As I Am*, topped nonfiction bestsellers lists. It was Phyllis's ability to access both sorts of book that made her essential for everyone in publishing. She had to keep speaking clearly to the evangelical side of the religion publishing industry, whose books and advertising dollars still were the overwhelming force in the industry, but spiritual mediums were becoming the story of the day.

A decade later and even an evangelical Christian was becoming a bestselling oracle. A novel, *The Shack*, by Canadian evangelical William Paul Young, told the story of Mack, a grieving father, who meets "Papa" (God the Father) in a shack in the woods of the American Northwest. Mack also meets, at times, the other two members of the Christian Trinity, in the form of a Middle Eastern carpenter (Jesus), and an Asian woman named Sarayu (Holy Spirit). This shocking fiction was also originally self-published and Young's shoestring edition sold one million copies within six months, a new unprecedented feat, and became, still as a self-published book, the number one fiction title on the *New York Times* list, beginning in June 2008, for a whopping seventy weeks. It, too, was then bought by one of the giant publishing houses, which went on to sell millions more.

2

Back on the farm in 1995, Sam was beginning to wind down his medical practice, and looking for new ways to occupy his time, always with an intense curiosity. He decided to buy into a millwork shop. He had a longtime patient and friend by the name of Ralph Holyfield. Ralph worked for Owen Lumber running their window shop and he hated the boring work, his negligent employees, strict hours, and all those things that come with a nine-to-five job. One day Ralph turned in his resignation and announced he was going back to making doors in his detached garage. That worked fine for a brief time, but when Ralph's wife divorced him a few years later he needed a place to work. Sam convinced him to open a real shop off Summer Avenue in Memphis, to make high-end doors and cabinets using Ralph's equipment and Sam's good credit. They struck an arrangement whereby Sam would handle the financials and Ralph would do the woodwork. "Dad's going to the shop usually meant that he was going to pick Ralph up for lunch and the place never actually flourished," remembers daughter Rebecca, but that was okay with everyone in Lucy; it was more than enough to keep Sam's mind and hands busy.[1] The shop went through several permutations and locations before Ralph left Memphis in 2004. Rebecca and her father ran the shop until 2008 when Rebecca was diagnosed with MS and had to stop driving; then they moved it to the two-thousand-square-foot barn in her backyard. There it remains.

It was just as well for Phyllis that Sam had his shop; it kept him busy, and Sam was always in need of something to busy himself. Phyllis was traveling for *Publishers Weekly*, often three or four weeks in a row. The children were gone from home, Rebecca and Sam Jr. having been last to leave, and Phyllis was energized by her work in a way that she hadn't been since teaching poetry.

Still, she found time to pray. Ever since the early sixties, every three hours during every work day, beginning with prime (6:00 a.m.), she had followed the non-petitionary prayer of the Divine Office. When the appointed hour came, she would slip away from a meeting or an office—or into the bathroom, when the children were at home—hoping to go unnoticed and unremarked, a breviary in hand or in her purse. She did this, she said, in order to remember who God is and to forget about herself, and to be in sync with Christians around the world who did likewise. "Prayer has efficacy and purpose far, far beyond the lives of those called to it," she once said, "and its measure is to be taken cosmically, not individually." There is a sense of isolation, sometimes, in her praying; she also said, "We are, as Christians, together always in our aloneness."[2] Phyllis used a variety of prayer manuals including *The Short Breviary for Religious and the Laity* compiled by monks at St. John's Abbey in Minnesota. All of this was something her mother had given to her: the discipline, the desire to sit with God.

3

In the spring of 1997, in the suburbs of Chicago, bookseller and literary agent Joseph Durepos was formulating an idea for a book. He thought that someone should create a manual for daily, liturgical prayer easier to handle than the breviaries and books of Gospels and saint-a-days that one was then forced to juggle to follow the Divine Hours. "It came to me in a Catholic bookstore in Darien, Illinois," Durepos remembered. "I had gone to daily mass at the Carmelite Center and then went over to the gift shop. I remember standing there looking at the ungainly, almost unusable three-volume Divine Office with annual supplement. I wanted to observe a more formal, fixed-hour prayer experience in my life, but what was on offer didn't cut it for me. So I decided on the spot it needed to be done by someone and I would find that person."

Two weeks later, Durepos mentioned the idea to a few friends, including the experienced Christian author and book editor LaVonne Neff. They were sitting in Durepos's Downers Grove office, above the Hallmark Gift Shop, twenty-three miles west of Chicago. Talking about books and publishing on the day before the annual Religious Booksellers Trade Exhibit (RBTE) was set to begin in nearby St. Charles, Joe pitched Neff his idea. He wondered if she might be interested. Joe would agent it. "I could sell that," he told her. But LaVonne knew Phyllis and knew that Phyllis prayed the hours religiously already.

"You should talk with Phyllis Tickle," she told him.

"Do you think she'd do it?" said Joe.

"Ask her," LaVonne replied.

Durepos did; Phyllis leaped at the idea; and within a month Joe sent a proposal to Doubleday Religion.

Eric Major was the publisher of Doubleday at the time, and he was delighted with *The Divine Hours*, immediately seeing its potential. A devout Roman Catholic, more than anyone else Major is the one who foresaw how the books could build a large audience by appealing to people's desire to fulfill St. Paul's otherwise impossible injunction to "pray without ceasing." As Phyllis would explain in the introduction to the first book, those who pray a divine hour in one time zone then pass on the discipline to Christians in the next time zone, and so on, thus doing what they never thought reasonably possible. Also, as a Catholic, having lived long among people who pray, Major knew, as Durepos did, how difficult it was to follow the church year in prayer without being in a parish with multiple books at hand.

Phyllis had often admired Major's publishing acumen, as well as his religious commitments. She remarked to a friend after Major's death, "He was Roman and one of the most devout, holy, and energetic Christians I have ever known, while never losing his keen sense of humor, his humility, his edge, and his sense of wonder."[3] They made an ideal pair. It was, in fact, Major who insisted that the books themselves had to "look like a book and not some kind of precious religious artifact." "Faith is real, and the tools for it damned well better be real, too!" he said.[4]

The initial contract was for a single volume: *The Divine Hours: Prayers for Summertime*. When Phyllis set to compiling it, the work came easily. She had developed, unknown to herself, a yearning to see certain psalms set within the same office (prime, terce, etc.), as well as certain hymns or pieces of poetry or sections of scripture at a particular time of day. The readings in prayer manuals usually follow a pattern of Gospels in the morning office, Old Testament or Epistles at mid-day, and hymns at Vespers, but she relished being able to make these choices, now, for herself and others—including the juxtaposition of the psalms, the refrains, and so on, within each office, to the biblical texts. "I caught myself smiling over and over again, my heart light and my spirit soothed by the pleasure of dropping a psalm in place beside a section of the Gospels that had always somehow seemed to me to be its natural and euphemous mate," she said.[5] Phyllis set to work and for twenty-two months of ten-hour days, she and a research assistant (her daughter, Rebecca) completed the work. Mother would lay out the various texts, often clipped and taped in place on two-page spreads of a notebook, and daughter would type it all up.

After praying the hours five times a day (Phyllis often skipped the 6:00 p.m. office of vespers in her personal practice) for more than thirty years, stopping to pray throughout the day while compiling the first of *The Divine Hours*™ (she and Sam quickly trademarked the name) added layers to her experience. Eventually, even before the first book was published, Durepos went back to Eric Major at Doubleday Religion and pitched him the idea of two more. Phyllis and Joe knew that they had a successful idea. So, eighteen months after the first contract had been signed, but still nearly a year before *Summertime* was to be published, Tickle, Inc. was contracted to create volume 2, *Autumn and Wintertime*, and volume 3, *Springtime*. She was paid a whopping $350,000 advance against royalties for the three.

4

In the same sense of the medieval Benedictine monks, praying "the Hours" was, for Phyllis, "work for God." But spiritually, the best explanation she ever provided for why she remained faithful to this form of prayer throughout her life was to Bob Abernethy of PBS:

> It is a way of constantly keeping this open. Regardless of how much I sin, regardless of how many errors I make, regardless of how awful I perceive myself to be at times in my decisions and in my reactions to people and in my greed and lust, I've still got this core. I've still got, in the middle of my day, in the middle of all of my consciousness, this one passageway, this one place that connects me with the Divine, that's there, that's solid, that says, "Are you distressed by all these things you are? Are you heartbroken about all these things you have just done? It's all right. Come here." When I'm standing in that one place that is the Divine Office, I know God's in his heaven and I'm part of that heaven.[6]

Unbeknownst to her readers, to whom she was emphasizing the spiritual vitality of non-petitionary (non-Protestant) prayer in these books, and unknown to her closest friends, who simply never asked, Phyllis also prayed twice a day every day—post-nones and pre-compline—a series of prayers, which evolved and changed over time. These prayers asked God for help and guidance. She prayed them by rote, but they were of her own devising. She seems to have written them out only once, and at the request of her closest friend in prayer, when she was seventy years old. They "constitute a kind of private credo," she said, used "so to speak, to record the One to Whom I [am] praying, like taking a picture of the unpicturable."[7]

Emphasizing that the language of these private prayers has changed slightly over the years, she summarized it on this singular occasion this way. Notice the borrowing of language from both East and West.

Lord Jesus Christ, Son of the living God, have mercy on me, a sinner. (Several times)

Lord Jesus, forgive my sins (then named usually.) Take from me every thing, person, desire, pretension, and habit that keeps me from perfectly loving You and serving the Kingdom. I would love the Lord my God with all my heart and all my mind and all my soul and all my strength, and my neighbor as myself. Place Your yoke upon me and give me Your burden and take mine; and keep me on the narrow path and bring me through the straited gate. May that heart and mind be in me that were also in You, and may I be a living branch of the living vine. Give me clarity of vision, profundity, keenness and quickness of intellect, grace and effectiveness of delivery, humility, focus, energy, and passion. And grant that I may be like that piece of fertile ground You spoke of when You were here: the thorns having been raked away and burned, and the weeds have been pulled and burned as well, and the rocks and stones having been tossed aside, the word may fall, take root, and bear much fruit.

I ask grace. I pray as well for the guidance, correction, and instruction of the Holy Spirit. I pray for the protection, guardianship, communion, and all-encompassing, all-surrounding, total embrace of the Holy Spirit, love and discipline. Open me from the core out that this may be a life of praise and thanksgiving, obedience and charity, humility and service. Grant that I may be filled with the peace of God, the love of God, the fear of God, the Spirit of God, the kingdom of God, the presence of God, the favor of God, the wisdom of God, the ways/works/words/ and worship of God, the knowledge of God, trust and faith.

Oh God, with Whom all things are possible, save my soul, my spirit, my life and those of my husband into Your Kingdom here and hereafter, now and forever; and renew all the component parts of them—our bodies, hearts, minds, souls, and spirits—and grant that our strength may mount up like the eagle in accord with Your purposes and those of the Kingdom.

May the words of our mouths and the thoughts of our hearts be always acceptable in Thy sight.

I pray You as well to save the souls and lives and spirits of our sons and our daughters and their families (names here). Open the eyes of each of us that we may see and our ears that we may hear and our hearts and minds that we may understand and be converted and turn to You and be healed. And grant that each of us may be found worthy to stand with joy before the Son of God in whose most holy name I pray, even as He taught us, asking You to hear it as if coming from each and every one of us when I say, "Our Father. . . . etc., etc."

I raise to you my husband, that he may be filled with gratitude and joy and comfort, and that we may both be filled with discernment to spend everything You have given us charge of and everything You have allowed us to become for Your sake and that of the Kingdom as You would have them spent.

Make us better parents, grandparents, great-grandparents, godparents, adult friends, mentors, congregants, and co-congregants. Grant that neither of us may do or say or act upon anything about sexuality, ecumenism, or inter-faith relations that is not given us by Your Spirit to do or say or believe or act upon as You would have it done.

Help me to better understand the nature and role of prayer, church, work, love, marriage, and hospitality that I may perform in each more faithfully and speak and write about each more wisely. Amen.[8]

She was also experimental in her private prayer. The Jesus Prayer, of Eastern Christian distinction, was one that she often practiced, and there were times that she felt it had "worked" in her in the sense that she felt, at the end of a day, that those words, "Lord Jesus Christ, Son of God, have mercy on me, a sinner," had truly prayed themselves subconsciously within her, as a wordless prayer of the heart. These were all private experiences and none would be normally mentioned in a biography of a literary subject, unless that subject was one of her generation's most recognized experts in the area of prayer.

There were always tensions in Phyllis's life as a result of her need to spend significant time each day alone in prayer. Her private, spiritual life came with the demands of a husband, many children, then grandchildren (who were sometimes even living at the Farm in Lucy, and to whom Phyllis and Sam were often Gran and Paw Paw), a busy work schedule, and other commitments. Just six months after the first contract came from Doubleday for *The Divine Hours*, Sam became seriously ill with angina and weariness. He knew he had heart troubles, and carrying nitroglycerin tablets had become his usual habit. On April 30, 1998, he was taken to the emergency room at Methodist Hospital in Memphis, and triple-bypass surgery was scheduled for the following day. From that moment on, her partner's health problems would be a daily concern.

Beyond weariness, like those Benedictine monks whom she emulated in practice, Phyllis frequently craved more time alone. When, in her sixties and seventies, visiting family kept her from her routine of the Hours, she even occasionally felt physically ill.

On one of these occasions, after the little ones had left in their parents' cars, Phyllis retreated to her room to pray. Then, she "traveled" to a "place" that she describes this way:

> I was somewhere up above life and being shown that I had no idea of the mystery that kept it all going—millions of people and cars and roads and zillions of activities all making the "nexus" or complete body of Life and all frantically moving in response to some mystery. . . . I saw that what is, is like looking down on a marvelous constellation or nebula of infinite pieces all flowing like a mass of protoplasm and working away just like my own body is and does. We are it—all there is except God out there alive so long as He desires it. Living and dying and sloughing off and coming in, all held by the "breath" of God or the affection of God. And when we're gone—not us individually, but us in toto—it will all be rolled up like a spangled cloud and be not. It was wonderful.[9]

She was different from those whom the poet Robert Browning once described with the line: "So free we seem, so fettered fast we are!" Phyllis felt, rather, fettered by everyday life, but free in herself. Then and there, prayer was sometimes ineffable.

5

The first two years of the new millennium would be the most important for Phyllis's writing career. The first *Divine Hours* volume, *Prayers
for Summertime*, was nearly seven hundred pages, published by Doubleday in February 2000. Volume 2 followed quickly, that September,
and volume 3 in the following year.

Likewise, *The Shaping of a Life* was published in April 2001. For
this, too, she received what was then (and now, certainly) a very large
publishing advance for a spiritual book. The $250,000 was never
remotely recouped by Doubleday and yet Major doesn't seem to have
worried about it when he signed the contract in 1999. The autobiography reached many readers, mostly women, many of whom wrote joyful
letters of reminiscence to Phyllis, but it did not strike a popular chord
in the marketplace. *The Divine Hours* was a different story.

The Divine Hours became a phenomenon among Episcopalian,
mainline Protestant, and even evangelical Christians. Quite suddenly,
Phyllis was exemplifying with her own writing what she'd long been
predicting was happening, by accomplishing in books what used to
happen only in church. *The Divine Hours* is perhaps the best example
of "portable pastors" ever seen. The appeal to do this had always been
a motivation for her, to move beyond simply observing that this was
happening in the marketplace. Plus, she had long believed that "every
believer must be a kind of psalmist, either literally or privately."[10] In
this context we can also understand her long association with being
a lay eucharistic minister in the Episcopal Church: Portable pastoring
was deep in her bones, and always of more interest to Phyllis than simply being a congregant.

The Divine Hours was introduced by PBS's *Religion and Ethics
Newsweekly* with Bob Abernethy in a five-minute segment on March
31, 2000. The video interview was shot, not with Abernethy in her living room in Lucy, but with another reporter asking the questions. For
this reason, Phyllis was unable to correct Abernethy's voiceover when
he said, "For hundreds of years in the West, Christians' fixed-hour
prayer has been offered almost exclusively by Catholic monks and
clergy. Now, according to Phyllis Tickle, more and more Protestants,

like her, are discovering the discipline." No self-respecting Episcopalian, especially one as cognizant of the religious landscape as Phyllis, would allow Episcopalians/Anglicans to be lumped in with Protestants. She often quarreled on this point with other historians and theologians. (Although, oddly, there was one instance—an essay from 1996—when she wrote, ". . . for me as a Protestant. . . .")[11]

At that point in the interview, however, Phyllis spoke of the renewed appeal of spiritual discipline and why it was appealing to many people:

> Discipline is a growing of muscle. And this is discipline, and it's the growing of the spiritual muscle. It's the discipline that allows you even to check out sometimes when you're in the middle of a meeting, for instance, or in the middle of a high-pressure conversation and that watch beeps I know I drop back, and I'm doing two things at once. It's kind of organized schizophrenia, but I'm praying. If I cannot get away from the physical situation, I'm praying and talking at the same time.[12]

She plumbed many sources, ancient to modern, in order to populate the nearly two thousand pages of the original three volumes of *The Divine Hours*. There is an artistry to her work that was easily noticed, and often remarked upon. That is why John G. Whittier's hymn "Dear Lord and Father of Mankind" is found beside prayers and poems from the Sarum Primer of 1527, and fundamental English prayers blend well with others from Syrian, Celtic, and Latin sources throughout the centuries. Most of the Psalter is also carefully excised for precise purposes, including under headings such as "The Request for Presence" and "The Call to Prayer."

She knew Catholic sources, but turned to them rarely. She would always bear some of the anti-papist attitude that she learned at home and in the Presbyterian churches of her youth. One saw this in the sometimes disdainful attitude she had toward religious authority and ceremony. As an American Episcopalian, she also showed a surprising lack of interest in the Church of England. Just as she once dismissed the guru status of the Dalai Lama, she tended to view any elevated ordained person as a possible threat to the faithful. Her view of religious authority never strayed far from the Protestant one; as she wrote in the foreword to Pastor Ken Wilson's *Jesus Brand Spirituality*: "The faith we Christians claim has been so dented and chipped and discolored by the centuries, so institutionalized and codified and doctrinalized, so written upon and then so overwritten into palimpsest, that there are few Christians who still can discern the contours of the original."[13] Again, books as "portable pastors" were not simply an observation; it was a practice she favored. Fifteen years earlier, she'd made this remark in the prologue to a book of essays, which she then removed two decades later when the book was republished: "I am not a cleric. I have never wanted to study in a seminary or even to have access to one." She valued individual ways of knowing, and disregarded knowledge that is handed on. As she went on in that prologue from 1985, "[L]iving itself has been given, at least in part, as a way of knowing God intimately. . . . [T]here is no waste in experience. Every man and woman we meet becomes a metaphor of ourselves."[14]

This same anti-ecclesiastical authority attitude extended to the relatively new order of spiritual directors that was popping up during the years she was an expert commenting on the religious scene. She once wrote to a friend:

> You ask about spiritual directors as an entity or group, and I wince. . . . I have always been leery not only of having one, but also of the professionalized concept itself. . . . God knows I have been the blessed and grateful recipient of the informing and counseling work of many older and/or just wiser and more experienced Christians; but every time I have thought it might be time to go for a "Spiritual Director" in caps and per se, I have been told, "No."[15]

One exception to this attitude toward religious authority came in her response to being in the presence of Archbishop Desmond Tutu. This happened for the first time on Trinity Sunday, May 29, 1994, in a Los Angeles hotel room. Tutu was in town for BookExpo America, a trade show, promoting his forthcoming book, *The Rainbow People of God*. His publisher at Doubleday, Thomas Cahill (who preceded Eric Major), invited Phyllis and a colleague to join them and a few others for a private eucharistic service.

When Phyllis spoke of this experience in subsequent years, as for instance, in *Prayer Is a Place*, she didn't seem to realize the contradiction between the blessed emotions she felt being in Tutu's presence and the revulsion ("disgust") she experienced in the presence of the Dalai Lama's devotees less than one year earlier. First, she remembers and describes inane details: "To his left was an octagonal lamp table and beyond that, the other and matching high-backed chair, still empty. To his right was another table—the low, square kind that hotels put in corners to fill up the incongruities between overstuffed low sofas and overstuffed high-backed chairs." Then, Tutu's private mass in an ordinary hotel room is turned, by her description, into a holy space: "[T]o enter that badly lighted, long-nosed room with its pseudo-personal furniture and its glass-topped everything was, as nothing in life before or since has ever been for me, like entering the imagined catacombs of Christian history." Earlier in *Prayer Is a Place* she had briefly considered, then discounted, the notion that her "disgust" at the Dalai Lama might have been culturally conditioned. But surely that's what her reaction to Tutu was all about, as this lifelong Western Christian felt that "what we experienced there [with Tutu] . . . will always be God-with-us."[16]

6

She often heard from readers and pray-ers that they took her books with them into the restroom, or some other quiet, secluded place, at noontime to "pray their hours." In fact, this was Phyllis's own teaching; before the first volume of *The Divine Hours* appeared, she wrote an article for *Spirituality & Health* magazine, at the invitation of its editor, Bob Scott, in which she included this bit of advice:

> Stay Free of Religiosity and Piety: For lay observants like me, ordering a secular day by a liturgical clock is frustrating enough at times to invite a little self-congratulation on its accomplishment or a little devout explanation to one's fellows for one's strange mini-absences or faintly odd schedule. The same Jesus who straightened out the Sabbath, however, also straightened out prayer. When you do it, he said, go into a closet, shut the door, and pray in secret to your Father in Heaven. The trick, in other words, is not just in the doing of the prayers, but in the addressing of them as directed by the Recipient.[17]

This form of prayer was something that she'd watched her mother do alone at home, and it was solitary for Phyllis, as well. She was alone in her own praying the Divine Office each day. She would pray Prime at about six in the morning, alone in the bathroom, where the necessary book rested, waiting, on a shelf. After the children were grown and gone, she would then usually return to bed, and, she believed, God spoke quietly to her in her rest or return to slumber. As she explained to a friend, "It is in that hour and a half . . . that I 'hear' most of that day's conversation. That is, it is during that time that the Spirit speaks and shapes and suggests most."[18] By nine o'clock, she was usually ready for work and observed the office in an armchair that sat beside her desk. The noon hour, too, usually saw her there, and so on throughout each day.

Had she been less gracious, she might have expressed private thoughts she held about the primacy of the spiritual discipline of spoken prayer over various form of meditation, or "centering" prayer, which were also then popular. She might have written to the audience of *Spirituality & Health* as she wrote to a friend who asked about the difference:

The thing that frustrates me a lot is talking to New Agers (that's a derogatory and I don't mean it in that way) and eastern gurus or aficionados who think moving the attention and awareness around in subjective country is praying. It's not. Half the time it's just resting, letting the intellect check out for a while—or to put it cognitively, to allow the left brain a chance to work out what the right side is flubbing. Pure psych, in other words, not theology. I mean I do that a lot, too. . . . A lot of times I just quit and let the old mind wander into undisciplined and/or non-verbal awareness, usually with a benefit that seems to me a lot like what meditation or yoga or whatever is supposed to give one, but I don't know. . . . [A]lso, there are other times when I just have to pull up stakes and go rest a while. It's the same place as prayer, roughly, that is, but it's not prayer as a working session; it's conversation. Remember that old "I come to the garden alone, while the dew is still on the roses" hymn? Man, I love that thing. That's where I rest, in that garden. And yes, Jesus is very definitely there and always has been; and I guess I'm being taught something, but it feels too gentle to be more than affectionate counsel.[19]

7

The Divine Hours was published at the right time, at the height of the spiritual book renaissance that had begun in the 1970s and galvanized in the 1990s in the U.S. They were also volumes soaked with personal experience, and readers seemed to grasp that intuitively. But Phyllis was not only someone who had prayed the hours privately for decades: She was experienced in prayer in ways that neither her native Presbyterianism, nor her adopted Anglicanism, could have anticipated. Perhaps when one spends thousands of hours praying silently and alone it is inevitable that religious experiences take place. She didn't talk about these occasions, and she certainly didn't write about them in the prayer manuals. Episcopalians rarely speak of such things. However, she told one or two friends who happened to ask that she knew speaking in tongues, jaw trembles, trembling by the Spirit, and ravishment (the feeling of being erotically enjoyed) firsthand in prayer.[20]

Among Charismatic Christians, speaking in tongues is almost always reported as experienced first in a group setting, but that was not the case for Phyllis, and she never provided details of when and where it happened, other than to say that in her extended prayer times of nones and compline each day, she had occasionally experienced what she called "speaking beautiful sounds that were not English or any other tongue I have ever known."[21]

Phyllis had an easy familiarity with personal, religious experience, and always accepted her own unquestioningly. Such experiences were, for her, as Thomas Hardy describes the effect of a certain heath at twilight, "[N]obody could be said to understand the heath who had not been there at such a time. It could best be felt when it could not clearly be seen. Its complete effect and explanation lay in this. . . ."

As she entered her eighth decade, personal, intense religious experience became more frequent. In direct proportion to her husband's descent into dementia, Phyllis became more spiritually and passionately alone. She didn't mind the transition, apart from the accompanying sadness of watching Sam in confusion and illness. Returning to Hardy's heath, "The storm was its lover; and the wind was its friend. Then it became the home of strange phantoms. . . ."[22] Phyllis began to covet time alone—something she had never had in her adult life, and more than ever she explored prayer as a "place" that one can "go," both interiorly and visually. She meant this literally—beyond any Ignatian sense of using the imagination. It was during her private times of praying the hours that she "traveled" in these ways, and she spent years pondering where this non-locative place actually was. Sometimes these experiences of soul seemed absolutely real to her. She pondered them deeply, in theological and metaphysical terms, but privately: "[I]t is to me as if the soul, supposed always to be beyond knowing or the probing of awareness per se, were now seeking to be knowable within and to human consciousness," she confided to the only friend to whom she spoke of these things.[23]

It was common for Phyllis to experience mystical moments on the other side of praying one of the hours, particularly after 1994 when Lyme disease made it necessary for her to lay flat, on doctor's orders, for a minimum of twelve hours each day. This meant that she would eat dinner and soon afterwards retire, alone. There, quiet and in bed in the dark she would "travel" in prayer—or in what others would call contemplation. She joked seriously that she would never allow her physician to alter his diagnosis nor his prescription. At *Publishers Weekly*, Phyllis had tracked the bestsellers of Redfield, Walsch, and Williamson in the 1990s. Now, a decade later, she was experiencing a similar sort of direct contact with the Creator, complete with personal messages, although hers remained private and were left unpublished.

Phyllis's spiritual experiences were extensive in the middle of the first decade of the new century and included sensing the presence of spirits and ghosts, even in her own home. After a series of experiences, she accepted such presences as personal truth, although she knew that such claims smacked of Spiritualism, a theosophical heresy born in 1848 in upstate New York. She also frequently heard Jesus speak to her, and occasionally felt that God as Shekinah was hovering over a place, signifying God's blessing.[24] Like one of the authors of those books relaying divine revelations, she once remarked to her friend: "[In prayer], I go somewhere. Forced to elaborate, I would say I walk about on a plain, but never alone. There is a Teacher there and a Holy One. More than that, I don't know, except that I am because of that."[25]

This was her own personal Sinai. On another occasion, she went into detail to relay a vivid prayer experience involving another non-locative journey. This took place after she finished praying the liturgical hour of terce, when she would commonly lie in bed, allowing herself to go deeper into her prayers in just this sort of way:

> [W]hen I finished terce and set the book beside me on the bed, I went in. . . . [A]fter terce, I am almost oppressed by the need to lay my prayers aside—or certainly to not follow the normal pathway of them. Instead, I am taken to this place of no-thought, all-image. It's a half room caught between and on the underside of two encased stairwells—the kind of hole you used to love to hide in as a child. . . . Except that this one was larger and appeared to be on a back porch in which one flight rising above my head went up into the attic and the other up into the second floor of whatever it was they served. The walls were of bead board and the whole could have come straight out of Faulkner—in other words, out of a South I never knew as a kid. And sitting there in the corner that was the crux of the undersides of the stairwells was as sweet and fresh and unsullied as any place I have ever been—just me and the good Lord. And we did what I think my father used to mean when he said, "We communed." I always wondered what that meant, but I think I sort of know now. Then, gradually, there was a window behind me with only one stairwell still in place, and the window opened onto immeasurable vistas. I have no idea when I came back or how.[26]

Confiding these mysterious experiences to only one friend: Ken Wilson, a Vineyard pastor in Ann Arbor, Michigan, and an evangelical Christian who had no hesitation asking the kind of personal, spiritual questions that elicited her honest responses. How ironic that hundreds of thousands of people knew her as the compiler of *The Divine Hours*, as an exemplary of the routine of liturgical prayer, and yet she was leaving on mystical journeys, off-script, in the privacy of her bedroom each morning.

When she did talk about it once, in cautious terms, while leading a retreat for fellow Episcopalians, it didn't go well. On that occasion, during Advent 2004, she began by giving her then-standard talk on the origin of the divine offices, where they came from and their history in the Abrahamic faiths. For Phyllis, this was rote. Then she "veered over . . . to prayer as a place and the offices as chapellettes along the road and as holy places and as transparent ones with side doors that open into other realms," she explained to her friend later.[27] "They all looked somewhere between blank and curious," she said. At the same time, she was writing *Prayer Is a Place*, and penned this sentence: "Prayer is a nonlocative, nongeographic space that one enters at one's own peril."[28] She meant this literally. Perhaps she expected this statement to open doors whereby she might begin a new "career" in prayer, and in teaching and talking with others about the miracles of where prayer can take them. This didn't happen. Few if any took her seriously. She went back to keeping her experiences to herself and compartmentalized her spiritual life even more. She feared being embarrassed.[29]

Ten years later, Phyllis made oblique reference to her ongoing experiences in prayer when the organizers of the 2014 Christianity21 Conference, where she was to speak in Denver, asked a series of interview questions including, "What's one of your most meaningful spiritual practices?" She responded, "[T]he most meaningful practice to me—or better put, the dearest practice—is setting my alarm for 4, or on some days 4:30 a.m., in order to observe the Office of the Night Watch and then, the Office having been observed, to lie in prayer and meditation and listening for another hour or so." No one followed up, to ask what she hears during that hour.

None of these mystical experiences were subjected by her to evidence or to any sort of burden of proof. Knowing God remained deeply intuitive. Just as Sam had long doubted the reality of the near-death experience she had in the hospital after a miscarriage, which she relayed in her first autobiography, she knew that most of her colleagues in the church would doubt her as well. One saint to whom she looked for affirmation was Teresa of Avila in her descriptions of a place of prayer being like an "Interior Castle"—but it was unlike her to quote the saints. More like her, Phyllis quoted on the final page of *Greed* from the prophet Isaiah: "I am the Lord, and there is none else. I form the light, and create darkness: I make peace, and create evil: I the Lord do all these things." And then she follows the quote by simply saying, "Such knowledge is too wonderful for me."[30]

8

Phyllis was standing in the kitchen on the Farm in Lucy on the sunny Tuesday morning of September 11, 2001. Her phone rang at about 8:15 a.m. central time. Knowing that her mother was flying in and out of New York City all the time, Rebecca wasn't far away, in Memphis, but immediately concerned. She wanted to reach her mother. "I'm at home," Phyllis told her youngest.

"Something has happened in New York. Turn on the TV," Rebecca told her.

The north tower of the World Trade Center was on fire. Phyllis turned on her set, and like millions of Americans, watched the second plane live on television as it hit the south tower. Meanwhile, her *Publishers Weekly* colleagues at 17th Street in Manhattan were watching the same scene out of the south-facing windows in their downtown offices. Phyllis would learn a few days later that at least two of her colleagues at *PW* died on one of the planes.

She had work scheduled at the offices in New York for mid-October and Sam wanted to come along. He wanted to see for himself what had happened and brought his camera. When they arrived at LaGuardia, Phyllis was anxious to see her colleagues, but first, as she said to Sam at the airport, "I have to see *it*." Their taxi dropped them off south of Trinity Wall Street Church, and they walked the few blocks to St. Paul's Chapel at 209 Broadway in lower Manhattan, between Fulton and Vesey. St. Paul's had become a place of respite for the workers at Ground Zero, and a place of pilgrimage for the people of New York. The two walked around, among the hundreds of others that day, in silence, in tears. "Ash and debris were everywhere, the odor of smoke from the burning buildings pervasive; but so too was the silence," she remarked the following spring in a talk at nearby Trinity Wall Street. After an hour, Sam remained, taking pictures, and Phyllis went to the office.

"Death is philosophy's dark gift to the human spirit's formation," she also said in that talk at Trinity, just a few hundred yards from Ground Zero, only six months after 9/11. And, "Death is no more than the rood screen between our flesh and our assumption to union with that spirit."[31]

She would return to St. Paul's Chapel many times over the next year, on each occasion when she traveled to New York for work. On the first anniversary of the cataclysm, she joined Muslim theologian Ingrid Mattson and Quaker author Parker Palmer on Krista Tippett's *First Person: Speaking of Faith* radio program to discuss what happened that day and what it meant. The segment was titled, "The Spiritual Fallout of 9/11."[32] Phyllis spoke of the acts of compassion she'd witnessed over the year, and of the event itself in connection to other tragic events in American history as only a Southerner would do: "It takes a very long time to understand, first of all, that both sides [in the Civil War] thought they were right. Both sides were Bible-quoting . . . God-citing, believers in their cause," she said, "and 150 years later I don't know a single Southerner who doesn't say 'Thank God slavery is over.'" She cautioned any sort of claiming of moral victory in the aftermath of 9/11: "We [Southerners] know what it means to feel betrayed by your fellow countrymen, your fellow human beings, but we also know that good things came out of that—that we're better as a country, as people, as Christians, and as people of other faiths—so it takes away part of the edge of hysteria . . . makes it easier to look at this with the long lens of history."

The value of prayer also felt keener than ever to her in the aftermath of 9/11. As she told that audience at Trinity Wall Street six months after the tragedy:

In extraordinary times like the ones through which we are presently passing, the discipline of fixed prayer balanced by work becomes even more necessary to the soul's health; for without it, we can readily veer off into despair or—perhaps even more deadly for the soul—veer off into a neurotic absorption with horror, which is not to say—which is never to say—that we should not honor the horror we have seen.

CHAPTER 13

The Shaping of a Life

At the turn of the millennium, Phyllis again wanted to take a step back from her work at the magazine. The first of the prayer manuals was compiled for Doubleday, and the others were in the works. She wanted to stop being a journalist and return to writing about her own faith.

The writing of her autobiography, published in April 2001, was a deeply emotional experience. It was also passionately received by many readers, who wrote long letters of appreciation. Fellow writers resonated with the work, too, for the most lyrical and original passages were about the writing life, the mind, and creative process. There was, for instance, this passage about writing early in the morning: "I discovered . . . to appreciate the clarity of early morning for seeing the true edges and definition of things; the imperative of sustained writing even if the phrases and sentences are as uninspired as finger exercises; and the skill, like a beagle in the autumn hunt, of following without question the scent, the perfume, the irresistible musk of Keats's truth that is beauty."[1]

Fellow pray-ers loved the book, as well. *The Shaping of a Life* was first proposed by Phyllis to her agent as *And I Live Here: One Christian's Account of the Life of Prayer*—it was to be a memoir about her vocation to prayer, a book, she said, that for many reasons she could not have written before. But by the time her agent sent the proposal to Eric Major at Doubleday it was retitled *Prayer Is a Place*, picking up on a phrase that Phyllis used repeatedly in it. Prayer is locative in her life, she explained. Eventually, Doubleday asked her to reconsider the title again, feeling that even the word "prayer" would limit the audience. Even so, Phyllis always maintained that the shaping referred to in the final title is the real business of prayer.[2] So the book was written with an agenda, and not originally as an autobiography.

It was not a great commercial success, as her boss at *PW* playfully predicted. Eighteen months earlier, when Phyllis told Maryles that Doubleday was paying her an advance of $250,000 for an autobiography, Daisy's response was, "Why?!" Paying such an advance against royalties, the publisher must have calculated that at least a hundred thousand people would buy the book. Less than seven thousand ended up buying it in hardcover.

Shaping received many glowing reviews, but there is a lack of candidness and revelation in the writing. Beyond the grief of the death of her child, there is little vulnerability or surmounting, important qualities in successful memoir. She actually writes about her spiritual development in a way that is almost tortured at times, as when attempting to describe her first non-Protestant worship experience:

> What happened to me on my first Sunday among the Anglicans, though I didn't understand it at the time, was the substantivization of a tenet. I had slammed head-on into the realization, in physical objects and forms, of what saying, "I am Christian" just might really imply. More than the Eucharist itself, I suspect, this lifting out into the exterior world of the furniture of the interior one had been what so terrified me—that and the fact that giving flesh to human lives that had dared to believe gave flesh to the mass and thereby made it alarmingly more actual.[3]

It is as if she is bursting to express something personally vital, but cannot. At other times, she seems at pains to describe minutiae of her internal processes, including, a few pages after the above example, when she goes on about the different feelings welling in her, during college, between reading the psalms in the Gideon Bible versus the psalter she discovered in the Book of Common Prayer.

Her discomfort in writing about herself is evident throughout. The tone and feeling of her personal essays from the 1980s are absent. Maybe the journalist and scholar had caused the poet to lose her confidence.

She never lacked for anecdotes or analysis to explain where she came from or who she was, but she comes across as a writer who is not puzzled by the mystery of herself. Neither was she uncertain about God in her life. This is not to say that she thought God explicable, but she always knew what she knew. To some, that tone came across as the journalist coming out of the closet; to others, it simply disappointed. At other times, she uses philosophical language to distance herself from what was obviously personal. She had done this earlier in the preface to her edited collection of Christian women writing on the subject of abortion, noting: "For its readers a book can be a sharing of human-ness with impunity, a vicarious expanding of possibility with small risk; for its authors and editors it can sometimes be a Promethean agony of exchange between one's privacy and one's sense of community. For me, at least, this has been such a book."[4] Abstraction was often her way of entering a topic.

There is also a kind of dishonesty that prevails, as she has nothing critical to say of anyone. And when she attempts to speak of her own sins, she tells of using a slug to ride the bus as a teenager, framing the tale to resemble St. Augustine stealing pears in the *Confessions*. Then she spends four pages bemoaning her untruthfulness surrounding the deed. There is also the lack of honesty about difficulties in her mar-riage, even in small things, like praising Sam's "life force" as "shaman-istic" since nothing is ever "allowed to die around him," rather than say he was a pack rat, which he was, and it drove her crazy. It was as if she wrote *Shaping* for who her audience knew her to be, rather than who she really was. She was by then the compiler of *The Divine Hours* and so also found herself writing sentences such as, "As was true of many another young adult in America's mid-century, I had not yet learned to pray by the time I was nineteen years old. . . ."[5] What a different book it might had been if she had written it ten or twenty years earlier.

2

Chapters thirty-five and thirty-six form the heart of *Shaping*. There, she tells the story of her near-death experience at age twenty-one, brought on by the experimental drug she was taking to prevent miscarriages. She speaks of the event as the pivotal moment in her life, and it was. But she couldn't help but then take a step back from the event and add glosses such as: "There are amongst us human beings and especially amongst our theologians and philosophers a veritable bevy of low-key but ubiquitous arguments about the standards and definitions of truth. . . ." This was her way of prefacing that, for her, the event was absolutely central, "truth" or not. She describes dying, Sam attempting to resuscitate her in the hospital bed, all the while, as she puts it, "I was up in the corner of the room" watching. Faithful to accounts of near-death-experiences everywhere, she describes literally floating down a tunnel toward a light and hearing, "Come." Then she brings that abstruse discussion of philosophical truth full circle and reveals how the event became central: "It is, as the philosophers and theologians have said, what I do remember and how I have remembered it that have shaped my life."[6]

There would be one more volume of autobiography a few years later, and this time it actually was titled *Prayer Is a Place*. But it did not pick up where *Shaping* left off: with Phyllis still in her late twenties. Its tone is completely different. More like the playfulness and information in her lectures, *Prayer Is a Place* focuses almost exclusively on the *Publishers Weekly* years, written for an audience of her friends and colleagues, going so far as to name and complement dozens of them in its pages.

3

In 2001, Phyllis signed over all performance and publication rights to her chancel drama *Figs and Fury*, about the prophet Jeremiah, to an intentional, religious community on Cape Cod in Massachusetts. She was also contracted by them to write a new drama, specifically for performance in its immense basilica-style church, the Church of the Transfiguration, in Orleans. As usual, she set out to suit the drama to the chancel. She conceived the project by inspiration and prayer, writing to the spiritual leader of the Community of Jesus in November 2001:

I have been convicted in prayer—and much to my surprise, may I say—that Ezekiel wants to come next. He completely dumbfounds me, and I haven't an inkling of an idea about how one even begins to start to commence rendering his cinematic visions and parables by means of the conventions of chancel drama. None the less, it seems in my soul to be Ezekiel.[7]

The work was never completed, but this sort of Spirit-led approach to writing carried throughout Phyllis's life—after she was introduced to the Community of Jesus.

She wrote in *Prayer Is a Place* how she first came to know the Community: she was stopped in the aisle at the Religious Book Trade Exhibit by Paraclete Press marketing manager Carol Showalter. Carol, like everyone working at Paraclete, was a member of this vowed residential community of some three hundred people, both lay and monastic, from a dozen or more denominational backgrounds, including Episcopal, Roman Catholic, Evangelical, Presbyterian, and Christian Science. They went from being a loose gathering of evangelical and charismatic Christians in the 1960s to a highly disciplined Benedictine, monastic-style community under the governance of a prioress. To this day, they keep the liturgical hours (in Latin), observe the liturgical seasons, fast, pray, operate a publishing house, and mount arts guilds of various kinds noted in North America and increasingly abroad, for their musicality and performance. They also worship on their own campus in the aforementioned church, completed in 2001, which is a close and studied replica of the Romanesque-style basilica in Ravenna.

By the time Phyllis was introduced to their publishing in 1994, Paraclete Press had been in existence for a decade. She quickly accepted an invitation to consult for them, and she joined their editorial advisory board, helping broaden their appeal to authors and media in the book industry. She also became quickly drawn to their way of life. She found their worship passionate and creative, the homilies heartfelt, the people not friendly with Christian nicety generic in the South and Midwest, but more brotherly and sisterly; they freely and graciously challenged each other, and Phyllis. She remarked at one point, "the Community members have honed one another into the most radiantly confessional Christian family I have ever borne witness to."[8] Soon, she had become an oblate as well as a close friend, and began communicating regularly with the publisher at Paraclete and the prioress of the Community itself.

She felt gratitude and welcome there, just as she began to feel less connection to the faith tradition that she had found in college. Phyllis's Episcopal Church experiences had never satisfied her desire for deep,

personal relationships. The lack was epitomized for her in the cliqu-
ishness of the "passing of the peace" at every eucharistic service. When
others turned and smiled and shook hands with those around them,
Phyllis would try her best to do nothing, to greet no one in what felt to
her like an artificial replacement for the real demands and possibilities
of church. She would refer to the Community as a place of joy for her,
and as a place of spiritual "homecoming." They even helped kindle the
monastic in her, and she began to reimagine her already robust prayer
life as that of an "uncloistered Benedictine."

4

Within two years of her first visit in Orleans, in October 1994, Phyllis
was turning what had become her personal involvement and love for
the people of the Community of Jesus, and life there, into a writing
project. It was to be titled *The Making of an American Abbey.*

She proposed to write the history of the founding and flourishing of the Community, in the process demonstrating that theirs was a
unique expression of a growing movement among American Christians
to re-form themselves along ancient lines. She wrote:

> We . . . begin to see, if still imperfectly, an emerging re-configuration of
> North American Christianity that is clearly post-Reformation as well as
> all the other "posts" we currently employ as self-descriptors. Whatever
> else it may turn out to be, our so-called emerging or "New" Christianity
> is most assuredly a coalescing of the faithful into ecclesial communities
> of the like-minded across all the old Reformation divisions of Protestant
> vs. Roman Catholic, of Protestant Confessing Churches vs. Protestant
> Reforming Churches, of charismatics vs. social justice believers. The prog-
> ress of this clumping together finds its most obvious expression in the
> growth of "house churches" and in the rapid expansion in this country
> of "community" or "non-denominational" or "independent" congrega-
> tions, by whatever name they may choose to call themselves. . . . In this
> case, the history of The Community of Jesus in Orleans, Massachusetts is
> a proof-text for what has happened and is happening in North American
> Christianity.[9]

The Community was honored that Phyllis would want to tell their story, even if she might paint their specific charism with a wide brush. And Phyllis was officially contracted to write that history. Already a member of the Paraclete Press editorial board, she began to make additional visits to the Cape to spend time doing research, including interviews with founding members. Occasionally, Sam would come along, and he too made friendships with Community members.

5

When the opportunity and demands of *The Divine Hours* came to dominate her writing life, Phyllis had to put *The Making of an American Abbey* on the back burner. She would take it up again for a while in 2002 to 2003, even conducting more lengthy interviews with principal characters in the story, and accruing two cartons of primary source materials in her office. Also at this time she began to ponder moving to the Community, as a sort of retirement. She believed that Sam, always more gregarious than her, might have plenty to keep him busy, even though the pieties of the place didn't suit him. Sure enough, Sam resisted. They visited together on several occasions, but Sam ultimately didn't feel comfortable, and he still wanted the farm.

In addition to being a homecoming of personal faith and experience, her experiences at the Community of Jesus brought Phyllis to an appreciation of Catholicism that she had never previously had. Her Methodist-raised father was opposed to "all things papist," as he would put it, and Phyllis's own Episcopalianism was never of the Anglo-Catholic variety, steering away from devotion to Mary, the liturgy of confession, and the ritual solemnity of the mass. At the Community—where she began to spend three to four weeks every year—she attended the praying of the hours and found in abundance artistic people who shared her growing love for religious and spiritual mystery. They also gave her space to be and pray and do her work, far from the noise of the farm and family.

They even caused her to reconsider her disinterest in Christendom and its edifices. *The Making of An American Abbey*, however, would never materialize. She would abandon the project for a variety of complicated reasons: Sam's illness and increasing disinterestedness in faith led to refusals to join her on Cape Cod; other projects kept taking precedence, beginning with *The Divine Hours*, and then *The Great Emergence*, which was years in the making. But also, after years of research and interviews, some former members of the Community contacted her to tell personal stories of unhappiness and even abuse during their time there decades earlier. Phyllis decided that the place and its people were too important to her in the present, and chose not to become the one who interpreted their past.

6

In the early spring of 1999, producer Judy Reynolds and reporter Kim Lawton of PBS's *Religion and Ethics Newsweekly* traveled to Lucy to interview Phyllis on subjects of popular religion that were gaining a strange new traction. One of these was gargoyles, which publishers were suddenly making the subject of new books, as retailers were opening shops selling them in many formats. "They play with the idea that just beyond the regular, just beyond the expected," Phyllis remarked on camera, "just beyond the realm, there hovers the world of the other. And the gargoyle said, 'Aha, look at me. I'm the other. And I won't hurt you, but I will scare you just a little bit. I will remind you that in the world of God, not everything is as everything seems.'"[10]

Phyllis was often still being utilized as the "last word," or as the detached, journalistic expert on all matters of religion in popular culture. This is a role that she usually embraced, and in which she excelled. Another of those short pieces filmed by the PBS crew that spring was on the resurgence of interest in Joan of Arc in film, books, a television miniseries, and on college campuses. In that piece, which first aired on May 7 that year, Phyllis remarks of Joan, "She becomes a real icon for our time, one who understood that organized religion has its place, it has its function, that it's where God and man meet and do the business of both. But there is another place where man meets the divine, and they're doing no business at all except the business of the divine."[11]

What took her the most time over the spring and summer months of 1999 was the preparation of a major talk she would give that fall at the Trinity Institute's thirtieth national conference, at Trinity Church Wall Street in downtown Manhattan: "Roots and Wings: Episcopal Identity and Vocation in the New Millennium." Fred Burnham, director of the institute, was responsible for bringing Phyllis to the conference. She would return again several times in the years to come, but this was her first. She immersed herself in diagnosing the state of religion and flux in the western hemisphere, as it related to the challenges facing the Christian churches in the U.S. (Her research for *The Great Emergence* had begun.) She prepared multiple, fully written drafts (unusual for her), submitting them to Burnham for review and almost approval (highly unusual), of what ultimately became a thirty-seven-page address. "Hated reading the damn thing to that poor audience," she joked years later to a friend, since "I don't speak from text or notes simply because I can't read my audience and a piece of paper at the same time."[12]

CHAPTER 14

Behind the Scenes for LGBTQ

Back in the early 1980s, pulmonary medicine was in its early stages. As a medical specialty, it had only existed for a quarter century, but Sam was a pioneer in research and practices in the mid-South. On that forefront, he was also one of the first physicians in greater Memphis to treat AIDS patients, at a time when there was great uncertainty about its contagions. He said to Phyllis one day in 1984, after describing the symptoms of this mysterious new disease, "I want to treat a particular patient." He was referring to a young man whom other physicians had been refusing to take into their care. "Fine," Phyllis said, unsure of the problem. "You don't understand," Sam persisted. "No one knows how this disease is contracted." He went on, "This may impact our lives together. It could affect how we make love, for instance. There may come a time when I stick myself or somehow contract this disease and it could impact our lives."[1]

During that time of uncertainty, when no one knew how it was contracted or how contagious it might be, Sam believed that it was important for older physicians who had already established families to treat AIDS patients. He didn't think it was fair to ask a young doctor just starting out to risk his life. But he could. "Okay," Phyllis said, not ready to argue with such conviction. Sam went on to build a large practice to AIDS patients in West Tennessee. Subsequently, he felt even more emboldened to treat those suffering from the disease on the many occasions when he heard clergy, as well as fellow physicians throughout the South, say that it was probably a scourge of God brought to bear on the gay lifestyle.

2

When AIDS was largely misunderstood, most of Phyllis's friends, going back to grad school and teaching, her work in poetry, and as a book publisher, were scholars, artists, and writers. These communities seemed to be touched by the disease more than others. Also then, Phyllis was serving as a member of the vestry of St. Anne's Episcopal Church in Millington, Tennessee. It was on that vestry that she first became sensitized to the fact that her denomination did not permit the ordination of gays and lesbians. The bishop of West Tennessee was staunchly opposed to changing this practice, as were the majority of voting members in the House of Deputies at the triennial General Convention of the Episcopal Church USA. Phyllis had many gay friends, but hadn't given the issues much thought until the gay community seemed to be embattled from all sides—disease decimating their lives, and acceptance of their rights in question.

Still, most of the impetus in the Tickle home toward the cause for gay rights came from Sam. Sparked by his work as a physician, aware firsthand of what was happening to the lives of gay patients and friends, Sam was prodding Phyllis to pay attention to a growing crisis. His anti-religion stance was simultaneously strengthening, the more he watched the leaders of churches speak uncaringly, unchristianly, on this subject. He also, in working with St. Luke's Press, knew many writers whose lives were touched by the growing epidemic. In fact, the press's accountant was transgendered in some as-yet-to-be-understood ways, and s/he and Sam became good friends.

Going back to his own school days, Sam never felt like he quite fit in. He was drawn to depressives, neurotics, misfits, and those who had been hurt or felt excluded. By the time the AIDS crisis erupted, it was already clear to Phyllis why Sam's love for LGBTQ people developed so easily— because he felt that he was one of them. It was a few years earlier when he came out privately to Phyllis as bisexual. This is how he described it to a physician colleague who was also a transgender friend: "After 15 or 20 years of marriage I told her I need a man. I need her [Phyllis] more, but I think I would have lost it had I not made that plea to her. She approved because that is who I am. Yes, I know it even improved our sex life. I leave the closet door open but do not advertise." From then on, at least, Sam enjoyed occasional sexual partners who were men. He goes on to speak of "Phyllis and our deep love," adding, "She approves of my men and knows each one and is best friends with them. She knows I need a man."[2]

Phyllis lived with this silent pain around her marriage for four decades. The first line of the poem "Hymen Broken" perhaps expresses the emotion: "Sometimes it sweeps over me in icy waves of quiet."[3] There was a degree of stoicism in how she managed it; there was nothing she could do. In this way, the following sentence from *The Shaping of a Life*, read by many as an anti-romantic musing, was actually a way of expressing that there are certain truths in life that she might have preferred not knowing: "Whatever clear otherness there was to him [Sam] in those long-ago days, whatever otherness there still is in either of us, exists now more as a particularity of the what-we-are than as the border marker of a neighboring territory."[4] She excelled at philosophizing around emotional difficulty.

By the end of Sam's life, all of his children would know about his sexual identity, whether or not they wanted to believe it. It seems that none of Phyllis's friends were aware, although it was often evident from comments she would make about her husband that there were ways in which she had to either acquiesce to his needs, or else leave him, and the latter was not an option. She at times counseled friends in bad marriages toward divorce, as for the greater good, but she always believed her own marriage vows were for life.

3

Phyllis and Sam felt called, together, to join an active LGBTQ congregation as soon as they heard about Holy Trinity Community Church in Memphis. This particular church family made the two of them feel at home for different reasons and in different ways. Phyllis entered into conversations theologically, with progressive intentions—but these were also the years when she was moving from being a detached journalist-observer of religion to renewed involvement as a partisan-participant. Sam was there for relationships. Together—finally, religiously together—she and Sam were settled and at home at Holy Trinity.

Phyllis often said to people who asked where she attended church that she and Sam were at Holy Trinity as missionaries of the Episcopal Church, but that was never really the case, and ECUSA never had any formal relationship or outreach at Holy Trinity. They simply felt more

comfortable there than they ever did at Calvary Episcopal in downtown Memphis. "The pain in that congregation [Holy Trinity] was at
fever pitch at that time," she said, "since it looked then as if it would
never be all right to be gay or hermaphroditic or just different." She
and Sam were there as simple congregants, "asking for a place within a
spiritual family, but we were also walking straight into a maelstrom."[5]

It wasn't uncommon, for instance, for a month to go by during
which at least one member or regular communicant at Holy Trinity
had died by suicide. Phyllis felt the necessity of the Gospel and experienced the presence of Jesus in ways that wouldn't have been possible
at most Episcopal churches. "I fell in love," she said, "with the passion
for Jesus that truly, truly broken and rejected and battered and publicly castigated people can have when they understand themselves to
have been accepted by Him."[6] Holy Trinity's then-pastor, Tim Meadows, describes it: "I think what attracted both Phyllis and Sam was this
church at that time was an exiled community whose members risked
their livelihood to be in the fold."[7] It was more than a place of refuge;
they had a voice resonant with pain and joy of exile and costly discipleship. She also loved the absence of pews.

For Sam, it was the first time that Phyllis had gotten him to attend
church regularly in years. Holy Trinity was a special congregation in
how it taught the Gospel. There was a sense that it was possible to
embrace people from all faiths for the benefit of the Gospel that wasn't
defined by any one particular faith or tradition. This suited Phyllis, as
well, who was always more than Christian in her own spiritual identity.

4

This was a time in Phyllis's life when it seemed that every spirituality
author with an eye to advancement wanted a pound of her flesh—
for endorsements, introductions, or favorable coverage in *Publishers Weekly*. She seemed to know everyone. She had sat with the Dalai
Lama, and was unimpressed by his guru effect on devotees. At the
other end of some spectrum, she'd met Roy Rogers and Dale Evans,
authors of a now forgotten memoir that was nevertheless something
PW was obliged to cover. She even spent what she later remembered

as "a hideous afternoon being taken by police guard into a conference room in some hotel at some meeting in Florida so the Attorney General could fill my ears in safety with his importance as well as his religious insights."[8] Attorney General John Ashcroft had a new book, *On My Honor: The Beliefs that Shape My Life*, and the event Phyllis remembered took place in early March 2001, two months before the book was published. During this same time period, however, and on behalf of Holy Trinity Community Church, Phyllis became the one asking favors.

She had met and immediately admired Tammy Faye Bakker Messner, who was the opposite of these others. Not only did Tammy Faye want nothing from Phyllis, but she was, then, also without pretense. "I don't even remember when or how we met, but it was way after the break-up with Jim and after her marriage to Roe, and way before she got sick," Phyllis recalled.[9] Tammy Faye had fought colon cancer in 1996, but Phyllis was remembering her famous announcement and discussion of her lung cancer on *Larry King Live* years later. Then, at the tail-end of the twentieth century, either despite or because of her fundamentalist background, Tammy Faye came out in full support of gay rights and LGBTQ people. She began to march in gay pride parades, and for many reasons—most of all, a documentary narrated by drag queen RuPaul, *The Eyes of Tammy Faye*—she became a gay icon.

Phyllis said, "She didn't want anything except to talk about the situation in which we found ourselves and to swap tales that might allow each of us to elucidate something for the other."[10] With the blessing of Pastor Meadows, Phyllis began to curate a series of talks on Sunday mornings before worship. She called them "Pancake Theology," and Sam loved working in the kitchen at the griddle actually making the pancakes. Her first big "get" was to ask Tammy Faye to come to Memphis. It was the spring of 2003 and Holy Trinity was then meeting in an old bank building on Summer Avenue.

"Boy, did she come! The place was packed with TV ancillary spots set up all over the building and parking lot, there was a totally jammed street outside, cops everywhere trying to control the flow, and so on. But the point is that she came at her own expense. I think the church maybe had enough money to help with the hotel, but I'm not even sure of that, and it wouldn't have mattered to her any more than no stipend did. She believed in it and them, and everybody in that place knew it." Phyllis remembered, "We stayed in touch until she became too ill. I think I even still have a carton of her books downstairs [at Lucy] that she gave me from her stock and signed, so that anybody who didn't get a copy and wanted one could have it."[11] Tammy Faye would die in July 2007.

Next, Phyllis turned to her old friend, Bishop Spong. He wasn't the "gay icon" that Tammy Faye was, but Phyllis described him to her fellow congregants as the most eloquent and determined advocate for full LGBTQ rights that the church of the last half-century has seen. He, too, brought out big crowds at Holy Trinity, speaking over pancakes there the following year, also at Phyllis's personal request, apparently understanding that it was good work in the world, and probably that he owed Phyllis a favor or two. That Sunday, traffic on Highland Avenue, to where the congregation had moved when the old bank building was no longer suitable, was more congested than anyone had ever seen. People were double-parking in the road to hear Spong, who they quickly realized was indeed their champion—a genuine hero of gay, lesbian, bisexual, and transgendered people.

"Those two were the ones the folk most wanted to hear from, be assured by, and be affirmed by. It was just pure grace or luck or both that they were willing to come," Phyllis remembered with a grin.[12]

5

Curiously, however, there was a way in which Phyllis could not fully commit to Holy Trinity. Her experiences there would be both profoundly rewarding and somewhat painful, as she hoped anxiously that her Episcopal Church would move swiftly toward full acceptance of LGBTQ members, including the ordination of clergy who so identify. She clung to her identity as an Episcopalian, a lay reader and eucharistic minister in that tradition, as she so often reminded people, despite the fact that her own congregation lay outside of it. She became a close friend of her pastor at Holy Trinity, Tim Meadows, an openly gay man who wanted a sustaining affiliation himself with a mainline denomination. She deeply hoped that that denomination might one day be her Episcopal Church. Meadows had already left one denomination, when the United Methodist Church would not allow a gay man to pastor one of its churches.

One Holy Trinity member recalls how Phyllis was regarded at Holy Trinity: "She brought an intellectual component, as a scholar. She was a rock star in the religion world, which most of us did not know, at first. But Tim did. I also think that having straight allies, a long-married couple, attend, love, worship, alongside us, as one of us, was a great component to the congregation."[13] By that point, of course, Phyllis and Sam knew that they were not simply a straight couple—but that was mostly an understanding between them. And Phyllis watched as Sam quickly moved his official church membership to Holy Trinity, just as she felt that she could not. This caused another small emotional split between the two of them, and even between Phyllis and her own conscience. She wasn't willing to give up her license in the Episcopal Church as a lector and lay minister. From time to time she would tell the rector at Calvary Episcopal in Memphis who she was going to visit, and when, and he would in turn provide her the consecrated bread and wine that she needed from the Calvary ambry.[14]

She was nevertheless assiduously working behind the scenes to lobby the Episcopal bishop of West Tennessee to change his mind regarding acceptance of LGBTQ people. Then she lobbied leaders at the national level. She believed that the Holy Spirit led her to do these things, and she would talk that way about them to friends who understood evangelical language, its power and potential. Yet, she worried. The colophon she chose for her autobiography—an obscure passage from the Book of Common Prayer's translation of the Psalms, speaks to this in a way that she never did: "Let not those who hope in you be put to shame through me, Lord God of hosts; let not those who seek you be disgraced because of me, O God of Israel" (Ps. 69:7). More than anything else, she wanted her beloved Holy Trinity to become Holy Trinity Episcopal Church. But it would never happen.

6

Phyllis was not one for causes, but this was different. Never giving lectures on this topic, or coming out and endorsing specific candidates for positions in the church, she and Sam made a powerful point by worshipping at an openly affirming congregation and speaking openly about it in personal conversations.

But she didn't feel called to play an active part in the intellectual or doctrinal debate on the issues. In print, she wrote: "Whether any one of the combatants likes to admit it or not, either of the opposing positions of proscription or progressive revelation may be assumed with credibility." And in private, she said: "[Y]ou follow the love you're led to by every whit of Jesus' teaching and life and the Spirit's voice. Somewhere along in there you just begin to assume the doctrine thing will work itself out, but that the folks who work it out will have to be somebody other than you yourself because you're much too busy just being part of them to be able to separate out and objectify enough to parse the thing intellectually."[15]

She often advised colleagues who were preparing to out themselves in support of LGBTQ acceptance in the church. For example, theologian Tony Jones, before he accepted an offer from Beliefnet to publicly debate Rod Dreher, the "Crunchy Conservative," on the issue of gay marriage wrote to her asking for advice: Should he do it? If so, how? Phyllis wrote back:

> I have been in some prayer about my response since getting your note yesterday. I think the answer, if I am discerning correctly, is that you do have to accept this challenge or request or whatever it is. . . . If that be true, I would probably go in sideways through parables and/or stories rather than head-on. And I might even go sideways via Church history, a la James Boswell and *Same-Sex Union* etc. But I'm pretty sure that head-on would be (almost always is, in fact) a wreck waiting to happen.[16]

A few years later, when acceptance of LGBTQ Christians in churches of all kinds was still a "red line" issue (to cross the line was to move from being evangelical or United Methodist or whatever to something else—often Episcopal), one of Phyllis's closest friends, Ken Wilson, the founding pastor of the Ann Arbor Vineyard, began his own process of reevaluating his stance. Wilson was one of the most respected Vineyard leaders in the country, a real theologian-pastor, and one with a publishing track record with Thomas Nelson, a relationship that had been initiated for him by Phyllis. She and Ken began talking about LGBTQ acceptance, and Ken began a quiet, serious study of the Bible in order to reevaluate his position, which had been, according to evangelical doctrine, exclusionary—a sort of "love the sinner, but hate the sin" approach. After his period of study, Ken was considering coming out with a new understanding. He told Phyllis that he wanted "a hush-hush by invitation only hermetically-sealed conversation with pastors . . . to discuss homosexuality and the church," asking, "Are there a few evangelical pastors that you think we ought to invite? People who might be in a position of assessment on the issue similar to where I'm at? The higher level the better, and pastors is what I'm interested in primarily."[17]

Phyllis wrote back two days later. She was stuck in a snowstorm in the North Carolina mountains with Sam.

> I have struggled off and on during the night to try and come up with just one even, but no luck. . . . I was and am alarmed to realize that I don't— which, of course, speaks volumes about the problem, doesn't it? . . . If you . . . can pull this thing off and come up with rhetoric or exegesis that makes it possible for pastors to do what has to be done, it'll be the greatest gift to the Church of the last quarter century at least.[18]

Over the next several years, Ken would send bits of research, and passages from his sermons, to Phyllis asking for her response. His final coming out wouldn't take place for several more years, when he asked his entire congregation to discern along with him by reading a book-length study paper he'd prepared on the subject. The following winter that paper was published as *A Letter to My Congregation*, with Phyllis writing the book's introduction. Ken lost his church as a result.

She also fumed occasionally behind the scenes, as in this email after the Episcopal Church failed again to reach positive, progressive conclusions on these issues: "My episcopakin have delayed and delayed so many times over on grappling with the biggies, that I'm truly leery of delays anymore. Though of course I am also clueless about how to out maneuver them."[19]

At the same time, she sought to understand what it was like to be LGBT or Q, in private conversations, even in private prayer. At one point she felt that God had told her that full acceptance of LGBTQ

Christians was correct, even if it couldn't be demonstrated according to biblical teaching. She would say, on occasion, that she wasn't going to make theological or biblical arguments for gay equality. Her job, instead, was more pastoral. It also seems she may have asked Sam what gay sex was like, in her desire to understand, and this might explain how she came to believe that gay sex was less unitive and complete for those who engaged in it, when compared to heterosexual sex. She said to her closest spiritual friend: "I am persuaded that they [LGBTQ people] are devout and Christian and beloved. I am also more or less persuaded (I lack first-hand experience, after all) that the joining or coupling is a different and less complete one."[20] One can almost hear Sam explaining it to his wife this way in order to emphasize his commitment to her and to their marriage.

She was effective advocating quietly, speaking with would-be delegates of the 2003 Episcopal Church General Convention, where Gene Robinson was confirmed as the first openly gay bishop in the Episcopal Church, and later, on a smaller scale, playing an affirming role at the Wild Goose Festival in 2011, where other luminaries such as Jim Wallis of Sojourners, evangelical evangelist Tony Campolo, and singer/songwriter Michelle Shocked all spoke against inclusion. (By 2015, Wild Goose had evolved to become a completely affirming venue for LGBTQ people, and even saw the re-emergence of Campolo as a surprise guest, just one month after he finally came out with an affirming stance. Already ill, Phyllis was sorry not to be there when Campolo publicly apologized to the Wild Goose community in early July 2015.)

7

Meanwhile, at Holy Trinity Community Church, Sam was settled and active—planting trees and bushes, cooking pancake breakfasts—while Phyllis was often away over weekends. Then it came time for the congregation to vote on whether or not to affiliate with a mainline denomination, or remain an independent, community church. Many in the church prized their independence. Even Phyllis argued this point, saying to some, "Holy Trinity needs to be careful not to end up another rabbit pelt on the belt of some denomination." But the dominant view was that they needed the financial safety net that comes with being a part of a denomination. Membership would enable them to take advantage of loans, insurance for their pastor, and so on.

Both Pastor Tim Meadows and Phyllis wished that Holy Trinity could join the Episcopal Church, but at the time the bishop would not accept either the church or Tim, an openly gay pastor. The United Church of Christ—the mainline denomination most actively accepting of LGBTQ people, evidenced by an overwhelming "yes" vote at their 2005 General Synod in favor of gay marriage—did. Phyllis didn't want the UCC for Holy Trinity. Sam disagreed. One year later, the congregational vote at Holy Trinity was in favor, and in 2007 the church officially joined the UCC. Soon, the congregation found themselves doing the work of denominational structures, which offered them a chance to participate with the larger church in an intellectually welcoming community. Additionally, the vestry at Holy Trinity was replaced with new bylaws and a church council. Worship changed, to the disapproval of both Phyllis and Sam. Holy Trinity started looking and feeling like many other congregations look and feel on a Sunday morning in Memphis. The anti-episcopacy of the UCC was moving in, which might have been okay, except that what had been edgy about Holy Trinity in liturgy, worship, and style, was soon gone, too. Phyllis's warnings about denominations came true and, in the words of Timothy Meadows, "we all knew the beautiful season was over."[21]

8

Phyllis often struggled with religious hierarchy and organization. Such struggle played a role in her cofounding The Canterbury Roundtable, a collegial working group that came together twice a year on either side of the Atlantic to discuss the future of the Anglican Communion and the theological and liturgical priorities in which its members were actively involved. Phyllis co-founded it with Megory Anderson, an American theologian who was finishing a PhD at Canterbury Christ Church University in Kent. Gareth Jones, the head of theology at Canterbury Christ Church, spearheaded the English contingent, and participants in the U.S. included Donald Schell, Lizette Larson-Miller, and Bob Scott from Trinity Church Wall Street and The Trinity Institute. As one of those participants remembered, "It was fairly early in the time of stress within the global Anglican Communion over sexuality, so we were also aware of the importance of keeping informal lines of communication and relationship open."[22]

Perhaps unknown to the others, Phyllis possessed a keen sense of anti-clericalism and was interested in how the Roundtable might help flatten teaching authority in the Anglican Communion. A short anecdote illustrates this: While dreaming up the Roundtable, Phyllis was also one of a distinguished group of board members of a new website, funded by a millionaire in Memphis, called Explorefaith.org. At a board meeting in 2005, the marketer for the new site asked a group that included Phyllis, the Rev. Barbara Brown Taylor, the Rev. Dr. Fred Burnham, the Rt. Rev. Frederick Borsch, and the Rev. Michael Battle, PhD—how the site might reach a wider audience with its content. Someone suggested that the religious and educational titles of those writing for the site (people like Taylor, Borsch, and Battle) might be jettisoned. "People in the pews, or those who have left the pews, don't want to see 'The Right Reverend so-and-so.' It's off-putting," he said. "If teaching is good, it doesn't need the authority of job titles to say so." A lively debate ensued, including some consternation, until the marketer gestured to Phyllis, who was silently grinning in the corner of the room. "What do you think?"

"I couldn't agree more," she said.

Throughout 2007, at Phyllis's urging and instigation, The Canterbury Roundtable began to brainstorm and create what they offered as a potential fourth vowed order within the Communion: an order of teachers composed of secular (non-religious) scholars. As stated in a proposal that was submitted by the Roundtable to then-archbishop Rowan Williams, the purpose of the Canterbury Order of Teachers (COT) would be "so that every parish or diocese or province within the Anglican Communion, for the benefit of its clergy or laity or their associates, may have access to authoritative scholarship that is both secularly validated as academically sound and also delivered by scholars who, in making the vows of membership into the Order, have attested to their belief in Jesus of Nazareth as the Christ and Son of God." The proposal went on to stipulate that members of the COT would be paid for lectures, and that this process would be "administered by the Office of the Principal of the COT." Phyllis wanted to help educate the laity, as well as find new means of employment for her friends and colleagues. The expectation was that the archbishop would formally commission the order and then appoint said principal to oversee operations. This never happened. After the formal proposal was made to Lambeth in early 2008, the idea fell quietly away.[23]

9

The Holy Trinity season in Phyllis's life is ultimately a demonstration of how uneasily she made her way as a religious leader. Her license as a lector and lay eucharistic minister aside, she was usually doing very different work in religion: judging, evaluating, and explaining. But, at times, she was called upon to lead with her spiritual and religious gifts. These were tremulous but exciting moments for her. Vineyard pastor Ken Wilson remembers one of these occasions:

> I invited her to speak at my then church, not to do her usual 50,000 foot assessment of what's happening on the religious landscape, but to be the Phyllis I was getting to know. She seemed terrified, which was so difficult for me to accept at the time because I viewed her as so capable and confident and to use an old charismatic term, anointed. But she was clearly conflicted and it just didn't make sense to me. She came in February 2005 and did narrative preaching about Melchezidek. A non-religious visitor brought by my daughter had a classic Pentecostal initiation experience during Phyllis' talk. On Sunday, I invited her to pray over people one at a time, give a blessing with anointing of oil, like old line Pentecostal healer-line style (something we'd never done before) and she did it for maybe ninety minutes after the service ended. People just lined up and stayed like they would for a famous healer holy person.[24]

The "50,000 foot assessment" would remain the most comfortable position for Phyllis. She would never participate again in a religious service in those more intimate capacities.

CHAPTER 15

A Rapidly Changing Church

As the turn of the millennium approached, evangelicals Doug Pagitt (Minneapolis) and Chris Seay (Houston) were talking about icons and liturgical seasons, making many people in their churches nervous. Lauren Winner, a young convert to Anglicanism from Orthodox Judaism, was talking to fellow Christians about the richness of Jewish spiritual practice, including the Shema. And an evangelical pastor named Brian McLaren had just published *Reinventing Your Church* (1998); he wasn't advocating reinvention of style (the sort of things that had been done by mega-churches since the early 1980s), but wanted to pay attention to the changes of postmodernity. Phyllis, who was still at *Publishers Weekly*, quickly took notice of all of this, realizing that it was part of what Robert E. Webber of Wheaton College had predicted much earlier in his 1985 book, *Evangelicals on the Canterbury Trail*. She also realized that the numbers were growing.

None of these people were questioning evangelical orthodoxy in those early years. McLaren "organized his treatment around strategies for a postmodern context," and Webber, in his own turn-of-the-millennium book, *Ancient-Future Faith* (1999), "stressed paradigm thinking and showed how classical Christian theology, worship, spirituality, and mission were well suited to postmodern ministry"—as it was explained by David Neff of *Christianity Today* magazine.[1] That would change. But, at the beginning, emerging church leaders focused on how to be church and do ministry in a new paradigm.

Gallup and other polling organizations began to take note of the spirituality revival going on. For example, the number of people responding affirmatively to the statement, "I feel the need for spiritual growth" increased from 56 percent to 82 percent between 1984 and 1998. PBS's *Religion & Ethics Newsweekly* quoted these statistics in a seventeen-minute segment on changing attitudes toward organized religion and the boom of individual spirituality. They interviewed luminaries Wade Clark Roof, Robert Wuthnow, Martin Marty, and Marianne Williamson. And after a lengthy interview with Phyllis from her home in Lucy, they quoted her—as a journalist and critic—reflecting on the lack of response to human suffering and need in many of the new spiritual movements and teachers: "It asks nothing. It makes no demands. You can only live in that so long before its sure sweetness will kill you. It's like eating too much icing."[2] Her opinion would soon change, and she would see what was happening in the churches as much more than candy.

2

People will debate for years to come whether Phyllis was an evangelist and catalyst for change in the American church, or simply a historian and sociologist telling of changes taking place. As a biographer once said of Thomas Merton, one might say of Phyllis: "He wrote at a time when the very foundations of Christian life and culture were being shaken. One of the reasons he was sometimes misunderstood was that he was doing a bit of the shaking himself."[3] Curiously, she once said, "Books are strange things, both proactive and reactive. That is, they both engender change and respond and adjust themselves to it."[4] The truth of Phyllis as evangelist or mere sociologist probably lies somewhere in the middle. Throughout her late career of interpreting Emergence, she would often encounter in Q&A a question resembling: "What you describe is not exactly good for us, right?"

She would respond by saying something like, "I know that it feels uncomfortable from where you stand. . . ."

Her enthusiasm, as always, infected. It was the mystic in her that communicated a sense of *wow!* when sharing knowledge with others. The incident recounted in the prologue of this book, when she was accosted after giving a lecture, was uncommon with respect to its physical confrontation, but not in the way that Phyllis walked a line between reportage and advocacy. It was often difficult to tell the difference between the two in her work, even as she was hesitant to pronounce judgment, or lose her journalistic or academic prerogative for impartiality. Soon after that occasion when she was accused of belittling the authority of scripture, she would publish *The Great Emergence*, in which she expanded upon what infuriated the man in Atlanta. She would track the issues in the church that demonstrate an assault upon *sola scriptura*, the doctrine most precious to the evangelical worldview and faith:

> The next assault in this progression of assaults [upon *sola scriptura*] was the ordination of women to the Protestant clergy. . . . The ordination of women was followed, of course, by their elevation to the episcopacy in the Episcopal Church in the United States. Clearly the battle of "Scripture only" was being lost. Now there was only one more tool left in sola scriptura's war chest. . . . Enter "the gay issue."
>
> To approach any of the arguments and questions surrounding homosexuality in the closing years of the twentieth century and the opening ones of the twenty-first is to approach a battle to the death. When it is resolved—and it most surely will be—the Reformation's understanding of Scripture as it had been taught by Protestantism for almost five centuries will be dead. That is not to say that Scripture as the base of authority is dead. Rather it is to say that what the Protestant tradition has taught about the nature of that authority will either be dead or in mortal need of reconfiguration.
>
> And that kind of summation is agonizing for the surrounding culture in general. In particular, it is agonizing for the individual lives that have been built upon it. Such an ending is to be staved off with every means available and resisted with every bit of energy that can be mustered. Of all the fights, the gay one must be—has to be—the bitterest, because once it is lost, there are no more fights to be had. It is finished. Where now is the authority?[5]

She was, at that point, akin to a Faith Popcorn, the trend expert who consulted with dozens of Fortune 500s (*Clicking*; *The Popcorn Report*), of American religion. Between the closing years of the millennium and the publication of *The Great Emergence*, Phyllis was transforming her focus onto American churches, rather than American religion more broadly. This would preoccupy her for the rest of her life. And when she said, "We are in the midst of radical change" it often felt somewhat like "Change is coming" as well as, "We should embrace it."

3

There is nothing more difficult for people to hear than prophecy, and Phyllis reveled in delivering it. From her young days in the academy she had taken "big picture" approaches to answering ponderous questions. From the education she received from her scholar-father, and then at Shorter College, she had a broad, sweeping understanding of Greek and Roman history, Latin and other languages, the decline and fall of great civilizations, and world literature. Her subtle mind refused to see facts in isolation. Her brain always made connections, at a faster rate, and with more stored data with which to assimilate the new information, than others.

And yet, she wasn't a scholar. She never cleared new ground and rarely plumbed truly original sources. Her work was derivative, unapologetically so: She knew what was best to repeat, dissect, and explain.

To distance herself from scholarship, she would use humor. She would make fun of Martin Luther before Protestant audiences, for instance, knowing that she would raise eyebrows and get a few laughs. On one of these occasions, she said at a conference in Ireland that by having five "solas" Luther must not have understood Latin very well. Then she suggested that it was naïve of the Protestant reformer to assume that *sola scriptura* might ever be enough to guide Christians. "I love to tease Luther. I have to sometimes temper it with the remembrance that he died a horrible death, a lingering death, of colorectal cancer, which probably explains something of what's wrong with Protestantism," she added.[6] If most anyone else said such a thing, they'd probably be criticized, but Phyllis could get away with it.

Another time, she poked fun at Baptists as a digression while explaining the genus-species distinction between Protestants and the various denominations within Protestantism: "Nobody thinks that all Protestants are Baptist, right? Baptists tend to think so, but no. I'm very fond of Baptists, I have a Baptist degree and my mother was a devout

Southern Baptist."[7] (She didn't actually earn a degree from Shorter College, a Baptist school, but no matter.)

Then there was the time when she was being interviewed by mainline clergy for a mainline clergy magazine and she used this analogy to explain why Emergence Christians are so nervous about buildings and hierarchy, the two things traditionally most associated with church: "The minute you own a piece of real estate, then you have to have somebody to clean it, then you have to have somebody to be sure that it gets clean, then you have to get somebody to be sure that it's insured, and the next thing you know, you've got a bishop," she explained, with a grin.[8]

4

Two other things happened as the millennium was closing that turned Phyllis's attention to the emerging church. First, there was a July 1998 article in *Mother Jones* magazine. It was the first national magazine to attempt to describe what was happening. Lori Leibovich's "A Look Inside Fundamentalism's Answer to MTV: The Postmodern Church," ran in the July/August issue.[9] It drew a compelling portrait of Mark Driscoll's new Mars Hill Fellowship in Seattle: "Postmodern leaders walk effortlessly between the secular and religious worlds, talking about the new Radiohead album in one breath, Jesus in the next." Leibovich also drew attention to how Christian innovators were gathering together:

> Postmoderns receive crucial support—financial and otherwise—from the megachurches. These postmodern ministries are loosely organized by the Leadership Network, a Dallas-based umbrella group for many of the nation's megachurches. It's the Leadership Network that keeps Driscoll's bohemian Mars Hill ministry in touch with the fast-growing, but more traditional, University Baptist Church in Waco by holding conferences and seminars. For the past three years the network has sponsored national conferences that bring together postmodern leaders. The first one attracted nearly 300, the second 500, and the next one, this fall in New Mexico, is expected to draw 1,000. The network also helps arrange necessary seed

money, for example, setting up key contributions from megachurches for the University Baptist ministry in Waco. "We target young, innovative ministries because they are the future of the church," says Doug Pagitt, 31, of the Leadership Network.

Words like "postmodern" were the rage. This was an active, exploratory time in evangelical churches and organizations like Leadership Network in Dallas, for whom Pagitt, after a decade as youth pastor at Wooddale Church in Eden Prairie, Minnesota, moved to Dallas in 1997 to head up their Youth Leaders Network. Soon, he was disseminating Tickle wisdom in a weekly subscription fax service called "Helping Church Leaders Make the Transition—From the Present to the Future." An interview with Phyllis appeared in a late 1998 issue and one of her answers shows how she was reading the signs: *What is happening generationally?* "The ones that fascinate me are the Mosaics . . . kids born since 1985. There has been a real change in how they think, in how they organize and process information. They interact with everything, they have an inability to read just a flat page, and their attention span is shorter. Their hierarchy of information has been flattened."[10]

The other thing that happened to capture Phyllis's attention took place while she was giving a talk in Atlanta. She met a young man who said something that proved more important to her than any other comment she received in a career of thousands of Q&As. Her talk was her usual on the trends in religion, as witnessed in what spiritual and religious books were doing. She mentioned the Jesus Seminar and its strange new ways of determining what Jesus may or may not have said, and she mentioned the Virgin Birth as one of the traditional doctrines under assault by their researches. "After the lecture was over and the general questions finished, a young man—probably no more than eighteen—came up to me, shaking his head, 'I just don't get it,' he said. 'Of course I believe in the Virgin Birth. Why wouldn't I? The whole thing's so beautiful, it has to be true, whether it happened or not.'"[11]

She hugged him. What he said functioned like a holy revelation to her. She told a colleague that "she felt as if the universe had shifted." "I felt like I was standing on holy ground," she said.[12] Years later, by the time she told the story for the first time in print, she had fully formed it into her theological perspective. This happened seamlessly, in part, because what the teenager said crystallized what already made sense to her. Phyllis had written decades earlier in a chancel drama these words for the Prophet Jeremiah to say to his scribe, Baruch: "God is beauty. Oh, Baruch, God is such awful beauty. If I am angry, it is that we too may all be beautiful." To which Baruch replies, "I don't understand." Jeremiah answers, "Nor do I, nor do I."[13] So the flash experience with the teenager around the Virgin Birth became the framework for what had first come to her in these fictive words for Jeremiah. That anecdote about the Virgin Birth would, in fact, become a foundation plank for the Emergence Christian notion that truth is "actual, not factual." Over the next decade and a half, Phyllis was often frustrated when others would retell it, taking it out of context, and outside of her experience. Many people even co-opted it for themselves on the lecture circuit, and in print.

She'd been talking about how Euro-American Christianity was in the midst of a time of reformation, or "re-formation" as early as 1995 while writing *God-Talk in America*. She was referring to "emergence" as the nascent term for a movement afoot as early as 2001, citing as an expert the historian John Lukacs. And by the time her ridiculously brief, 176-page masterwork, *The Great Emergence*, was published on October 1, 2008, she was already at the center of describing and interpreting the nascent movement.

She shared podiums with many of emerging's leaders. Diana Butler Bass and Phyllis, for instance, keynoted together at many conferences during the years before and after the publication of *The Great Emergence*. These were gatherings which, in many ways, prepared the ground for the publication of the best books written by the two women. Clergy and church professionals would come together to puzzle over what was happening around them, and Phyllis would say memorable things such as: "Postmodern, post-Christian, post-Protestant, and post-denominational. What do all these posts mean? That we know where we have been but that we have no idea where we are going!"[14]

Phyllis often used a page from *Parabola* magazine, whose editorial board she sat on for many years, as a demonstration tool. On it was an image of a rather standard Rorschach test.[15] "Do our perceptions alter reality?" she would read from the handout, and then describe how the brain has to choose which reality to see. Then she would add how the brain sees both figures in the drawing, at times, as true.

Then, a quadrilateral diagram became ubiquitous. It was a mnemonic device to demonstrate two of her central theses: that all who care deeply about the Christian faith are ultimately revolving around the same center, and that the old categories of "left" and "right" no longer adequately describe what's happening in the churches. The four quadrants were, starting in the upper left, Liturgicals, and moving clockwise: Social Justice Christians, Conservatives, and Renewalists. Each quadrant touched the other at the center, and each also touched the two that adjoined it, meaning that Liturgicals were sharing with Social Justice and Renewalist Christians; Social Justice Christians were sharing with Liturgicals and Conservatives; Conservatives were sharing with Social Justice and Renewalist Christians; and Renewalists had things in common particularly with Liturgicals and Conservatives. Phyllis referred to the meeting in the middle—the center point—of all four quadrants as "The Gathering Center," a pragmatic phrase for those who, despite real differences, are looking to cooperate towards a future.

5

Prayer Is a Place was published in June 2005, to coincide with a major luncheon talk Phyllis was to give at the annual Religious Booksellers Trade Exhibit. This gathering was a veritable love-fest for her each year. She received a standing ovation after the talk, and copies were given out by her publisher to everyone in the audience. She recommended a book that had just been written by Brian McLaren, whom she'd never met. *A Generous Orthodoxy* helped to forge the Emergence ethos. Its subtitle says it all: *Why I Am a Missional, Evangelical, Post/Protestant, Liberal/Conservative, Mystical/Poetic, Biblical, Charismatic/Contemplative, Fundamentalist/Calvinist, Anabaptist/ Anglican, Methodist, Catholic, Green, Incarnational, Depressed-yet-Hopeful, Emergent, Unfinished Christian.* Tony Jones, a mutual friend, was in the audience. He reported the compliment back to McLaren and before the year was out McLaren and Phyllis were sharing a dais at a conference where Phyllis was giving an early version of her every-five-hundred-year-rummage-sale talk. She said to McLaren, "My daddy always said a man is best known by the enemies he keeps, and in light of all the people who are mad as hell at you, you're someone I have great respect for."[16]

She was often sharing a dais with evangelical "stars" such as McLaren. Others included John Ortberg, former teaching pastor at the original megachurch, Willow Creek Community, outside Chicago; Anne Graham Lotz, daughter of the famous evangelist and the president of Angel Ministries; evangelical Bible scholar and writer Scot McKnight (*The Jesus Creed*, etc.); founder of Gateway megachurch in Austin, Texas, John Burke; and Dan Kimball, one of the first to write at book-length about the emerging church (*The Emerging Church*, 2003), which included a foreword by the most popular pastor in America at that time, Rick Warren of Saddleback.

When Phyllis and McLaren started working together, Burke, Kimball, and Pagitt were all writing essays for a forthcoming book, *Listening to the Beliefs of Emerging Churches*, edited by Robert E. Webber. "Ancient/future" was how Webber was talking about how evangelicals were increasingly interested in the teachings and practices of the early church. The often controversial pastor Mark Driscoll contributed to that book, as well, just before he publicly left the movement. In fact, his essay—denouncing any attempt to reconcile homosexuality with faithful Christian discipleship, and buttressing a traditional understanding of atonement in salvation history—showed how far he was from the ethos and approach that would soon come to characterize the movement.

Emerging leaders were focused on influencing and reaching Generation X. Most of them were Gen X themselves and saw their generation as the first one prepared to leap past modernity's preoccupations with propositional truth to recover the mystery and wonder of faith they believed characterized the early or true church. The 2006 National Pastors Convention was a turning point, not only because Rick Warren and Mark Driscoll publicly turned away from Emerging/Emergent within the year, but because other prominent evangelicals like Scot

McKnight began to distance themselves from it, and LeRon Shults soon left to take up atheism. Jones and Pagitt, meanwhile, would continue at the movement's center, as its prime movers, by virtue of charisma and entrepreneurial spirit.

6

During a break between sessions in San Diego in February 2006 at the National Pastors Convention, Phyllis was sitting in one of the resort's tired restaurants, eating dinner with Doug and Shelley Pagitt and Baker Books editor Chad Allen. At that time, Emergent Village, of which Doug Pagitt was a cofounder, and Baker were in league to create a series of books called "emersion," spearheaded by Doug and Chad.

This was what is referred to in publishing as a pitch meeting, but in this case it wasn't clear who was pitching whom. "Doug said something about how Emergent Village's detractors claimed the organization was hell-bent on designating insiders and outsiders to the movement. Before he could say another word, Phyllis pounced. 'Say what?!'" remembered Allen. "There's no castle building going on here!" Phyllis added, genuinely annoyed by the accusation.

"Doug responded by asking if she'd be willing to take up for Emergence by turning her verbal presentation into a book. I was crunching away on a breadstick, I think, eagerly awaiting her reply. . . . [S]he didn't need much convincing. If we'd given her five minutes, she likely would have pitched the idea to us! She said something like 'I'd like to do that,' and that was it. A quiet yes from one friend to another, and a terribly important book was born."[17]

7

In the months before the release of *The Great Emergence*, Phyllis watched with sadness as the religion department at *Publishers Weekly* was slowly dismantled. The most serious economic recession since the Great Depression was underway and advertising hit rock bottom in the spring of 2008. On June 1 of that year, Lynn Garrett was let go. Four months later and two key editors in New York, Isabell Taylor and Dick Donahue, were fired. By January 2009, even the great Daisy Maryles was let go, despite her nearly forty-five years with the magazine. *PW* had become a shell of what it had been. Phyllis grieved over this, and exchanged frequent emails with former colleagues and friends who were affected.

Sam's health also grew increasingly worse, and Phyllis found it difficult to do the work to get *The Great Emergence* done. A new mass was discovered in his thyroid, and on October 16, 2007, he had surgery to remove it. Preparing for that occasion, plus trips to see doctors while they tried to titrate him onto synthetic thyroid, were trying for Phyllis. She was supposed to deliver her book to the publisher by January 1 and had never been late with a manuscript before—a point of pride. The book's message was also so urgent, she believed, that postponing publication was unthinkable.

A few weeks after Sam's surgery she wrote to Chad Allen at Baker: "Given what Sam's physician told us yesterday, I am as sure as anybody ever can be that I will be done by 7 January. I may make 1 January, but I don't want to commit to that, unless you too are comfortable with it; but 7 January is not a problem. Please let me know whether that extra week is acceptable or not."[18] Chad responded ninety minutes later with gratitude and assured her that they would still publish the book, as planned, in October.

But this wasn't at all the end of personal problems at home relating to Sam and his needs. It was also while Phyllis was wrapping up *The Great Emergence* that one of Sam's friends, Art, came to stay in his RV on the farm. "RV" is really too generous a term for the vehicle; he was living in an old bus on the site of their unused garden plot. Writing to a friend, Phyllis referred to Art as an "eternal hippie . . . a confirmed, bright, unrepentant, uncompromising hippie" who they'd known "as a fellow-congregant for five years."[19] Sam and Art knew each other from Holy Trinity. Art couldn't afford to pay lot costs for the vehicle anymore, so Sam (and Phyllis) allowed him to park, semi-permanently, on their property. Art made it possible that Sam wasn't alone all the days and weekends when Phyllis was traveling. After less than a year, Art moved away from Memphis, but left behind the RV. There it remained in the garden between the yard and the barn.

Next, ailing and lonely, Sam reached out to a teenager who lived in the neighborhood, giving him money and advice. As a result, the boy hung around the farm and occasionally helped Sam out. Eventually, kicked out of his father's house, he came to live in Art's abandoned RV. He brought his problems with him, and burglarized their home one night in the spring, taking everything he could find, even managing to carry away a safe that was mostly full of papers, but also silver dollars from the 1930s and '40s that Sam had collected. Over the years, Sam had filled socks with the silver and placed them in the safe. There were about a dozen socks in there. None were ever recovered. The boy also stole an Indian peace pipe from the fireplace mantle—a relic from a great-grandfather. He probably stole it to smoke crack from, but it wouldn't have worked for that purpose. Eventually, the teen's father got it and some other items back to Sam and Phyllis, and soon thereafter, the RV caught fire and burned to the ground.

8

Journalists, trend-watchers, and those whom her analysis impacted directly—clergy and anyone making a living by delivering faith and spirituality—saw immediately the importance of *The Great Emergence*. Bob Abernethy, the executive editor and host of public television's *Religion & Ethics Newsweekly*, a personal friend to whom Phyllis sent an advance copy, read the book straight through while waiting for his Subaru to be fixed at a garage. In a handwritten letter, he wrote to Phyllis, "I thought, as I read, about how we could include your grand survey in our program. I see your story as the basis for a terrific documentary, but I have not figured out yet how to make your overview work in a short piece. We will have to find visible examples, and I will work on that."[20]

Scholars did not embrace the book, what with its assigning of decades, years, and even specific dates to great moments of transition and change in the world and the church. Academics frown on that. But Phyllis was more of a "macro-historian," and had a valuable and even pastoral role to play.[21] For her, writing with broad strokes was the product of a mystical imagination, and a desire to speak directly to people who were actively involved in professional religious work. Readers have always embraced such an approach, and those who help readers find books that help navigate conundrums do, too. The American Library Association's *Booklist* gave *The Great Emergence* one of their coveted "starred" reviews, writing, "Somehow . . . diverse strands come together in a seamless fabric that, at fewer than 200 pages, is small but full of big ideas, a remarkable achievement of synthesis and thoughtful reflections."[22] It is also possible that the woman who as a girl was reared on dispensational theories in the Scofield Bible, dividing all of human history into distinct historical eras, was particularly open to assigning specific moments in time to divine turns of history.

9

"Did God put a period at the end of [the book of] Revelation, or did he put a comma?" Phyllis asked audiences, to emphasize what she still believed was the central issue at stake: *sola scriptura*. Does a Christian believe every word of the Bible precisely as written, without interpretation? Is that even possible? And when we realize that it is not, then, what's next? Whichever side of this issue you were on, she would explain to audiences, you at least must understand that *sola scriptura* and its aftermath are what we're talking about.

The issue of slavery was the first to split Christian churches in the mid-nineteenth century. "It was scriptural differences of opinion. The Bible doesn't say 'go own people,' but it certainly recognizes slavery as a possibility, and it even provides for it. We got over that, because it didn't make sense," she said to activist Andrew Marin in 2009. Next, she explained, "We got over feminism—or, we got over the need for equality of the genders. Again, the Bible is pretty clear—Paul is certainly clear—about the role of the genders, and it didn't work in our society." Then, the church "got over," or made accommodation for, divorce, a subject about which Jesus teaches quite clearly, in contrast to sexuality, as wrong. "So there is a progression, if you will, of sociological shifts, over the last one hundred and fifty or sixty years." Full rights and inclusion of LGBTQ people in the church is, she said, "the last 'playing piece' in a deadly game. We will make this change, there is no question about that. We're going to 'get over' this. It is the last stance for *sola scriptura*."[23]

She continued to take her combination of sociologist and evangelist to churches and associations of religious professionals to explain the emerging church—and then a few years later, what she herself coined Emergence Christianity—as the reason for their professional, personal, and spiritual unease. She began to describe the unease that people felt as a natural outcome of what every "rummage sale" in the history of the faith goes through and feels like. Repeated hundreds of times before hundreds of thousands of people over a decade, she would explain:

> About every 500 years, the cultures within which latinized Christianity has found a home go through a time of total upheaval in which everything—everything including religion, that is—undergoes re-definition and reconfiguration. We are in such a time now. 500 years ago in the sixteenth century we call our upheaval the Great Reformation. 500 years before that, in the eleventh century, their ancestors had called their own time of tsunami the Great Schism. Their forebears, 500 years earlier in the sixth century, had named their given time of deconstruction and reconstruction as the Great Decline and Fall. And as we know, 500 years before that, in the first century, our forebears had passed through a shifting so dramatic that even the dating of human history would come to be recorded in terms of it—in terms of before and after the Great Transition—or Great Transformation.

And when emerging leaders began to have disagreements over important and trivial matters, she would explain that splits in congregations, even between friends and family, make a certain sense. "When the authority begins to give way and something new starts, one of the signs that it's maturing is that it begins to develop internal discord," she said. This was a decade and a half after Pagitt had started working at Leadership Network, and McLaren had started publishing books. "It is so easy to love a baby," she went on, "and it's hard as hell to like a two-and-a-half-year-old. Right? The same thing happens here and it's happening in Emergence Christianity. . . . There are now at least eight, ten, to twelve divisions within [it]."[24]

10

A sense of urgency began to rise in the mainline denominations to find a way forward without abandoning what they loved about who they were. This is when Phyllis began to talk about "Angli-mergents," or, Anglicans who were also emerging. She called them "the hyphenateds," although soon the hyphen itself was removed.

The first meeting of Anglimergents was held in February 2008 in Minneapolis. Called the "Nicodemus" meeting, it was convened under the radar by non-Episcopalian organizers Tony Jones and Doug Pagitt. Confidential invitations were sent to Howard Anderson, Fred Burnham, Bob Carlton, Wendy Johnson, Dixon Kinser, Lallie Lloyd, Sara Miles, Eliacin Rosario-Cruz, Bowie Snodgrass, Phyllis, Michael Tippett, Robert Two Bulls, Carol Ward, and Karen Ward—only four of whom were actively serving congregations: Miles in San Francisco, Rosario-Cruz and Ward in Seattle, and Snodgrass in New York City. The seniors present were Burnham, from Trinity Church Wall Street, and Phyllis.

They discussed what emerging was and what it was not. One thing it wasn't was new forms of worship designed to appeal to Millennials. Phyllis was strong on this point. Emerging was a sensibility, a mindset, a worldview, a theological place at which they had arrived, and being Episcopalians added certain distinctives and commitments to these features, such as love for the rhythms and language of the Book of Common Prayer. Then they talked about how best to move forward within the Episcopal Church: Should they actively recruit bishops to support their efforts? Should they lobby the church for an "interest desk" at the Church Center? Phyllis wasn't in favor of either approach, seeing the emerging sensibility as depending on continued organic ways of growing. To bring it under any official or firmly-established aegis would be to kill it. Others disagreed—others, perhaps, who had a more vested interest in making a living within this new framework.

That summer, a similar group met again, in Seattle, without the non-Episcopal facilitators, and with the addition of a few invited others including Tom and Christine Sine, and Tom Brackett, who had been hired by the Episcopal Church specifically to encourage emerging conversations in churches. Phyllis was asked to provide some historical analysis at the outset and there was much discussion of how important *The Great Emergence* would be for schooling Anglimergents in what they were experiencing "on the ground." Karen Ward shared what she had recently learned from Fresh Expressions (the Church of England's name for its official efforts to encourage emerging communities) pastor Ian Mobsby as to the challenges going forward; these included a lack of funding for ordained missioner posts; needs in training; and the fact that the movement had too great a top-down approach, with a lack of consultation with on-the-ground practitioners. Everyone agreed that these problems were similar to those facing the Episcopal Church in America.

A few months later, most in this group were at the Episcopal cathedral in Memphis, along with a few hundred others who were there to hear Phyllis talk about *The Great Emergence*. The gathering was organized by JoPa (a company started by Tony Jones and Doug Pagitt), on behalf of Baker Books, who published Phyllis's book. There were separate talks among the Anglimergent insiders focusing on institutional issues, questions of authority and where it rested, how to handle resistance to change, and what Presiding Bishop Katharine Jefferts Schori was prepared to do from the top in order to encourage the Episcopal Church to keep emerging. One of the more prominent clergy who was there summarized in a memo to her (highly sympathetic) bishop afterwards: "Leadership will come from people who are actually doing things . . . and though there's a role for prophets and messengers (as Phyllis Tickle shows) I believe we can largely resist the desire to follow spokespeople unconnected to communities of practice." Then she adds: "Of course the temptation to brand emerging will remain: as will struggles over resources and visibility."[25]

All this time, while there were entire Episcopal dioceses reading and discussing *The Great Emergence*, Phyllis was also interested in the possibility that Anglicanism worldwide could be the future solution for what many of those in the emerging church were seeking. In 2002, Robert Webber had published a post-9/11 book titled *The Younger Evangelicals*. He had pointed to story-telling, performative symbols, and community as old-new ways that truth was being discovered anew among Christians. He wanted to move theology "from propositional-ism to narrative," and apologetics "from rationalism to embodiment."[26] What Webber wrote confirmed what Phyllis had witnessed as a religion journalist, but also, her own experience in her communities of faith.

She rarely spoke of those experiences, however. Whether it was her own prayer life or her struggling with friends who wanted to be LGBTQ and Christian at one and the same time, she had her own per-sonal reasons for being present within what became Emergence Chris-tianity—and her explanations, in public talks and interviews, would always turn to the historical and theological. She would tell anecdotes of others, past or present, rather than speak of her own experience.

11

In 2012, Phyllis was a main stage speaker at the second annual Wild Goose Festival in 2012 at Shakori Hills Campgrounds, south of Durham, North Carolina. Vincent Harding, one of Dr. Martin Luther King Jr.'s speechwriters, was present, as were activist and soon-to-be former Jesuit John Dear, Sojourners founder Jim Wallis, and icon of the post-evangelical crowd Frankie Schaeffer. Phyllis was there because she loved the people who attended the Goose and because she was pro-moting the sequel to *The Great Emergence*, due out that August: *Emer-gence Christianity: What It Is, Where It Is Going, and Why It Matters*.

In that book, she extended the story of Emergence by broaden-ing her analysis even further. The roots of Emergence shouldn't be seen as evangelical only, or dating back only a couple of decades. Instead, Albert Schweitzer's investigations into the historical Jesus in 1900 turned into Albert Einstein's physics and its resulting uncertain-ties, beginning in 1905, and then came William J. Seymour, a pastor born to former slaves in Louisiana, who moved to Los Angeles and started the Azusa Street Revival in 1906. It was Seymour who began the rallying cry among Christians, that hasn't ceased to this day, to experience again what was told of in the Book of Acts. Historians had always focused on Azusa Street as the founding of Pentecostal Christianity, focusing on the gifts of tongues and miraculous healing that took place there, but Phyllis was the first to make it an essential link on the way to twenty-first-century Emergence, with or without the charismatic gifts.

Every movement recognizes its leaders, and then it begins to form a civilization. Emergence Christianity was no different, and by the end of the first decade of the new century, its most recognized leaders were Brian McLaren, Diana Butler Bass, Frank Schaeffer, Tony Jones, and Doug Pagitt. And then there was the issue of nomenclature. Before "Emergence" became common currency, there was "Emergent" and "Emerging." Phyllis told the story of how the movement's earliest name was created by a handful of these leaders back in 2000. This email from Pagitt formed her raw material:

> The name [Emergent] actually came from conversation about forestry. In determining the health of the forest one can look at the "old growth" as seen in the tree tops. You can climb a hillside and look down on the trees or fly over in an airplane. Healthy tree tops tell of the history of the health of the forest. Emergent growth is found not in the tree tops but on the forest floor. One must get into the forest, move the pine needles and see the growth that is coming.[27]

Characteristic of all new movements, there is a lot of disagreement as to what should be emphasized most. And what to call it. In the spring of 2012, United Church of Christ pastor and author Eric Elnes began circulating to a sub-group of Emergence leaders what he was calling "The Characteristics of Convergence Christianity." He was posing a list of twelve characteristics to describe: "What people like myself, Brian McLaren, Frank Schaeffer, and Phyllis Tickle are talking about when we use the term Convergence Christianity." Phyllis wasn't exactly using that term, but she and the others in the named group gave Elnes permission to promote his declaration and Elnes went on to announce them, saying, "[This] is a phenomenon primarily among post-evangelical and post liberal Christians who have left their native traditions behind—or remain within them but have let go of what they consider to be the 'baggage' of their traditions—and are now discovering each other out in the wilderness. They're finding that each group has gifts to share that the other has been yearning for, and minus the baggage, these folks are great fun and inspiring to be with."[28] Each of the twelve characteristics began with the phrase, "They are letting go of . . ." and included "old hierarchies" and "literal and inerrant interpretations of their sacred texts." Some of the leaders, particularly Schaeffer, were concerned that the list was too much an argument from the negative, focusing on what adherents do not believe. (Schaeffer's objection on this point was odd, given his own pugilistic approach in lectures and in print.) Phyllis countered, "I think that such [arguing from the negative] is far and away the better way to begin something like this. Once you begin writing from the positive—the 'They believe' stance—you approach doctrine and creed and fences yet once again . . . or you make the whole thing so general that it is meaningless and/or spineless."[29]

Interestingly, however, despite being included in Elnes's group of Emergence leaders, Phyllis was rarely mentioned as *one* of them, since she rarely spoke of her personal involvement in the movement. She was perceived as one who stood apart from what was happening in faith communities themselves. One of very few instances in which an Emergence leader spoke of Phyllis as an insider (and not simply as a historian or pundit) was Brian McLaren in the introduction to *We Make the Road by Walking*. This wasn't until 2014. He listed her with William Barber, Tony Campolo, Dorothy Day, John Dear, Martin Luther King Jr., Oscar Romero, Jim Wallis, and others, as one who over the last century helped give birth to a reform movement in the worldwide church.[30]

She was booked out eighteen months in advance to venues who were happy to pay her hefty fees to come and deliver her rummage sale talk. It was so popular that when Brian McLaren was traveling in the fall of 2013 to the Mesa Gathering of church leaders and community builders in Bangkok, Thailand, he asked Phyllis to record on her phone a three-to-five-minute version for him to share. To a different gathering of seminarians and would-be preachers, she concluded a talk by saying: "[W]e must look—indeed, we cannot faithfully refuse to look—at a new grandeur that lies before us, resplendent with its more communal and unstudied praxis and its pulsating worship ripe with expectation, dangerous with its untried pavement and unmarked lanes, seductive with its perfume of prophesy and promise, untried in its devotion and earnest in its passage."[31]

12

One wishes that Phyllis would have returned to verse late in life. Wallace Stevens published these lines in *Harmonium*, before the First World War: "Rationalists, wearing square hats, / Think, in square rooms, / Looking at the floor, / Looking at the ceiling." Throughout the century, the modern project would unravel further. Phyllis might have given poetic image and emotion to the uncertain present as well as the new frontiers of knowing.

History will tell whether or not she was correct in her reading of the signals and signs to identify a great emergence of Christianity in the late twentieth and early twenty-first century. As McLaren put it in *A New Kind of Christianity*: "[N]ot everyone agrees with Phyllis [Tickle], Harvcy [Cox], Doug [Pagitt], Tony [Jones], Diana [Butler Bass], Marcus [Borg], and the rest of us."[32] Theirs was a club of bright lights, but one that perhaps did not then grow into something more identifiable.

Essential to Phyllis's interpretation of what was happening was an optimism that there was a purification and clarification going on in the faith that held hegemony for millennia, soon to produce something that looks different and is transformed—a new way of being Christian. On the contrary, many said then, and still do now, that what was and is actually happening was and is a great decline, rather than a great emergence. To them, particularly those who are lovers of the church and active in churches, it has seemed more productive to cherish what is, for as long as that might be possible.

CHAPTER 16

Navigating Gratia and Jesus

Phyllis once said to an interviewer from PBS's *Religion & Ethics Newsweekly*, speaking from the porch of the Farm in Lucy:

> Out here, we're not the measure of anything. We're never going to win out here. Do you know what I mean? The whole enlightenment in Western civilization in the last three hundred years has been built on the notion that man is the measure of all things. That's bull. Man's the measure of absolutely nothing. But you forget that when you're in the city and everything is scaled to man. Everything I touch here is alive. Out here nothing is an object. You're caught in majesty that doesn't require anything of you except just the sense of yes, it's here, and God bless me for the time I'm part of it.

With roots firmly planted in land that was hers to tend, Phyllis felt that she knew who she was. And whether it was a Tennessean, a Christian, or a country woman, she believed she was of a people apart.

She enjoyed the interruptions of life, for the remove that they offered. On one occasion, while writing a letter to a colleague about poems in process, and challenges she was experiencing in rewrites, suddenly the typewritten letter ends abruptly with, "Must close. Sick cow and Sam needs help. All love. . . . p."[1] This was common. She felt the desire to eschew many of the conveniences of modernity—to the betterment of herself, her children, and the world. There was something deeply monastic about her approach to life both on and off the farm.

2

But if she was monastic, she might best be compared to Copernicus or William of Ockham—vowed religious with a passion for science.

In the new century, her focus was increasingly on contemplating how recent experiments and conclusions in the sciences could be brought into theological conversation. She was well-served as a child learning science in school, and then by marrying a physician (who was also an engineer, mechanic, and physical scientist all his years), and living on the farm, she was regularly putting scientific thinking to the test.

For many years, she was quoting and recommending the articles and books of Antonio Damasio (*The Feeling of What Happens*; *Looking for Spinoza*; etc.), a professor of neuroscience, then at the University of Iowa, now at the University of Southern California. The two never met, and in truth their fields of influence were widely apart, but Phyllis probably garnered Damasio more readers than any other single person through her advocacy from the lectern. She was often introducing the man and his ideas, as when she said to a large audience at the Trinity Institute-sponsored Spiritual Formation Summit at Kanuga in 2003, "This man is head of neuroscience for the University of Iowa and he's making a huge impact upon plain old folk who are reading his books right and left. What he's talking about is the fact that mind *is* body, and body *is* mind. It is not anymore mind-body-and-spirit. It's body-spirit-and-soul, as it was in the beginning, before we got to the Reformation."[2]

Her purpose in recommending Damasio's work was to exhort audiences to realize two things, one intellectual, the other spiritual. First, she wanted to communicate that they were living in a post-Cartesian, post-Enlightenment world. Second, she wanted them to see that they were more than thinking beings. Referring to another of Damasio's books, *Descartes' Error*, she said in that same talk, "You are not just because you think. You are more than that."

Damasio's books were written as popular science—distillations of years of research. In *Descartes' Error*, he wrote in the Introduction, "The strategies of human reason probably did not develop, in either evolution or any single individual, without the guiding force of the mechanisms of biological regulation, of which emotion and feeling are notable expressions." And, "The physiological operations that we call mind are derived from the structural and functional ensemble rather than from the brain alone: mental phenomena can be fully understood only in the context of an organism's interacting in an environment."[3] Still, Phyllis distilled the ideas further.

Her argument was subtle, but she communicated it beautifully to lay audiences. That was her great gift—for instance, when she used the African understanding of Ubuntu theology, taught by her old friend Archbishop Desmond Tutu, to explain what contemporary physics was pointing toward. She did it like this: "Those of you who are taking a workshop in Ubuntu theology . . . it is a theology of Africa that basically, stripped down, says 'I am because you are.' The reason we are post-Cartesian is that there was a huge error in Descartes . . . because until there is an observer, there is nothing observed."

Then, "Physical science, which began looking like the enemy . . . much of what they now tell us about the universe is exquisite theology. The great chaos mathematician, Frank Tipler [professor of mathematical physics at Tulane; author of *The Physics of Immortality*, 1994], wrote some four or five years ago, 'If anyone ever told me, as a young physicist, that I would be a believing Christian after all these years in my laboratory, I would have said he was a liar. But I now believe that, oh God, there is an Omega point." Phyllis was always giving talks sans notes and her ability to recall facts and quote from memory was remarkable. Several years later, Tipler would write another influential book, *The Physics of Christianity* (2007).

She went on to connect African theology and contemporary physics, eventually concluding, "Science has given us what Ubuntu does! We now know that a thing can be a particle in a way; that is, it is not what it appears to be because it isn't until it is what it is that it's doing! . . . And if that's true in the physical world, it is probably true of us. It is not there until there is someone there to observe it. . . . You do unto others because without others, you ain't!"[4]

This was also when Phyllis began to say to audiences that, if it were up to her, she'd make a college major or serious minor in physics or mathematics a requirement for anyone wanting to enter seminary in the new century. "I think it is impossible to conceive of the richness of scripture or of the religious experience without some real intimacy with the wonders of physics—with what we've discovered since Einstein."[5]

3

Philosophical questions were also a delight to her. She pondered them often, and posed them to audiences like Zen koans. "What is a soul? Can you tell me where it is, as a part of you?" for instance, she asked, expecting no answer. But she pondered it, as Christians have since ancient days. ("We are weighed down by the needs of the body and yet, as it is written, 'We overcome through him, who has loved us,' but going forth from the body and leaving behind every burden and nimble sin, who are we?" a fellow bishop once asked St. Augustine.)[6]

She was reading in new physics for answers—and sometimes her reading gave her new ways to discuss the perennial questions. "Physics . . . has become the poetry underlying much Emergence theology," she believed at that time.[7]

Occasionally, these pondering questions became part of her conversations with other theologians, as well. On one occasion, she had this back and forth with the New Testament professor and author Scot McKnight. Remembering reading the account of her near death experience at the age of twenty-one, McKnight asked Phyllis: "I think I know what you will say but let me ask it: Do you think there is a 'consciousness' (soul, spirit, whatever) separable from the body and brain?" She responded:

> I believe to the point of absolute, militant fervor in the oneness of all—or perhaps I believe in the Oneness. There is nothing apart from it, nothing that is not of it, nothing that is other than it. To stand there, of course, I have to take up as my sword and shield that honorable question of "Can the pot say to the potter, 'Why madest thou me thus?'" Personally, I find that better, anyway, than trying to "justify the ways of God to man," but it's not just laziness on my part; it's conviction. Nothing else makes sense to me. As for consciousness . . . I think consciousness (and I have never said this to anybody else) is rather like digestion. Both connect the organism to the requisite sources of energy and sustenance, though neither "is" as a "thing," but only as a function dependent upon its own functionality to be. And of course, as we both know, pushed to its logical conclusions (though "logical" is becoming more and more a death-trap to me) makes

me something of a Calvinist—or at least it plants a lot of damned tulips in my front yard, doesn't it?

OK, more than you wanted to hear; but durn it, you shouldn't have asked! Which means, nobody ever asks these questions in the world of socio-history or whatever it is I do, and I miss them—miss knocking heads over them, miss growing because of them.[8]

4

The online, virtual world of Second Life was a hot topic among clergy and religious professionals, then. Those were the heady days of Internet entrepreneurship when it was common to assume that every aspect of life could easily be rapidly and satisfactorily relocated to the web. By the second quarter of 2007, Second Life (www.secondlife.com) claimed seven million members worldwide. Six months later and that number had increased to twelve million. As applied to faith, some of these people were "meeting" for regular worship through their avatars, which, many then said, was no less real than visiting brick and mortar houses of worship. Pastoral care, education, evangelism, and outreach were all taking place online. Even eucharistic services were tried. There was talk of creating a Second Life seminary for training future spiritual leaders of this type of church. Theses and dissertations were written on this controversial ecclesial subject. It became common to speak of SL (Second Life), as well as RL (Real Life), as a way of noting their rough equivalency. By then, it had caught Phyllis's attention.

One topic of controversy was whether or not sacraments were possible or effective in a virtual reality. Did bread and wine and water have to be tangible in order to be real? Many—including those who were deeply involved in the early years of Second Life excitement—thought that prayer and pastoral care was one thing, but sacraments were something else. Worship, too, was hotly discussed. Was virtual worship a sort of "playing" church, or was it somehow a new or evolving form of ecclesial reality that needed to be understood and utilized? One clergy advocate put it this way: "People tell me that it's not real church if it's not real brick and mortar. But my hunch is most Christians would agree that a building is not the church either. The community of believers is the real church."[9]

Given her rough experiences with church over her lifetime, her native anti-clericalism, and her endless curiosity about new technologies, Phyllis was—if not a ready convert—eager to try. She became fascinated by Second Life and its potential, which is why, when she described it in *Emergence Christianity* as follows, she had a smile on her face: "[T]he 'people' living in Second Life are pixel-made projections of people who physically are in physicality while being psychologically or subjectively in virtuality and engaging that experience through the avatar who is their presence while there."[10]

5

An Episcopal priest of the Los Angeles Diocese, the Rev. Melissa McCarthy, introduced some of the worship spaces in Second Life to Phyllis beginning in June 2007. McCarthy had been present at a talk Phyllis gave at a clergy convention in Long Beach, California, a few months earlier, when she had talked about trends in the church including the experimental virtual church, Church of Fools, that had recently been created by the United Methodist Church in Great Britain. Afterwards, McCarthy wrote to introduce her to the new realities of SL, a much larger and more ambitious effort. The two then had a rapid back-and-forth on the topic, with McCarthy sending Phyllis sample texts of SL sermons and snapshot worship spaces as they appear in SL.

At one point, Phyllis wrote back to say, "I cannot even think of how to tell you what a gift you have given, and are giving, me. I spent an hour at least this a.m. and time yesterday as well as a lot of time Saturday just hopping around and learning and enjoying. At some point I may sign up for citizenship; but anything you can send me on all of this is so gratefully received."[11] Her interest was, as often, passionately involved as well as journalistic. In her talks on the road, Phyllis often then mentioned Second Life, usually to the horror and groans of the church professionals who were in her audiences.

Then she met Mark Brown, CEO of the Bible Society of New Zealand and leader of the Anglican community on Second Life that "built" the first Anglican cathedral, there—a virtual one. Brown's blog first announced this cathedral as a place "to create an awe inspiring church that stands out for its brilliance and beauty," where "we regularly come together from around the world to worship and pray together in the Anglican tradition." That was in April 2007. By the following January, Brown reported that the Anglican group in SL had 328 members, with about ten additional joining each week.[12] For the next two years, Phyllis was mentioning SL in all of her public talks on trends in the church. She was intensely interested in "what it's doing and can do and almost surely will do to and for religion," as she put it. "This is the first real breakthrough to cyberspace that I have been able to believe in."[13]

Kimberly Knight, one of the other original creators of Second Life, eventually created an avatar for Phyllis, about three months after McCarthy's initial introduction, so that Phyllis could move around in the sacred space of SL. Phyllis was excited to try it. She gave her avatar a name: Gratia Raymaker. *Gratia* is Latin for "grace," and "Raymaker," well, it isn't clear what she had in mind with it. She began to go online often as Gratia, wandering around in this digital version of church, pausing to pray, seeking out new friendships. She would then talk with Knight about the experience when they were together at Emergent Christian conversations.

6

At this time, Phyllis appeared on Krista Tippett's *Speaking of Faith* National Public Radio program to talk about the Second Life phenomenon. She said in its defense, "[E]very time one of these kids logs on, they step through the back of the closet into Narnia. And they live with ideas of different levels of reality. There's virtual reality and this reality, and that they all have some substance, and that they don't have cognitive dissonance about taking all of that seriously."[14] This was, for her, a new mode of using the Christian imagination.

She wrote in *Emergence Christianity* with more than curiosity—a sense of adventure—about these developments, mentioning specific examples such as the 1st (not First) Presbyterian Church of Second Life (www.1pcsl.org). She referred to Emergence Christians on the forefront of these new expressions of church as akin to "apostles" of "a vast new mission field in what we call virtuality."[15] She would be surprised, perhaps, to see that today, virtual congregations have not progressed much since her explorations of them several years ago. The homepage of 1pcsl, for instance, still reads, as of this writing, "We currently meet for conversation & prayer, but aspire to eventually incorporate service, evangelism, education, and worship into our activities." There are a few active SL congregations, including Presbyterians and United Church of Christ, but the boon for expressing the faith, it never became.[16] SL today is mostly linked with online, role-playing games. Asked if most of the hopes for Second Life have so far gone unfulfilled, Kimberly Knight says, "To a degree, it is safe to say that. I do believe for some it has been a personal revolution of reality in so much as they have been able to explore parts of themselves and a way of life they might not otherwise have been able to." In our age of exploring gender identity, Second Life has been particularly important.[17]

Whether Second Life ever becomes what she predicted, Phyllis was definitely correct about the sensibility of Emergence Christians when she pointed to these:

> deinstitutionalization; non-hierarchical organization; a comfortable and informed interface with physical science; dialogical and contextual habits of thought; almost universal technological savvy.[18]

7

In March 2009 Phyllis's book *The Words of Jesus: A Gospel of the Sayings of Our Lord* was published in paperback by Jossey-Bass. It had been released in hardcover the year before. She had never been particular about Jesus in defining her faith in the past. Her first theological/philosophical book, *Re-Discovering the Sacred*, had ruminated in much broader religious terms: "Whether the sacred is seen theistically or nontheistically and whether it is approached ecstatically or cerebrally makes no difference to that one immutable principle with which we began: Admission to the sacred presupposes reverence."[19] So, her writing about Jesus caught some Tickle readers by surprise.

But in the year *The Words of Jesus* was published, she wrote this for the Sierra Club, narrowing the field: "When I say I am a practicing

Christian, what I am saying, among other things, is that like a large part of the earth's population—the larger part, in fact—I am what technically is called an Abrahamic or, put another way, a member of the Abrahamic faiths. That is, Jews, Christians, and Muslims. . . . For Abrahamics, the great gift in Eden was that of receiving soul, of our birthing as creatures formed in the image of God."[20] And then, of course, it did not surprise anyone who had been listening to her talk about her faith since *The Divine Hours* published, that Phyllis was passionate about the historical Jesus and the Christ of faith.

Just as she was beginning work on the book, an Episcopal friend made the comment to her that Jesus and Christ are not the same, to her. Phyllis responded:

> I'm not sure, of course, that I understand exactly what you mean by those words, but I know what I mean by them. I mean that "Christ" is a hole in temporal reality set there from Eden on as a rift and/or passageway and/or window that was promised and now is, and that is the way through to the kingdom of God both here and whenever (if there is a difference in those two, and I am not sure there is, btw). That "rent in the Temple vail" was a mechanism which is and was assumed by Jesus of Nazareth and by means of which He became God when God is incarnate, as well as becoming the being through whom we become the sons and daughters of God, as promised, as well as gods ourselves, as re: the Psalms. Because I believe this is to be true, or an accurate-for-now grasp of what Scripture is saying, then indeed no man or woman can enter the Kingdom save through that door. Beyond that, salvation is of the Jews. I see no reason to question either of those lynch pins within the structure of the story.[21]

(Is it any wonder that so many people enjoyed corresponding with her?) Sadly, however, there would be little of this sort of personal perspective offered in *The Words of Jesus*.

8

She took a risk in writing it: deciding to speak on a subject that was outside her areas of expertise. But all those years of enjoyable debate with Jack Spong, Marcus Borg, and Robert Funk made her want to make a contribution herself. She'd also become well-versed in the non-canonical gospels of Jesus, such as Thomas and Q, over the previous decade of reviewing books and trends. As she put it in an interview at that time, her purpose in writing *The Words of Jesus* was to make "the case that the historical Jesus and the actual Jesus have to be blended together in some kind of recognition that the Gospel of Jesus is the one we've got. We have to come to a point of respecting the tradition of 2,000 years of Christianity that have proceeded from the Received Jesus."[22]

What Phyllis meant by "the actual Jesus" came directly from the personal experience she had had with that Jesus. She didn't want to write anymore as one detached—certainly not on a subject as important as this one. And so, when writing about the need for different (not middle) ground than that established by biblical literalists and non-literalists, she said, "[T]here is a third way of knowing the Scriptures. There is—for want of a better word—*actualness*. There is anterior to Scripture a holiness that is subject neither to literalist nor to metaphorical translation, but rather is the irreducible, ineluctable cohesion of it."[23] She fully believed in that holiness, because she knew it.

9

Her process was the same as it was when writing any of her books. She started by gathering reading materials and surveying the literature. She would designate a place on her large desk for stacking materials that were being gathered—from among her own books and files, then clippings of what came across her desk, what her editor might send her to read, and then email responses from friends to specific questions of interest to the project. These were all treated as pieces of evidence that then led to other evidence, and the piles grew. Eventually, she would obtain an accordion folder and begin carrying that folder with her when she left town for a few days. She'd also jot notes all over her desk blotter, as well as on large pieces of poster board fastened to the wall on either side of the desk: names of authors, book titles to check out, signal phrases that would eventually become chapter titles, headings, or simply points to be made in the book.

Prompting her to write a book on Jesus, she believed that the members of The Jesus Seminar and others like N. T. Wright hadn't yet made historical Jesus research and thought accessible enough to people who wanted to engage with Christ in a twenty-first-century way. She took a philosophical tone on page one, aiming past those who would pick up a book about what Jesus said for purely devotional reasons: "When I began this project almost two years ago, I was innocent about what it would cost me. . . . I lay sleepless and wrestling . . . with new perceptions about what it is to be both Christian and a self at the same time." She was most comfortable when taking the widest view possible.

But she went on to explain her purpose: to compile the words of Jesus—from the four Gospels as well as the first chapter of the book of Acts—into a "cohesive whole." This meant removing "the duplications and . . . connective tissue" of the various narratives in those original New Testament texts: the biographical material. Such a project, indeed, might be a way to fuse the Jesus of history who lived, died, and rose again, with the Christ whose teachings fashioned a faith. She took on this task with a desire to recover something that might have been lost, since, as she put it, each of the canonical gospels "began as 'Sayings' gospels." And, she hoped, "Devoid of narrative context, the Sayings come straight at us like so many bullets, piercing all our armor and destroying all our carefully thought-out prior convictions."[24]

10

Phyllis had often been asked to comment on the work of The Jesus Seminar. For a time, she made comments as part of her regular stump speech about the trajectory of changes in Christianity that included her being fascinated by their modernist project. On a personal level, she deeply disagreed with what they were doing, primarily because she did not accept the premises of the work.

The Seminar was an association of scholars, some independent and others attached to universities, devoted to scrutinizing the sayings of Jesus as recorded in the Gospels and elsewhere. They began meeting in 1985. Their most influential work took place in the late 1980s and 1990s, when their members and the Seminar itself were frequently quoted in popular media. Their work continues today, albeit on a lesser scale. Their theological journal, *The Fourth R* (as in, Religion is the fourth R necessary for basic literacy), still publishes original scholarship as well as reports on the voting of the members of the Seminar. In a recent issue, for instance, votes from their annual meeting in San Diego were reported, including these:

> Scholarship now needs a less blunt tool/analytical category than gnosticism for examination of the Jesus/Christ(ian) literature of the second and third centuries. (Voted Red)

> The Secret Revelation of John is Christian. (Voted Pink)[25]

This needs some explanation. Jesus Seminar members use colored beads to collectively and democratically vote on the historicity of the deeds and sayings of Jesus, and then increasingly, in more recent years, on other issues of interpretation of events, movements, and the documents from the first centuries of the Christian era. Taking Jesus's sayings as the example, a red bead is a vote "yes," that Jesus indeed spoke as quoted. The votes noted above from 2014, one indicated as "Red," the other as "Pink," represent the majority opinion given that day in the voting. In the early days of the Seminar, voting was always tallied with numerical values, as follows. Red beads earned three points in the final tally. A pink bead was a "probably" vote, and earned two points. A grey bead was a "no" but with qualification that the quoted saying contains authentic ideas of Jesus, and earned one point. And a black bead was an unequivocal "no," for zero points. Thus, the first findings of the Seminar were published in Robert Funk's book *The Five Gospels: The Search for the Authentic Words of Jesus* in 1993.

When asked what she thought of their work, Phyllis would reply that it was deeply important, as well as powerfully significant as an example of people's desire to get at or under or behind the real Jesus of history. "As you know, you can get side-tracked almost immediately down the rabbit hole of personalization personalities and lose both your audience and your point. So deliberately I kept it light and general and as impersonal as possible when it came to Marcus [Borg] or Elaine [Pagels] or Jack [Spong] or Dom [Crossan] etcetera," she said years later.[26] Those figures more or less lumped together as The Jesus Seminar in what they were about in their work, and that was easier to deal with effectually, as opposed to distractively, when Phyllis was lecturing. That way, she turned the theology and ecclesiology into a generalized mind-set as opposed to individuals and their particular slants on things or in specific books. She did, however, speak directly and almost always in the Emergence talks about Spong and Borg standing like book-ends reaching back over five hundred years toward Martin Luther and, metaphorically, encapsulating that period. What Luther opened, they were closing or marking the logical completion of.

11

To the end, the older she became, and the more immersed she was in Emergence sensibilities, Phyllis was convinced that the future for Christian vibrancy would lie in a spirituality with Christ at the core but including all religious traditions and ways of life. It would be cosmos-focused rather than congregationally-focused. The "new way of doing church" that filled emerging church talk in its early days would be replaced by something much more mystical and universal.

She expressed this eloquently late in life:

> I can't articulate exactly what it means or is or is going to be—none of us can, yet, of course. But we are about the business of stripping the mythology off of the mythos, and that's dangerous work, as well as exhilarating. Just now, I am more deeply into reading physics and neuroscience than religion, though I am not sure I would say that to just anybody. But therein lies the next message—the next revelation. As sure as Sinai or Tabor, this is our next moment of pivot and holy, frightening grandeur. It's going to mean everything from re-adjusting and re-assessing the universe and the canon to doing the same to basic theology and communal life. I am both glad I shan't be here to see it, for it terrifies me for those who must be Moses to it. But I yearn achingly towards its beauty and truth and revelation.[27]

CHAPTER 17

Trouble at Home and on the Road

P hyllis had become the breadwinner for the Tickle home, something that Sam had thought was never possible. He was retired
from medicine and there were still children, and now grandchildren, with needs. Their youngest daughter, Rebecca, for instance,
had recently been diagnosed with Multiple Sclerosis, and needed her
parents' help with hospital bills. So it was helpful that three publisher advances, over a twenty-month period at the end of the millennium, paid Phyllis $600,000 minus agent's fees. And her earning
potential as an author and lecturer seemed to be growing. Sam had
to eat his hat.

She loved the travel. She was fed by the stimuli of conversation
and she learned easily from others. Eschewing most of the finery in
hotels and restaurants, she simply relished her freedom. Getting away
from Lucy was a retreat from the mundanity of domestic and family
life. She expresses this quickly to a friend one evening in early summer: "I'm off to CA in the a.m. Back Saturday and then off again
on Monday for Boston and DC for ten days. Ain't life fun! Come
to think of it, it actually is."[1] Years earlier, she'd written to another
friend, "*Shaping of a Life* pubs 17 April and that means on the road
again, but sometimes that's better than being trapped in the office
actually working. It's *always* better than sitting in the studio actually
writing!"[2]

Phyllis had been ambitious going back to high school. When she
was a young mother, she left the house to teach at Furman, in the
Memphis high schools, at the Memphis Academy, and then Rhodes
College. She never stopped writing poems, plays, and essays. The writing of so many books—the number would reach more than forty—is

never done by people who are not possessed of enough ego, and a desire, to be heard.

She knew that her ambition led to accomplishment, but also that it sometimes strained her most important relationships. She also believed, at times, that her ambition ran contrary to the desires of God. Late in her seventies she prayed:

> Lord, I was ever greedy of life, my attention always straining toward the parts of it that had not yet come. . . . I plotted, with myself but despite myself, about tomorrow. . . . You know how I worked, Lord, recklessly but prayerfully, to set time's courses and, in Your name, to sculpt them to my intention, to my definition of good. But I am old now, Lord, and my prayers grown old as well. So it is that daily I am drawn, as here, to pray, "Deliver me, My Lord, from this my great sin, and take me, free of doubt and other longings, into Your good plan."[3]

But the reality was, if she was going to accomplish anything now, it helped to be away from home. Sam was increasingly difficult. His health was fragile, and her career seemed only to exacerbate difficulties that were native between them. One person close to the family observed, "He was very damaged and those cracks in his psyche wore mountains out of her plateaus and made her spinier than nature intended. She developed all sorts of new imperfections and defenses in response to his."

2

Few people knew the range of what occupied her mind while she was away. It could be an essay, emails with friends, or some new book. Sometimes, it was even more personal. One November, while in southern California at a conference, meeting with editors, book publicists, and authors, analyzing trends and giving interviews to other media who were covering the event—she was all the while jotting down poems to share with Peggy Ingraham later. For instance, it was while "covering" a Buddhist meditation service that weekend that she began to compose the following in her notebook. They were never published.[4]

Evening Prayers

Buddha's monks are going mindful to their prayers.
Female and Christian-born, I go as paramour,
both mindful and holy-time aware,
and my prayer? Love me, Lord,
and above all else,
grant this final grace to me:
Make my love more than will,
our time together more than my intention.

Watching a Monk Strike the Temple Bells

Who hears these bells
hears me.
Their bongs and trills
are matters
of a lifetime,
not in their sounds,
but in my knowing
that who hears these bells
hears me.

With all the delight of the road, though, she was frequently forced toward home. Her favorite long weekend of the year was the meetings of the American Academy of Religion/Society of Biblical Literature, where nearly ten thousand religion academics gathered, usually in one of the more enjoyable conference cities such as San Francisco, New Orleans, San Diego, or Chicago. The AAR/SBL meets each year from Friday to Monday before Thanksgiving. Phyllis sometimes arrived early and stayed late. It was while at the 2005 meetings in Philadelphia that she received word from Rebecca that Sam was back in the hospital. He had cellulitis in one of his legs. She changed her flight and made it home by early afternoon Tuesday, going from the airport directly to the hospital.

The atmosphere was grave. Phyllis was prepared for the situation to worsen. "The children are gathering," she wrote to a friend, "as was planned for the holiday [Thanksgiving], so this is good." Mentioning one of her grandchildren, who was then four, by name, she continued, "[He] lost his other grandpa about a year ago, so it seems important for him to see Sam (Paw Paw) alert and perky, although in a hospital bed. . . . So that's the news from Lake Woebegone, dire as it sounds."[5]

Sam would recover, but the increasing frequency of such moments caused Phyllis to ponder leaving the farm altogether. There was a ranch-style house nearby, still in Lucy, that she looked at several times. Without stairs to climb, she would worry less about Sam falling and hurting himself during her absences. Also, she wanted to remove farm temptations such as the tractor, which Sam could easily turn over on top of himself someday if he suddenly decided to ride it. But Sam refused to budge. And Phyllis responded by entrenching herself in the lecture circuit so that, where she lived near Memphis didn't matter so much. It was a way station.

Four months after that Thanksgiving trip to the hospital, Sam was admitted again, this time attached to a cardiac monitor in an attempt to determine what was wrong with his heart rhythm. Before summer 2006, he was diagnosed with congestive heart failure and had a stent put in. Phyllis was actually joyful. "All is going swimmingly here for a change," she wrote. "I look back over the last three or so years and wonder that we ever made it through. Horrible to do and horrible to recall. But he's up and working full days every day. The shop is flourishing once more, and he's joined the American Orchid Society. . . . [I]t's keeping him happy."[6]

3

Of all her books, Phyllis was probably the proudest of *Greed*, written as part of an Oxford University Press series on the Seven Deadly Sins. She was in fine company in that series, with the Buddhist scholar Robert A. F. Thurman writing on *Anger*, novelist Francine Prose on *Gluttony*, African American intellectual and academic Michael Eric Dyson on *Pride*, British philosopher Simon Blackburn on *Lust*, the Jewish intellectual and literary giant Joseph Epstein on *Envy*, and the Tony award-winning playwright Wendy Wasserstein on *Sloth*. Phyllis was Phyllis A. Tickle (using the middle initial as if to emphasize the importance of this one) on *Greed*. And each book was published, with ample marketing resources, and creatively. *Greed*, for instance, was released on tax day, April 15, 2004. *Lust* released on Valentine's Day, the same year. No book of Phyllis's has had, or probably will have, as much longevity in public libraries throughout North America as *Greed* has, and will.

Each book was launched with a major lecture at the New York Public Library in Manhattan—which was the dressing in the turkey for Phyllis. She said, "I am grateful, very, very grateful, to have been given the assignment of wrestling with sin in so exquisitely public and permanent a milieu."[7]

She reveled in the freedom to pursue these opportunities, but then bristled when that freedom was hampered by domestic responsibilities. She believed that she had spent most of her life as a Martha, to use the analogy of the two female friends of Jesus mentioned in a story in the Gospels, "wondering indeed who was going to make life go for all the Marys out there doing nothing," as she once explained to friends.[8] And yet, she was drawn to Mary life more and more.

Sam was nearly deaf by this point, making conversation difficult. Also, problems on the farm surfaced and resurfaced regularly. One day, while she and Sam were away from home, Phyllis wrote to complain to a friend:

Three of our kids live in Johnson City, so we are in the home of #2 daughter who presently is at the doctor's office seeing if indeed she is about to produce a couple of new grandchildren. Plus which, it's Sam's 71st birthday. Beyond that, #7 child, Rebecca, who with her husband always oversees the Lucy environs when we are gone, just called to say that Crabby, Sam's favorite cat, has disappeared and been unseen for two days, the dam that holds the pond seems to have washed out somewhere in a place yet to be determined, and the truck has lost its driver's side mirror.[9]

At these times, the road looked most appealing.

She was trying to retire from *Publishers Weekly*. Having attempted to do so twice before, this time, in the spring of 2004, she didn't inform her boss, Daisy Maryles, that she wanted to retire; she simply said that she was resigning. There was writing she wanted to do, and Sam needed her at home. This tack seemed to work. She would be done at the end of August. The religion team took her out to dinner in July and paid their respects for all that she had done. At a final staff meeting, Daisy asked Phyllis to explain again what she wanted to do in retirement. Phyllis stammered out something about slowing down and being able finally to pray. "Don't you pray enough already?" Daisy quipped.[10]

Then, on September 2, Phyllis received word from New York that she could close the office the following day in order to prepare for a long Labor Day holiday weekend. This was confusing, since she'd resigned effective the end of August. The following day, a copy of the magazine arrived with Phyllis's name still on the masthead. Then, someone in accounting called to ask why Phyllis's last expenses invoice was marked "final." "Because it is?" Phyllis offered. "Well," the woman replied, "your September paycheck is on its way anyway. Cash it." She did, but they then finally let her leave.[11]

4

The Divine Hours, by this time, was recognized as one of the more important religion publishing projects of the decade. It was time for spinoffs. Oxford University Press produced *The Night Offices*, gathering in one volume the late evening and early morning prayers from *The Divine Hours*. A year later they also published *The Divine Hours: Pocket Edition*, a small, portable selection from the three-volume work. And an editor at Dutton Children's Books, a division of Penguin, asked Phyllis if they might publish a book for children. Their request was triggered by queries from young parents seeking breviaries their children could use as the adults were using theirs. *This Is What I Pray Today: The Divine Hours Prayers for Children* was born then as Phyllis rewrote some of the Psalms to create suitable material for young children. It was illustrated by Elsa Warnick. The Oxford volumes sold fairly well, but the children's book did not. A modest $5,000 advance to Phyllis still remained to be "earned out," as publishers say, a decade later.

By the spring of 2009, the demand for Phyllis on the lecture circuit reached its zenith. She loved the income but began to regret the time away—not because she missed Lucy or Sam, so much as she began to miss writing. For the fourth or fifth time in her life, she began to plot a way to be a full-time writer. On tax day, 2009, she wrote to a former colleague at *Publishers Weekly*, "I'm booked solid through 2010, but have no intention of living the rest of my life this way; so we'll be posting a new policy soon that I will do public lectures only in March, April, and May of each year. That way the travel is yammered together into one quarter, and I can be back here writing the other 9 mos."[12] It would never happen.

One month later, on May 3, 2009, Phyllis traveled to Grandville, Michigan, for a weekend at Pastor Rob Bell's Mars Hill Bible Church. It had been on her calendar for eighteen months, since she'd last been there to give a Great Emergence talk. Her topic this time was in tune with William Young's blockbuster spiritual novel, *The Shack*: the feminine side of the Holy Spirit. She said, "The part of the Trinity that we are asked to most intimately know is the Holy Spirit." She spoke of the Creation, told in Genesis, and reminded her audience how God said, "Let us make humankind in our own image . . . male and female . . . in the image of God." She went on to describe attributes, or parts, of God, in the Bible that are feminine: for example, Sophia in Proverbs, and the Shekinah in Rabbinic Judaism, which she explained was a feminine understanding of the presence of God roughly equivalent to how Christians came to know the Holy Spirit. Towards the end of her talk she added that "from Pentecost on [the Holy Spirit] came and entered us, came into us, lives in us, and we are the container thereof. And it is an erotic relationship, and that, too, is part of the feminine nature of it. It is an erotic relationship and the most intimate one that a Christian or a human being can ever have." She also added, as she introduced the service of communion which was about to commence: "Let us remember what we are doing. We not only celebrate that death and that promise of return, but we are feeding by eating God—by eating the body and blood of our God, we are feeding the God within us. For as we take those elements, the Spirit also feeds within us and is reinvigorated as he, or she, or it is by our faith."

The blogosphere erupted with cries of heresy. Conservative radio hosts, bloggers, and podcasters mocked her gender (not one for teaching in church), her message, and the notion—now commonplace in her talks to evangelicals—that *sola scriptura* was past. "It's just way too constricting," one sarcastically said, as if that summarized her position. She was also described as "seductive"—an ancient dog whistle of Christian men for tagging smart women.[13] By October of that year, she was confronted during Q&A at a rummage sale talk in Winnipeg by evangelicals protesting a wide range of what she teaching, and of what she wrote in *The Great Emergence*.

5

In 2007, Mother Betty Pugsley, abbess of the Community of Jesus, asked Phyllis if she would compose a new play for the tenth anniversary of the consecration of their church in Rock Harbor on Cape Cod. Building the Church of the Transfiguration had been a huge task, involving fighting the town for zoning permissions, and Phyllis had been present for the original celebrations around it. Now, she was an oblate of the Community, a longtime member of the editorial board at their publishing house, and a good friend. She had personal relationships with dozens of the Community's members and was still, supposedly, writing a book about this remarkable American religious community.

She jumped at the opportunity to return to the genre that first engaged her as a writer, and work was begun on *The Doorway*. From the beginning, the playwright knew that she wanted to return to midrash on biblical stories. The characters of Moses, Elijah, St. Peter, and St. John filled her imagination as she brought them to life. The instructions she was given were simply to honor the Feast of the Transfiguration, and after the initial draft was done, Phyllis spent a week with Sr. Danielle Dwyer, artistic director of the theater program at the Community, in the church, going through scripts, talking about the space, using the frescoes and spandrels. The art in the chancel and the push to finish the drama for the anniversary became a catalyst for the script, even giving rise to one of the main characters, Madeleine, and her struggle to finish a work of art that her heart was having trouble letting go. Phyllis took other inspirations from the building, as well: including its architecture and art, and the mosaic floor and its two owls, which Phyllis used in order to bring another character, Theodore (Madeleine's muse and inspiration), to life. The collaboration between playwright and director made Phyllis visibly nervous, at times, and there was tension whenever one of Phyllis's ideas was demonstrated to be unworkable on stage.[14] They haggled, argued, and wrestled to the end, but the resulting performances in June 2010 were dazzling to audiences.

6

By 2010, every active, progressive Protestant and Episcopalian in the U.S. was a Tickleite whether they had read Phyllis's books or not. The cumulative influence of *The Divine Hours*, *The Great Emergence*, and her lecturing was such that Phyllis informed the ethos of the emerging church and defined the zeitgeist of Emergence Christianity for its first and second generations of practitioners in North America. It would remain to be seen—and she feared for this—whether a third generation would follow in their footsteps.

Throughout the decade that she devoted to evangelizing and educating on the subject, she became entangled in many arguments and debates. One of these was the assignment of value in her analysis of what was happening. In other words, audiences, as well as colleagues in the field, often wanted to know from her: Do you think this is good, or bad? She was always hesitant to go too far down that rabbit hole and preferred to stick to the meta-narrative, saying what was happening in the churches, in the culture, and so on, rather than making value judgments.

But sometimes, judgments were unavoidable. When necessary, she would plant her flag in the organized faith of her Episcopalianism, without apology, saying essentially that she was willing to go down with the ship, if necessary, because that was the tradition that was hers. For example, in the author questionnaire she filled out for Baker Books when writing *The Great Emergence*, she answered the question of church membership, writing tongue-in-cheek, "Rabid Episcopalianism." And then, a few sentences from a 2010 interview have her saying: "I'm not an emergence Christian; I'm probably an Angli-mergent. I've fooled with it long enough to have caught it. I have colleagues who are pure emergence Christians who don't like for me to say this, but one of the things is that emergence praxis does not allow for much transcendence. It allows for transport—and there's a difference."[15] In other words, the virtues of flat ecclesiology were clearly explained by Phyllis, but to the end she remained an active member of a hierarchical church.

She challenged the members of that church as often as she embraced them. She would say: "If we're in the business of trying to save the Episcopal Church in the United States, shame on us. Come Judgment Day, we *should* be found wanting. We're in the business of serving the kingdom of God."[16]

7

By 2011, Sam was finally diagnosed with dementia, which Phyllis and a few of the adult children who lived nearby had already witnessed. The telltale event came when Phyllis was driving down the road in Millington and Sam suddenly grabbed the wheel. It was a scary moment. She managed to pull the car safely off the road and into a strip mall parking lot, where he apparently felt that he had to visit a particular gift shop. Once inside, he seemed to want to purchase everything in sight. The irrationality of the whole event was palpable and frightening to Phyllis, as well as to the store clerk.

They arranged for Sam to have live-in, nearly full-time care from a young man who functioned as part nurse, part body man. His name was Dan Slover and he was a gentle soul, most of all a great companion for Sam. At this point, Phyllis had difficulty being with Sam for any period of time; it was painful for her to see her lifelong partner and lover reduced in these ways. She needed Dan's presence in order to alleviate her own sense of loss and guilt caused by what was taking place in her husband.

Dan lived in the house in a basement room with an adjoining bathroom, just around the corner from Phyllis's office and library. He drove Sam all over town, which allowed Sam to get out of the house anytime he wanted, and Dan even drove Phyllis and Sam across country on a few occasions, when Phyllis needed to speak at a conference and Sam wanted to tag along. These were awkward times in public for Phyllis, mostly because she never quite knew what Sam would say. One such occasion was the Wild Goose Festival in North Carolina in 2011. There, Phyllis remained at Sam's side every hour except for when she was speaking, and even then, Sam was sitting in his wheelchair right up front, with Dan nearby.

Phyllis knew that her writing work would likely wind down as she neared eighty, but her speaking schedule continued to book out more than a year in advance. For a decade, her going rates had hovered at $5,000 for a single talk and $7,500 for two to four, "as long as they involve one portal-to-portal and occur within a seventy-six hour period," as she or Rebecca would explain it. Always, too, there was the reminder that, "Due to a health problem of many years' duration, Phyllis Tickle has to have ten to twelve uninterrupted hours of rest during every twenty-four hours. At a practical level this means that evening programs should not extend beyond 7:30 p.m. or should not be either preceded or followed by morning appearances before 10:30 a.m."

The wear of travel and troubles at home began to have their impact on her. She had been observing her twelve-hours-a-day rest ever since the Lyme disease diagnosis, but now she began to enjoy those times even more for their recuperative value. She bought an iPad and began to watch movies in bed at night, streaming Netflix. She also loved *Downton Abbey*. She would explain, when necessary, that it was important to keep up with culture, but these were also simple times of rest.

Meanwhile, a kind of simplicity came out in Sam in those final years that reminded those who loved him of his roots. He seemed again like the student who couldn't read straight, rather than the in-demand pulmonologist. He seemed again like the man who was more comfortable hanging out with down-and-out characters on the farm or in the shop, rather than the mensch who insisted on treating some of the country's first AIDS patients, despite the personal risk, and who willingly accepted venison roast and chocolate pie as payment when making physician house calls. Anger was his real nemesis, both before and after the dementia was finally confirmed. And the truth of the matter, for both Phyllis and the adult children, was that daddy had been dying for quite some time.

8

In January 2013, friends and business partners Tony Jones and Doug Pagitt organized a conference in Memphis on the topic of Phyllis's latest work on Emergence, just as they had done five years earlier around *The Great Emergence*. The new conference showcased Phyllis at the podium delivering three days' of talks. There was also a session at which several of her prominent friends: Nadia Bolz-Weber, Jones, McLaren, Pagitt, and Lauren Winner honored her by reading portions of essays-in-progress they were writing for a festschrift honoring her, to be published the following year.

On the final day, she made a point that she often made in those years, that one of the signal events that brought rapid change to the faith was the creation of the birth control pill and how it spawned new opportunities for women outside the home (women were finally controlling their own reproduction), and this, in turn, contributed to the breakdown of traditional ways of transmitting the faith. Some women in the audience took offense at this suggestion—that, in any way whatsoever women might be to blame for what shouldn't have been their sole responsibility in the first place—and certainly not by virtue of staying home, making babies, raising them, and teaching them the faith, while their male partners pursued other things. Blogger and author Julie Clawson wrote on January 14:

> There's no denying that the final session was just weird. Even those who weren't offended by what was said there thought it was a very odd way to end a conference. . . . While most of us there would agree that the fall of Christendom is a very good thing and that women's liberation signifi-cantly changed our culture, it was where Phyllis went with it from there that caused the discomfort. . . .
>
> Phyllis described the freedoms working outside the home in WW2 and the ability to control our cycles the Pill brought women and argued that such things led to the destruction of the nuclear family and there-fore the foundation of the civil religion of Christendom. While it is a narrow assessment of causality, I can agree with the descriptive obser-vation that such things changed our culture. But then she jumped from

these changes as that which brought an end to Christendom to describing how such changes led to the destruction of the ways the faith is passed on to new generations which thereby resulted in a biblically illiterate society. . . . Phyllis ended the session by encouraging us to discover ways to be back in the kitchen with our children and finding crafty ways to import the rhythms of the church year to them. Essentially to focus on the family and all that. That is the great emergence. . . . You can see why people left bewildered.[17]

Now, Phyllis was, throughout her last decade, not unlike Aunt Eller in *Oklahoma*: country-bred, worldly-wise, blunt, and comfortable more among men than women. She also was not easily bothered by accusations of any kind. Self-effacement and a stiff spine, she learned growing up in the mountains. Neither was she concerned with charges of political incorrectness. Consider a much earlier experience from the mid-1970s: She was in a butcher shop in Memphis with her children, one still in the stroller, when a young black woman began to talk aloud about Phyllis as a woman who obviously has lots of money to buy pork shoulders (which she'd just placed in her cart). "Man, if I had nineteen bucks it wouldn't be for that!" the woman said for all to hear. Phyllis's blood boiled, but she kept her mouth shut. Then the woman commandeered Phyllis's shopping cart, complete with child, and ran it into some nearby shelves. Phyllis was about to rush her, ready to fight, when the woman was quickly gone from the store. "She could have taken me had she stayed. . . . She was young and tough, I am middle-aged and winded," Phyllis wrote. And then, "The mountains of my growing up years are probably the only part of this pluralistic country where blacks aren't hated. I grew up neutral and I knew. . . . It was economic and it was political, but it was not racial." Phyllis wanted to say to the woman, to whom she felt "drawn" as a human being in need, "Hey lady, you don't hate me because I'm white. You hate me because life hurts and you can ease the pain by blaming me."[18]

In her talk in Memphis, Phyllis might just as easily have reached back further to make her point, to the invention of electricity and central heating as the time when the family unit began to break down. Scholars have said, "bedchambers became studies and playrooms . . . and the family dispersed itself and its activities throughout the house at all hours."[19] But that wouldn't have caused people to pause and think in the way that her intentionally provocative remarks did.

She was consistently pointing, during these years, to moments in American history that brought changes in religious observance. She wanted her audiences to understand the organic reasons why the faith of their parents, grandparents, and the like, often seemed more profoundly felt and practiced, compared to their own. For instance, she once responded to a reader who asked her when local laws began to ease around the country regarding activity—or forbidden activities—on the Christian Sabbath:

> I usually stop at 1908, and point to it as very significant in the re-definition of Sabbath practices, i.e., it's the year the Tin Lizzie comes out—first car that's cheap enough for almost anybody to afford and first car that could be bought on credit. You can, sociologically speaking, trace, from the Lizzie on, that change or shift from Sunday afternoon at home reading and worshipping to "Let's go for a Sunday afternoon ride" to "Can we get ice cream at XYZ," to "XYZ's" having to be open to sell said ice cream. Likewise, there is the equally informing shift from Sunday lunch at Grandma's after church, to "Let's go for a ride right after Church and have lunch out somewhere," again with the pressure of all the "somewhere's" to be open to meet said needs, etc.[20]

Also in the audience in Memphis, Jerusalem Greer, an author whom Phyllis had encouraged, wrote to her when the storm began in the blogosphere:

> I do not believe that you ever intended to blame women for the "demise" of Christendom in America, nor were you suggesting that all of American women now leave their jobs, don an apron and get back in the kitchen where they belong. . . . As best I can tell, by reading *The Shaping of a Life*, The Farm in Lucy series and even in *Prayer Is a Place* you were never Donna Reed yourself. . . . You are a most liberated woman and your experiences of juggling family and work is one I wish you talked more of . . . even if it is messy and complicated as most honest domestic tales are.

Phyllis responded the following day:

I would that such confusion had never happened and such bitterness never been experienced, much less vented. . . . [A]s you so kindly and beautifully say, anybody who has tracked me for more than five minutes, much less twenty or thirty years, should know that what is being laid to my door is about as far away from everything I have ever said and lived as anything could be. . . . Attempting to respond to this just now would, it seems to me, be to grant it a credibility it does not deserve.[21]

She never did respond to the accusations of betraying the feminist cause, and it didn't concern her.

9

Eventually, her writing began to slow. Her creative energy was waning. This is common for writers who live long and start their careers early. Critiquing one's work or another's, lecturing on themes that one has already published on, correcting and rewriting previous work, are work that often occurs after most of the creativity has been spent.

From the outside, it appears that this may have been true of Phyllis. A close look at her oeuvre reveals relatively little that was new after *The Words of Jesus* and *The Great Emergence* were both published in 2008. *Emergence Christianity: What It Is, Where It Is Going, and Why It Matters*, from September 2012, was not a derivative work, but it didn't break any new ground. In Phyllis's own words, it was an "interim report," or "at best, no more than a dispatch from the field," aiming to bring *The Great Emergence* up to the present. Then, *The Age of the Spirit: How the Ghost of An Ancient Controversy Is Shaping the Church*, released January 2014, was prompted by me, her co-author. Phyllis had said that she wasn't sure she had any books left to write, so I suggested co-authorship as a way to keep her pen going and as a way to extend *The Great Emergence* once more, creating what would essentially be book three in a series.

Our topic would be the split between East and West in the church a millennium ago. That was the "hook," the notion that we were approaching the precise thousand-year anniversary of the historic split. Phyllis loved the idea and we began talking about this "hinge of history" (borrowing from Thomas Cahill) in excited terms, back and forth, her exclamation points multiplying. We ended up using a revised version of one of my original emails to her on this idea in the opening two paragraphs of our proposal to Baker Books editor Chad Allen:

> As Phyllis Tickle has said to hundreds of thousands of people in lectures around the world since 2008, the only way to understand what is currently happening to us as 21st century Christians in the Great Emergence is to first understand that every 500 years or so the latinized Church feels compelled to have a giant rummage sale. Not only are we now living in and through one of those 500-year upheavals but we are about to honor the anniversary of one of the great ones from the past.
>
> The Great Schism of Christianity East from West has its roots in the fourth century, is memorialized in seminary courses as taking place in the year 1054, but as every historian of the faith will tell you, happened for all practical purposes in 1014. It was in that year that the Emperor Henry II insisted that Benedict VIII, the Bishop of Rome, begin reciting the Nicene Creed with that infamous additional Latin phrase: *filioque* ("and from the Son"). We are about to come upon the millennial anniversary of this momentous and inauspicious occasion—which is why we suggest that this book release in early 2014.

Phyllis always had subtle messages encoded in her writing. One message with this project was to explain that the disruptive chaos being presently felt in churches was of theological and providential design, her greatest meta-narrative of all: the revelation of God in three waves of the Trinity. Another message, which was perhaps more troublesome to some of her closest readers, was to validate the "gifts" of the Holy Spirit, as well as the centrality of the third person of the Trinity to the Christian life.

She wrote, to the surprise of many who were actively involved in a hierarchical church: "To know God without a priest or pastor either funneling and directing the experience or laying down the instructions for placing the call is exhilarating. It may be frightening, in fact, for the first time or two, but ultimately it is exhilarating, not to mention habit-forming. And whether one intends it or not, inevitably it leads to circumventing much of the system."[22] But it surprised none of her close friends. They knew that, despite her deep allegiance to the Episcopal Church and its hierarchical orientation, she was herself little impressed by bishops and the like. Some of her friends believe that, had Phyllis lived longer, she would have become a Roman Catholic; others think that she would have left hierarchical churches behind and aligned herself with a house church or some other emerging expression of faith, of some kind somewhere. Neither was likely. She would have stayed put.

Also motivating the writing of *The Age of the Spirit* was her unease with what she viewed as post-evangelical clinging to the cross, and the atonement through Christ, as answers to all spiritual need. Like many of her colleagues, she was reading René Girard and mimetic theory as an alternative to traditional atonement. Lutheran pastor and theologian Paul Nuechterlein became someone she also read carefully and consistently, with his Girardian reflections on the lectionary (girardianlectionary.net). So, too, the books of the only out gay Catholic priest, and leading theological interpreter of Girard's work, James Alison. Years earlier, in one of the first emerging church books, Pastor Karen Ward had written of atonement in a way that became emblematically pithy, akin to the line about truth not being factual but actual: "We are being moved, as a community, beyond theories about atonement, to enter into atonement itself, or at-one-ment."[23] Given this sea-change, when old images and atonement language continued at gatherings such as the Wild Goose Festival, Phyllis referred to them privately as "the unconsidered Jesus as Word and atonement as a deal between God and Satan: mid-20th century evangelicalism gone stale."[24]

10

Contrary to the above thesis that her creative powers waned in her last six or seven years, it could instead be argued that she simply had little time for writing. This is also accurate and she certainly felt keenly the desire to retreat and write, as she once had, when Sam was healthy and productive, and when being a household breadwinner did not also weigh on her.

A measure of heresy filled *The Age of the Spirit*, which we soon came to realize. Neither of us minded the implication or accusation. My own reputation hadn't been orthodox for some time, and Phyllis, nearing eighty, perhaps had nothing to lose. The heresy was the suggestion of progressive revelation, those three waves of the Trinity—using the medieval theories of a monastic prophet, Joachim of Fiore, who interpreted history through the lens of epochs of God's revelation, from the age of the Father to the age of the Son to the age of the Holy Spirit. A decade earlier, Phyllis had suggested a similar schema without reference to Joachim, identifying the first fifteen hundred years of Christianity with the Father, the time of the Reformation with the Son, and the present with the Spirit.[25]

In lectures after *The Age of the Spirit* came out, Phyllis took to explaining the heresy by pointing to the story of Philip in the Gospels, who first saw Jesus and told his friends to come and see the Messiah; then, three years later, he turns to Jesus and says, "Lord, just show us the Father." The Gospel says: "Jesus said to him, 'Have I been with you all this time, Philip, and you still do not know me? Whoever has seen me has seen the Father.'"[26] That was heresy for a good Jew like Philip in the first century. In the same way, she would explain, we are probably now in the time when we are going to have to engage God the Holy Spirit, whereas most Christians before the twentieth century were oriented to God the Father and God the Son. She would also refer to others who have said similar things, emphasizing that this was not an original idea, mentioning Joachim of Fiore as well as retired Harvard professor of theology Harvey Cox, who is often quoted in *The Age of the Spirit*.

We saw the book as a way forward between the anti-religious, secular (even atheist)[27] strand of post-Christian expression, which was gaining steam in the work of many who used to identify as emerging, and the older forms of creed and piety that each of us were schooled in. There would be deep uncertainty in a Christian life focused more on Spirit than on Son or Father, but we also felt that uncertainty was now the only authentic expression of what we called faith.

11

While waiting for *The Age of the Spirit* to be released, we talked about other five-hundred-year rummage sales that might need single-book treatment. There could be volumes on the Great Transformation (or Great Transition), which is what Phyllis named the Christ era; on the Great Decline and Fall; as well as the Great Reformation. Ultimately, none of these went beyond simple descriptions, except for one. We both were passionate about considering the way that Judaism and Christianity might be coming together again, looking at the split of these cousins in faith two thousand years ago (when both the church and Rabbinic Judaism were born). Phyllis had been saying for years that Christians might rename their faith "Judeo-Christian," and had made frequent remarks such as this one after attending a Jewish service: "Those chanted and sung phrases were as natural to me as the cadences and intonations of my own worship."[28] For my part, I'd worked for many years, while an Episcopalian, for Jewish Lights Publishing; and since leaving their employ and converting to Catholicism, had married a rabbi. So together, we began to contemplate a volume on the Great Transition that would focus on more than what happened around the rabbi Jesus.

In February 2014, while in New York City to promote the publication of *The Age of the Spirit*, along with a festschrift in honor of Phyllis compiled by Tony Jones and published by Paraclete Press, Phyllis and I spent two hours at the offices of CLAL—the National Jewish Center for Learning and Leadership, with Rabbis Irwin Kula and Brad Hirschfield, the organization's co-presidents. In a fourth-floor conference room on Park Avenue South we opened by asking Kula and Hirschfield if they sensed an "emerging Judaism" happening in North America, and if it was at all similar to what was taking place in the Christian world. "Absolutely," Hirschfield shot back, "and we were hoping you were here to tell us all about it." We laughed, but that was how the CLAL rabbis regarded both Emergence Christianity and Phyllis, as forerunners.

Kula and Hirschfield talked that day about both lay-led and rabbinic-led emerging communities in Judaism, most of them unaffiliated with any of the Jewish denominations, and how they shared traits in common with emerging Christian groups. There was, for example, The Kitchen in San Francisco, led by Rabbi Noa Kushner. "Judaism is about provoking awe and purpose. That's what we're here for," The Kitchen's mission statement (and website) read.

Phyllis and I began calling our book *An Interruption Healed* or *The Great Interruption*, followed by *Judaism and Christianity in the Great Emergence*. The title came from Phyllis, who woke up one morning and felt it as an epiphany. I then wrote the first descriptive paragraph for a proposal:

> This is the concluding volume in an Emergence complex that started with Phyllis Tickle's *The Great Emergence*. We—Christians and Jews—are all citizens of the same milieu. We are all moving toward rapprochement, especially Emergence Christians who are in a very real sense "coming back home." This is their story. But this is also a story about the conjoining of stories, and twenty-first century Jews and Judaism have a big part to play in it.

12

Again, difficulties at home, mostly the health of children and husband, tugged her back from the road. Sam's health issues intensified again in early 2014 and Phyllis began to cancel speaking engagements as well as personal visits. She wrote to one friend who had just reconfirmed a get-together: "I was going to write you first thing this morning, because I am having to cancel . . . filled with apologies, may I add, and regret, but nonetheless having to cancel. We are having a bit of a time of it here with Sam and his declining health issues these last few days, and I simply cannot get away."[29]

We nevertheless sent the new book idea off to the publisher of Phyllis's trilogy on Emergence, who showed little interest in the idea. Many of Phyllis's readers might have been surprised to see what she had intended to say in that final work. But it was not to be.

The idea of *The Great Interruption* did take one additional step. Church Publishing, Inc.'s Nancy Bryan, the editor who acquired this biography, approached Phyllis in the fall of 2014 to ask if she would co-author a book as part of a new series of "Conversations" between well-known pairs of friends and colleagues. Phyllis's response was that she had only one more book and it was something akin to *The Great Interruption*. In her meta-narrative style, she thought of it in terms of ancient history, similar to when Tacitus wrote of Pompey the Great and his soldiers entering the Holy of Holies in Jerusalem in 63 BCE and finding, to their surprise, "nothing" there: no statue of a god and no one guarding anything at all god-like. That was the signal gift of ancient Judaism to the world, Phyllis said, and to Christianity, its cousin: ultimate monotheism.

For several months, she was gathering surveys about changes among Jews in America, clippings of news stories and op-eds about the growing number of "Jewish Jesus followers," and other accounts of changes in Jewish identity. But the idea came to a stop when she was diagnosed with cancer. Just a few days earlier, on May 6, 2015, she had written to an Orthodox rabbi, a friend of a friend, saying:

> My work over the last two or so years has made me increasingly aware of a gradual rapprochement of sorts (for lack of a better word) between some parts of Western Judaism and Emergence Christianity. What will come of it, I obviously do not know; but I am very aware of the fact that this is not some kind of "inter-faith" conversation, valuable as those may be; rather it is a kind of yearning and recognition of a commonality that commands and informs at least the Emergence part of the discussion.[30]

She would have been surprised to discover, as I later did, that Thomas Merton, a writer whom she never appreciated much, wrote in 1962:

> [T]he antinomy [that Christians] have unconsciously and complacently supposed between the Jews and Christ is not even a very good figment of the imagination. The suffering Servant is One: Christ, Israel. There is one wedding and one wedding feast, not two or five or six. There is one bride. There is one mystery, and the mystery of Israel and of the Church is ultimately to be revealed as One.[31]

And she would have been delighted to see how the Catholic Church, in December 2015, would state that "the separation between Synagogue and Church may be viewed as the first and most far-reaching breach among the chosen people."[32] Even the enigmatic Leonard Cohen would write a song, "Treaty," on his final, October 2016 album that seemed to echo what Phyllis had been talking about for fifteen years.[33]

CHAPTER 18

Death, Again

By 2014, interest in Phyllis's big picture story of Emergence began to wane, not simply because the narrative of the Great Emergence, as she told it, was then several years old, but because many people were beginning to doubt the uniqueness of the event of the late twentieth/early twenty-first century in First World Christianity. There was growing uncertainty that what was happening then was as groundbreaking as Phyllis had described it. One of the points made by Lori Leibovich back in the *Mother Jones* article of the summer of 1998 began to sound more accurate: "Postmoderns repeat the word 'authentic' like a mantra. They seize on the tenets of Generation X—ennui, skepticism, cynicism—and use them as a way to attract members."[1] Their leaders were mostly Gen X, and if an attachment to the Gen X zeitgeist was the reason for their involvement, this also would explain why Emergence wasn't growing more quickly.

2

The year would be full of pain for Phyllis. On September 5, 2014, blogger David Hayward (Nakedpastor.com) wrote a post on the topic of abuses of religious authority among Christians. Hayward's post was titled "Tony Jones on Mark Driscoll: What came first, the thug or the theology?"—an analysis of a blog post Jones himself had written taking Driscoll to task for alleged abuses. (Jones and Driscoll knew each other in the early years of emerging, before Driscoll pulled away, deciding that the movement was too occupied with liberal theological ideas.)[2] Jones argued that Driscoll's conservative theology was to blame for his thuggish behavior. Hayward said to Jones that he should name abuse for what it was: simply abuse.

Jones's ex-wife, Julie McMahon, began commenting on Hayward's comment string six days after the initial posting, after Jones had three times defended his opinions of Driscoll. Her first comment was: "[W]hen my husband left for a 28 year old in the emergent movement it was Mark Driscoll that sent us money for groceries and prayed for us. I know a very different Mark." The following morning, McMahon's comments became targeted at Jones by name, offering details of the break-up of their marriage. In this public forum, then, over the next few weeks, McMahon almost daily accused Jones of a host of wrongs from the time of their marriage, and since. The firestorm that ensued was dozens of comments each day, mostly by people who did not know McMahon and Jones personally. Before the first week was out, some of these were demanding statements of support for McMahon by Jones's high-profile friends. McMahon herself demanded this, and Phyllis was one of the people mentioned and demanded to "appear" on this forum to explain her support for Jones since the alleged events were said to have happened. Certain leaders within the emerging movement, including McLaren, Mark Scandrette, and Pagitt, all of whom knew both McMahon and Jones, responded. Phyllis did not.

Almost two weeks after the whole thing began, Phyllis wrote to Jones personally:

> I knew nothing of the bru-ha-ha until I got this weird, accusatory note from Julie demanding a public apology for my sins and apparently my abuse of spiritual power, whatever that may be, and including a link to the site where I was to offer said apology. I went looking at the site and WOW! . . . Who knew this dumpster full of animus was going to find some tortured way to attach itself to such? So just a note to explain why there has not already been a note several days ago and to say, old friend, that I am sorry. . . . And also to say that the anger here is not just personal, as you know, but part of some strange kind of smoldering inferno that keeps cropping up but never seems to want to engage, only to rage. . . . So sad and pointless and wounding.[3]

The tone of Hayward's writing and his catering of the electronic assault on Jones was picked up by others, as well, over the next few months. R. J. Stollar, another popular blogger, even posted a lengthy survey of what he titled "The Evidence Against Tony Jones," including images from Hennepin County, Minnesota, court documents, where the obviously contentious and unpleasant breakup had taken place.

Phyllis looked upon her own remove from this unpleasant fracas, not as the right of an older person (she was the same in this regard when she was twenty, forty, or sixty), but because nothing good ever comes from quarreling with a wounded person. It wasn't until late January 2015 that she wrote a "Statement in Support of Tony Jones" at the prompting of a few close friends who were marshaling a campaign on his behalf. Similar statements were made by other Emergence leaders such as Nadia Bolz-Weber and Brian McLaren and posted as PDFs on a Scribd site called WhyTony. Phyllis began:

> Because of recent and current sadness in my family life, I have been at a considerable remove for the last month from the blogosphere and, as a result, from the burgeoning commentary about the failed marriage between Tony Jones and Julie McMahon Jones. Having just this morning had an opportunity to read some of what is being exchanged on the net and in the blogosphere, I come with a heavy heart to the business of sorting out my own thoughts and, even more to the point, with the serious reservations of a very old woman about adding anything to the cacophony already circulating.

She goes on: "First, I am moved by the irony of all of this. No contemporary theologian of my knowledge has more accurately or efficaciously introduced the work of René Girard to the Christian conversation than has Tony Jones. As most of us know, the keystone of Girard's line of argument is that scapegoating is a principal way among human beings of relieving communal guilt and communal anxiety. . . ." And then:

> My second reason is far more personal. I love Tony Jones as a friend and colleague, and also as a fellow Christian and astute theologian. While I understand that love can blind us to faults and errors—thank God for that. Otherwise, we would have no friend or lovers—I reserve the right to mourn the public flailing of one whom I hold dear, just as I roundly question the accuracy of many of the flails. To that end, may God have mercy

on all of our souls . . . both flailed and flailers . . . and may His Spirit
comfort us as we perceive and then endure the shame of what we do and
have done . . . every one of us. —Phyllis Tickle

3

A month later, in February 2015, a necessary eruption took place in
the evangelical world over LGBTQ rights when Brandan Robertson,
recently graduated from Moody Bible Institute in Chicago, came out
as queer and was jettisoned by Destiny Publishers, the evangelical publisher that had signed his memoir. This was further evidence of what
Phyllis had predicted: that gay rights would be the last straw of *sola
scriptura.*

Young Brandan had secured a promise from Phyllis to write the
foreword to his book. Upon hearing the news of the cancellation of the
contract, she wrote to him to say

> Talk about stepping into the whirlwind! But I have to say what I "feel"
> on this one, as much as what I think. That is, painful as this may be,
> it is probably going to end up by being a major step forward, not only
> for the LGBT community, but also for you and your work. It seems to
> me highly likely that you have just gained a remarkably well positioned
> podium from which not only to publish this book—because somebody is
> going to take it, believe me!—but also to advance the work you are just
> beginning as advocate and force for godly change within the evangelical
> communion. This is not to say that I am unaware of the cost you are pay-
> ing or the hurt you're enduring. . . . These next few weeks and months
> will effect and shape the next few years at the very least.[4]

Phyllis knew that the tide was turning for full acceptance, even
in evangelicalism. A poll conducted by the Public Religion Research
Institute found that 66 percent of all white evangelicals polled opposed
same-sex marriage—but that percentage went down by 17 points to 49
percent when only Millennial white evangelicals were asked the question. New books were coming out consistently, such as, in 2014, Millennial evangelical Matthew Vines's *God and the Gay Christian*, and
the aforementioned Pastor Ken Wilson's *A Letter to My Congregation*,

which represented the first time that the pastor of a large evangelical church publicly came out in favor of full acceptance. In June 2015, the Supreme Court made same-sex marriage legal across the U.S.[5]

4

Meanwhile, Sam was dying. The first of September 2014, he was moved to the Geriatrics Unit of Lakeside Hospital in Memphis, a psychiatric facility, and the third hospital in six weeks, each one passing him on to the other. "It seems we may not be bringing him home again, which is its own kind of agony, the worst, of course, being the business of never knowing what it is that he is feeling or experiencing or suffering himself in all his confusion," Phyllis confided to Brian McLaren.[6] Three weeks later, the family thought that they would be transferring Sam home, once more, and finally, for rehab, but that wouldn't happen.

For more than a decade, he had been dying. This was a time of prolonged sadness for Phyllis. She deeply loved her husband, and she also loved being married. "Marriage makes me . . . strong to venture (for there is another waiting to catch and repair me) and weak to dare (for there is another whose good rises and falls with my own)," she once wrote. "It makes me more sure (for there is another who has told me of the rightness of my thoughts) and less sure (for there is another who has demanded I see the error and selfishness of my ways). It makes me Phyllis to his Sam. . . ."[7] She slowly and surely watched her marriage die along with the man whom she had loved since he was a boy.

But this period of sadness was even more complicated, since she loved a complicated man who had many troubles and who brought them to their relationship in near-daily doses. There were other stresses, too, for example the increasing cost of maintaining the Farm in Lucy. Phyllis thought of moving back to town but stayed for Sam's sake. Many times, more than wistfully, while working at *Publishers Weekly*, she had said, "If ever I become a widow, I'm going to move into the Gramercy Park Hotel to live out my days." There was an anonymity about New York City that she loved, living in close quarters with so many. She got to be in the midst of a bustle without always having to engage emotionally. She loved to people-watch. And after living in the country, the pull of street vendors and knowing that everything you could possibly need was within walking distance was a joy.

She also missed the cleanliness and minimalism of apartment living—something that had also been a tension with Sam. The farm required an enormous amount of maintenance: a 3,000 square feet house needing to be kept clean and twelve acres of land to be maintained, all at a time when the child labor had long since moved out. It was too much space and work for a couple of retirement age. Sam was also messy and a pack rat. He was a creator, not a maintainer. He would plant beautiful flower beds that would rapidly be overgrown into weeds. He would cook a meal that left a multi-hour cleaning job in its wake. But when Phyllis contemplated compressing into a smaller space and throwing away the stacks of unnecessary things they had acquired, Sam dug in deeper.

So when Phyllis required quiet space to think through her writing, she spent it in hotel rooms and airport sky clubs for days or long afternoons at a time. She also extended her stays at the Community of Jesus on Cape Cod, where she had her own bungalow anytime she needed it.

5

However, "death" didn't mean to Phyllis what it means to most people. A comment she made in a 2002 interview, just after referring to the death of her infant son, revealed her perspective: "When you look death in the face, you realize that he's an old fooler. He's a charlatan. He's not real. We can't be killed. We won't die."[8] She may have been remembering the last line of Sonnet 146 by William Shakespeare: "And Death once dead, there's no more dying then." Several years later, she wrote in the introduction to her book on the sayings of Jesus: "What [the teachings of Jesus in the Gospels] share and rest on is the very simple principle that human life cannot end. Once we are born, we are. Always. Without end or hope of end, we are. Life is eternal; death is eternal. In life or in death, we are without hope of cessation. And if that is not a terrifying thought, I hope never to hear one."[9] This was a rare creedal statement for her and would soon prove to be both essential and inviolable.

CHAPTER 19

Her Final Year

Several hundred authors got their start through Phyllis's advocacy between the early 1990s and 2015. One was Joanna Seibert, who emailed Phyllis "cold" after walking up to her at a Kanuga conference. She then received this response:

Dear Joanna,

How good to hear from you and how generous a letter you have sent. Thank you.

It was a great pleasure to meet you. One of the side-benefits (that often takes center stage, in fact) of what I do is meeting other writers and swapping war stories and/or publishers, etc. I hope we have other opportunities to do so again and frequently. In the meanwhile, I am taking the liberty of showing your letter to a publisher or two to see what may be out there. Hopefully, we will hit our mark with one or the other of them.

Let us stay in touch, and may the dear Lord bless our work.

Cordially,
Phyllis

To complete the example—which is representative of hundreds of others—Phyllis then, over two decades, helped Seibert find her first publisher, contributed forewords to three of Seibert's books, had dinner with Seibert and her husband on several occasions in Memphis, and personally posted one of Seibert's books to the presiding bishop of the Episcopal Church, Katharine Jefferts Schori, at the offices at 815 Second Avenue in New York.[1]

On many occasions, Phyllis wrote glowing praise in personal letters and emails to friends and acquaintances. Most often, her endorsements made perfect sense. But there were times when she was "completely taken" with a book, somewhat inexplicably, allowing her tremendous kindness to take over. "It's very close to something of an American masterpiece," she wrote to one author, a close friend. "One could justify an entire lifetime by producing just one such chapter," she went on. Another colleague's book was "clearly magisterial." Enthusiasm came easily to Phyllis. As John McQuiston II realized after Phyllis wrote a foreword for the fifteenth anniversary edition of his book, *Always We Begin Again*, "Her praise . . . was classic, over the top, never to be doubted, generous Phyllis."[2]

There are many more prominent examples, as well. Nadia Bolz-Weber, now perhaps the most recognized Protestant clergyperson in America, was a missioner of the Evangelical Lutheran Church in America in Denver in 2006 when she wrote an email to Phyllis before the AAR/SBL was to gather in Washington, DC: "My name is Nadia Bolz-Weber. . . . I was thinking maybe we could get a group of emerging church types together for an impromptu theology pub during the conference sometime. Does this interest you?"[3] A former stand-up comedienne, Bolz-Weber wasn't shy and her spark immediately impressed Phyllis, who began shepherding a book idea into the hands of potential publishers. Soon, Seabury Books, an imprint of Church Publishing, published *Salvation on the Small Screen: 24 Hours of Christian Television* in 2008. Book two, *Pastrix*, a theological memoir, hit the *New York Times Best Seller* list in the fall of 2013. The two women would remain extremely close, even if their theological approaches were somewhat different. Phyllis wasn't as interested in sin as Nadia was. When Phyllis wrote one of her last endorsements of a book, for Bolz-Weber's *Accidental Saints*, it was: "If Saint Augustine were to return to life and live among us now, he would be Bolz-Weber." She meant it. She always meant what she wrote, even when it seemed to others to be an exaggeration. That book premiered at number eight on the *New York Times* list, one week before Phyllis died.

She wrote more than five hundred endorsements for books over the course of her career, and she gave serious thought to each one. One more instance from the summer of 2014 is representative of many others: She received a request from a Lutheran pastor to read his manuscript. She'd never met the author and had no relationship with him. He sent the printed manuscript with a cover note. Ten days after receipt, Phyllis wrote an email of surprising length that demonstrated she had read all three hundred pages, offering a detailed critique. It begins, "First, you clearly can write and have a gift for it," soon followed by ". . . then something happens. The other chapters all read like sermons. The voice shifts, and one can almost see in the mind's eye how you shift from addressing the reader to addressing the audience."[4]

Likewise, Phyllis met agents and partnered with them, at the expense of her time, to birth more authors and books. One of the best agents contemporary with Phyllis's years post-*Publishers Weekly*, Kathleen Niendorff, explained:

> I met Phyllis at the Trinity Institute at Camp Allen a decade or so ago. She was in the company of Desmond Tutu, Thomas Keating, Joan Borysenko, etc., but something unique to my experience happened when we were introduced: it was as if at that moment, our souls came out to play! . . . [S]he has sent me a bevy of wonderful writers to work with as their agent. Everyone is the beneficiary of her graciousness, not to mention her extraordinary storehouse of knowledge and her agile mind but also that—praise God—razor wit.[5]

Phyllis's energy for friendship, and the way that she fed off of the love and companionship of others, was similar to Thomas Merton's. A type-A personality who lived in self-imposed exile—in his case, behind a monastery wall—Merton was always, despite monastic rules of silence, receiving and inviting friends to his version of the Farm in Lucy, the Abbey of Gethsemani in Kentucky. As his biographer put it, "[W]hen Merton talked to you he made you feel—at least for a time—that you were his most intimate confidant, that he opened himself to you and you opened yourself to him in a way which made it an exchange like no other, and that this friendship could not be duplicated by either of you with anyone else."[6] Then there was the "pull" toward a more contemplative life, a yearning for quiet and space for writing, that the two shared. They both loved for friends to come, and then also for them to go. A depth of personal affection and a magic for friendship spill out in Merton's correspondence, as well, as it does in Phyllis's.

2

Sam died on Friday, January 2, 2015, at Saint Francis Hospital in Memphis. On Sunday morning, Phyllis wrote to one of her closest friends: "The time had come and at this point the prime emotion is relief for him and us. The mourning and the grieving had/have already happened, odd as that may sound. . . . And when the dust dies down, I suspect as well that there will be another time of mourning, sweeter than the first, gentler, quieter. We will see. . . . p."[7] A memorial service and Holy Communion was held at St. Mary's Episcopal Cathedral on Sunday, January 11. The Rev. Andy MacBeth, Phyllis's friend and former rector at Calvary Episcopal in downtown Memphis, presided. Phyllis was sick with a bad cough, trying to make it through the afternoon, greeting friends beside her four daughters, Nora Katherine Cannon, Mary Gammon Ballard, Laura Lee Palermo, and Rebecca Rutledge Tickle, and two sons, John Crockett Tickle II and Samuel M. Tickle Jr.

The cough didn't go away. On the morning of January 15, Tony Jones wrote to say "There are rumors of pneumonia. How are you doing?" Phyllis wrote back an hour later: "Yesterday I began to feel better and today I may even decide to live a bit longer. . . . haven't been that sick in years, if ever. Apparently I contracted something in those hours in the ER with Sam before he succumbed. A virus, obviously, and I strongly suspect the flu-like same one that finally killed him. I'm not running any races for a while, but at least I am dressed and upright."[8]

3

Phyllis and Sam struggled with their religious differences for more than sixty years. After he died, when asked to characterize her husband's religious or spiritual identity, she replied:

> I honestly didn't know after a while. He began as what I would call a more-or-less evangelical Presbyterian, absolutely hard-hard sure of the doctrines he had been reared with and aggressively defensive of them.

Served as area President of Youth for Christ rallies for a couple or three years, and so on. Once he even took on a professor at the university in a class we were both taking in a stormy attack on said professor's opinion of Buddhism—actually slammed his books down and stomped out of the lecture hall, to my absolute horror. It was the first time I ever saw the temper that was to become his nemesis.

She went on to explain some of the religious tension in their marriage:

[W]e would find a congregation whose theology and ecclesiology pleased him, join it, settle in happily, and then within a couple of years, there would be some kind of rupture or blow-up that made him want to move on to some other parish. He was, in other words, always disenchanted within five or six years, and we left a trail of "former congregations" behind us, much to my discomfort. After I got on the road, it was easier, for I was not expected to have strong parish connections in as much as I was in absentia most of the time anyway. But it always troubled me that he was never content or happy or "approving," though what he believed was never really spelled out, only what he opposed in some particular circumstance or other. It was very strange and somehow very saddening.[9]

This runs counter to the narrative that most of her friends and readers perceived. For instance, she once wrote, "Sam and I spend a good deal of time these days praying that the children and their children and, now, their children's children will keep the faith"—but the truth is, she was quite alone in that conjunction.[10]

A month after burying Sam, Phyllis's cough hadn't gone away, and she began to develop other problems. On February 17, she demurred about endorsing a writer's work, saying, "I have developed an eye problem—my doctor says from too much staring at screens, if you can imagine that!"[11]

4

"What do you see as the role in the spiritual journey of mortality, facing death, suffering, loss?" Bob Scott had asked Phyllis years earlier, when she was about to turn seventy, in the interview that concluded the last chapter. "What death does is it shortens the space between you and the Divine. There is a clarification of the issues," she answered, adding, "I suspect that death and loss are great gifts."[12] A few years later, at the end of an hour-long lecture at the Ann Arbor Vineyard Church, she said:

> Death is a very strange thing. . . . You have to be an old woman to get away with what I'm about to say. . . . Death always buys something, always buys something. If nothing else . . . when we are faced with death we are faced with that strange interruption of time. Just briefly, you're not to the grief yet; you're to that rip, that place where everything is so clear, so economical, so obvious, such wideness. Time stops.[13]

The story of Phyllis's own terminal illness was broken by David Gibson of Religion News Service on Friday, May 22, 2015. At the suggestion of Michael Lawrence of Orbis Books, the publisher preparing to release a collection of her writings that August, Gibson had flown from New York City to Memphis and spent the Tuesday prior with her on the Farm in Lucy in a lengthy interview, with a local stringer photographer. Gibson posted his story at noon eastern time, May 22.

Just before one in the afternoon, Diana Butler Bass posted a link on Facebook to the story, prefaced with: "Our sister Phyllis Tickle is dying. How much I love her and am deeply, profoundly grateful to her. Please include her in your prayers and intentions. That she may die well, even as she lived." This couldn't have been further from where Phyllis was in her own emotions. She was being driven to radiation treatment that very hour; her treatments had begun the day before in an attempt to deter the spinal lesion from growing and thereby to hopefully prevent the collapse of the vertebra; but while in the car, she was texting about the exciting projects she was contemplating, some of them mentioned in Gibson's reporting. Her response to her own pending death was stoical, and, as was often the case when talking about her private life, Phyllis went in the opposite direction from maudlin.

Not always, however. A month earlier, when she first saw the proofs for that Orbis collection of her writings in the Modern Spiritual Masters series, she wrote to me, as compiler of the book, saying, "I would call you, except I think I would mumble and stumble and probably cry, which is a totally non-productive response."[14] It was an emotional week for her. Only two days earlier, on April 21, she had informed her children of her diagnosis:

> In any report, there is the headline and then the storyline. So first the headline, which is that I have been diagnosed with a moderately differentiated adenocarcinoma of the left lung. The storyline is that, as you will remember, I caught some kind of flu or vicious virus in the ER when your dad died. By the day of his memorial, I thought I just could not make it and, that night, just gave in to the thing and was in bed with fever and a wracking cough for three or four days thereafter, days that Laura stayed over and helped us get through. Well, the cough would not go away, and I began to refer to it as "the cough from hell." Finally, in early March I made an appointment to see Forrest Ward, thinking that after two months the thing needed some kind of attention. I could not get into see him until the Tuesday after Easter, the 7th. He did an X-Ray, and we were off and running. He sent me immediately on that afternoon to the Radiology Dep't at St. Francis for better and more complete X-rays, which confirmed the presence of a mass. Then last week we did a guided needle biopsy, and I met with him yesterday to go over the pathology which confirmed the adenocarcinoma. I spent most of the day today getting the PET scan thing that has rendered me radio-active for a few more hours. Friday, once that report is in hand, I will meet with the oncologist and try to look intelligently at what is going on and what, if anything, needs to be done. Until then, when all the data are more or less in hand, there is really not much to say beyond the fact that, with a firm diagnosis in hand yesterday, I did not want to wait any longer to tell you what is going on. And yesterday, as I was leaving his office, Dr. Ward said, "And we never did do anything about the cough from hell, did we?" which happens to be true. It is better than it was, but I am still coughing up non-cancer crud and snorting down post-nasal drainage to beat the band. In fact, I think the damned thing may outlive me, at this rate. More when I have something more definitive. . . . love you guys, each and every one . . . p[15]

She thought then that she would keep the news of her illness within the family, and that she'd remain active for many more months, even fulfilling speaking commitments that she'd made through the following January. But within two more weeks, she knew better.

All day on May 22, the day that Gibson broke the story, there was an average of more than 250 shares on Facebook every five minutes, increasing as the afternoon wore on, with more than a cumulative 5,000 by 2:15. The number stood at 8,800 an hour later, and over 12,000 by 4:15. Twenty minutes after Butler Bass's post, Phyllis's friend, Sybil MacBeth, whose husband had presided at Sam's funeral, posted a link to the story with "Hard to imagine the planet without my dear friend Phyllis. May we all learn from her about her 'next career'"—much more in accordance with Phyllis's spirit.

The fact that Gibson had her mentioning three books she still wanted to write, rather than just one, was probably a surprise to her agent, Joe Durepos, and for good reason. In discussion with Phyllis, Joe was prepared to sell a last book, on her illness and dying and thoughts about what comes next, but that one would never materialize. Phyllis's heart was never in the idea.

At 4:15 p.m., Tickle's publicist sent out a release confirming Gibson's report, as well as the establishment of a literary trust. Also that afternoon, Wild Goose created a Facebook page for tributes to her. And Brian McLaren wrote on his website:

> The news became public today: Phyllis Tickle is writing her final chapter. . . . For all of us who know and love Phyllis, this is an emotional time. She's become a kind of patron saint and elder for all of us associated with "Emergence Christianity" (which Phyllis christened) and a whole array of inter-connected communities like the Wild Goose Festival. She has (in Diana Butler Bass's unforgettable terms) provided a needed alternative to "ignorance on fire" and "intelligence on ice." "Intelligence on fire" captures her spirit pretty darn well. If I could summarize her message in a single sentence, it would be, "The Christian faith is pregnant."

Characteristically, Phyllis took a mystic's approach to these moments and days. She quietly knew that for her all was well and would be well. She felt that she better understood some of the events of the last few years, as she explained to her eldest daughter, Nora (a devout Catholic) in an email just two and a half hours after announcing to all of the kids her illness. She knew, especially now, that God was telling her something important: "I began the retirement process in Jan.

2013 because I was beginning to sense some approaching closure, however spooky or irrational that may sound. More pointedly, between the two of us because you will know immediately what I am saying, I was told it was time and to do it."[16]

She was not only unworried about death, and felt comforted personally by Jesus in her dying, but she was actively looking forward to what she thought of as "passing permanently into Otherwhere."[17] She felt consoled by God in a way similar to the Ignatian understanding of that word: as an entirely gratuitous gift.

5

Coincidentally, one week later, a documentary on the subject of Tickle's life premiered across the Atlantic at the Corona Fastnet Short Film Festival, an annual affair in the fishing village of Schull on the southwest coast of Ireland. A small crew from Tiny Ark Productions had spent a week in Lucy the previous October filming Phyllis. The film had a stark beauty to it and pictured Tickle ruminating about her long marriage, life in a rural setting, and various spiritual topics.

Hundreds of people, throughout the spring and summer of 2015, were corresponding regularly with her. Cards and letters poured in, particularly in June after Gibson's article appeared. Many of these cards, letters, and emails included mentions or attachments of causes that Phyllis had been passionate about or copies of the latest article or blog post that the author had written, knowing that surely Phyllis would want to read them, as she always had before. One included a multi-page eulogy that the sender had given at his father's funeral a year earlier. Another—a Memphis author from the St. Luke's Press days—composed a poem dedicated to her that began, "When you venture through to that other side. . . ." Some included letters like those sent in Christmas cards, bringing Phyllis up to date on happenings in the sender's family, work, and spiritual life. Phyllis tried to respond to many of these via email and text, but nearly always, by this point, foregoing the telephone.

She wanted to keep writing, thinking, doing her work. I was in Italy in mid-June, taking part in a conference, when I wrote her after a session:

Just heard a remarkable paper given by a Jewish scholar from Jerusalem, who teaches at Tel Aviv University. Made me still want to write that book that we will not have time to do, on Judaism and Christianity. His topic was a midrash that apparently contrasts David, as reveling in wonder, with Moses, who somewhere in Deuteronomy says that we have to move beyond wonder to obedience and action. I wonder if the era of David has finally won.

"Exactly," she wrote back that same day, "and I'm still reading material for that book, crazy as that is."

Mother Betty Pugsley, the prioress of the Community of Jesus, told Phyllis that when the time came for hospice, knowing that Phyllis would want to stay at home in Lucy, the Community would send some of their religious sisters to care for her twenty-four hours a day. Phyllis received this offer with astonished appreciation but said she doubted she would take them up on it.[18]

She later estimated that 250 people, from April to June, wrote to ask if they could visit the farm and spend time with her. She said no to them all, most often by not responding, and that was a shock to her friends. Phyllis was a genius at friendship, able to communicate sincerity, warmth, and affection to hundreds of people, one at a time, in such a way that this many people—perhaps two or three hundred—may have, at any given time, regarded themselves as one of Phyllis Tickle's best friends. But despite the genius that allowed so many to know her and be known by her so intimately, there is a reason her children felt they knew their father better than their mother: Sam was the more self-revealing. Phyllis had her father's reserve. Her hundreds of close friends are an odd testament to this paradox: that perhaps no one really knew her.

6

To some who wrote, in her gracious way, Phyllis told some of the truth: Her time was being taken up by her six children and many grandchildren, who also wanted to be around. There even came a time in the early summer when *they* would have to be encouraged to visit a little less often. The radiation had been palliative, but a cough persisted and she couldn't talk in the way she was accustomed to talking after decades of projecting her voice. In one instance, she wrote a physical letter to her old friend Bob Abernethy at PBS and didn't completely close the door on the visit he proposed to make with a camera crew. He'd invited her to speak about "anything you want to say, and anything you think the many of us who love you might want to hear." She responded: "I would love to see you; but I must also be honest with you," and then laid out her physical limitations, adding, "That having been said, the doctors are making progress in controlling the spasms, and they also insist that the weariness is, in part at least, the consequence of radiation and will diminish. . . . I am wondering if we can postpone any decision . . . for a couple of more weeks?"[19] They wouldn't ever revisit it.

At the Wild Goose Festival in early July, I was asked to greet the crowd from the main stage during the opening session on behalf of Phyllis. In preparation, I asked her if she would write something that I might read. She did and sent it to me, asking me what I thought of it. "You might add a sentence about your current health and the status of any work," I responded hesitantly. "People will want to know those things, I'm sure." She wrote back with a new version that included this update: "The pneumonia that initially attended the cancer has cleared, much to my relief; and radiation, while debilitating, has also proved very palliative; although I still have difficulty with conversation, especially on the phone, I find myself once more at the computer part of each day and enjoying the sense of being back into at least that much of a familiar routine." I prefaced my reading of this statement with a few short comments about Phyllis. Anthony and Peggy Campolo were sitting in one of the front rows of folding chairs, just to the right of center stage. Tony had made news throughout the evangelical world one month earlier by coming out in support of full acceptance of LGBT Christians and gay marriage in the church. He had been immediately ostracized, including in *Christianity Today* magazine, by many who had long embraced him and his work as an evangelist. He attended the festival at the last moment because, as he said to a large audience that day during an interview with Brian McLaren, about 270 out of 300 of the speaking engagements on his calendar at the time of his coming out were cancelled within a month, and he suddenly had free time. More importantly, McLaren said, was the idea for the Campolos to attend the festival where they would receive a warm embrace and love for their stance. In my few opening remarks one was, "I know that many of you are personal friends with Phyllis. Is there anyone who has a greater gift for friendship than Phyllis Tickle?" And as I said that, I saw Tony nodding his head vigorously.

Phyllis's comments about the status of her health were followed by one more paragraph, which I then read to warm applause and a few tears:

> Most certainly, though, while illness may confine me a bit, so to speak, no illness could contain or restrain my joy now, during these few days of our observing the daily offices together. I have adjusted my clock here in the central time zone to mesh with yours there in the eastern one so that we may once more and for one more time come together before our God to pray as members of the Church Universal and as celebrants of the Wild Goose and all she stands for. Long may she fly. Amen.

When she'd sent me this greeting, I'd written back, "Marvelous." "Sez you. Gag me," she responded.

She was uncomfortable throughout the final six months with the flood of sentiment that came her way. All she wanted was to have the Farm in Lucy fold in around her as she lived quietly to the end. A good friend wrote to ask what he could pray for, on her behalf. She responded:

> Dear Friend, I got your note several days ago, of course, and . . . I was most struck—heck, I was stopped dead in my tracks—by your query of what should you be praying for—or more accurately, what would I want you to pray for in praying for me. Nobody had asked me that before, and it has taken me this long to discern what my answer is. I thank you for having triggered that process almost as much as I thank you for the prayers themselves. So, days later, what do I covet your prayers for? I pray and ask you to pray on my behalf for simplicity, clarity, and an easy death. Thank you, always, p[20]

7

She read detective fiction every night before sleep, which was nothing new. That summer she was plowing through the volumes in Priscilla

Royal's late thirteenth-century English monastic murder series (*Wine of Violence*, etc.), while she spent the mornings collecting her poems and revising a few. Pulling them together into a cohesive whole felt to her like tying loose-ends of her life together. In late July, consulting with friends at Paraclete Press on an anthology of poetry they were planning, she wrote, "We shouldn't restrict ourselves to 'religious' or 'religious verse'! All poetry is religious, for goodness sakes!"[21] As Wallace Stevens once said, "The poet is the priest of the invisible."

In early August, the evangelical publishers' trade association (ECPA) wrote to ask if she would allow them to come to Lucy and video her, so that she might address their upcoming conference. The request came through me and I was the one to discuss it with her. She thought and prayed about it overnight, she told me, but concluded:

> I can't talk now with any comfort at all, and the energy that I have must be conserved for what must still be done. The original prognosis of feeling really bad by mid-summer and gone by Halloween has so far been pretty much on track, which makes me think the drs. might just know what they're talking about. It's a concept I could ill-afford engaging while living with one of them, but I am now coming to appreciate.[22]

I passed that along.

She began to organize her poems as an autobiography. Others wanted her to write a last, spit-in-death's-eye sort of book, or an inspirational "Tuesdays with Phyllis," but she wanted to pull together something that had been precious to her, and to see how her decades of poems had charted the pits and peaks of her living. Back in 1974 she had written these words for the Prophet Jeremiah to say in prayer while kneeling. They were now her words in more ways than one:

> O, God, I would to Anathoth,
> To the silent land and the cypress lake,
> To the land my fathers knew,
> To die there with my poetry and my pen.
> O lovely land that holds my family dead!
> I would, my God, to Anathoth.[23]

The result would be *Hungry Spring and Ordinary Song: The Collected Poems* (*an autobiography of sorts*).

This return to the poems was prompted, in part, by the re-publication of several of her poems earlier that year in the *Phyllis Tickle* volume in Orbis's "Modern Spiritual Masters" series. I had made a point of singling out her poems in the compiling, and in my introduction, calling for attention to an important, mostly forgotten, aspect of her work. It seemed to me then, and now, that Sam led her to put poetry away, convincing her that there were more important things. She echoed this judgment once in a note to a friend, explaining why she didn't feel comfortable calling herself a poet. "I realized somehow that I had no gift, in the way of an Eliot or Virgil. I think I never could make myself believe that anything less than that should claim the laurel, almost like it's a god-bestowed crown and not a self-acclaimed one."[24] Yet, she *was* a poet, and had remained one. At some level, she realized this, as she said to a friend a decade before she died:

> You probably have figured out by now that I do better telling stories than trying to explain myself in direct prose. . . . I started life as a poet, and I think I never got over it. Metaphor rules in my head, along with simile. One of the reasons I could never be a preacher is that I just can't drive straight in like that. I have to tell a story and hope . . . p[25]

She may have had Robert Lowell in the back of her mind as inspiration when arranging her poems as autobiography. About his own *Selected Poems*, he wrote, "Looking over [it], about thirty years of writing, my impression is that the thread that strings it together is my autobiography, it is a small-scale *Prelude* [referring to Wordsworth's autobiographical poem], written in many different styles and with digressions, yet a continuing story—still wayfaring."[26] Phyllis was always attentive to Lowell's work, as well as to many of the Boston-area literati (Lowell, Plath, Elizabeth Bishop, Anne Sexton, etc.) and her own confessional qualities were inspired by the influence of Lowell and others like him. The return to poetry was also accompanied by a return to memories and love for her father,

Philip. Sometime after her cancer was diagnosed, Phyllis rediscovered her father's "poetry file"—a set of hand-written index cards of classic poems, mostly by the English Romantics, with his annotations on them. That file card box was in the bottom drawer of her chest of drawers when she died.

She organized the final section of the *Collected Poems* under the heading "Endings." She wrote none of these after her diagnosis, so in that sense they are not autobiographically about her final illness. But they deal with the deaths of loved ones: Sam's and others'. They address the awareness of the imminent need for an afterlife, something that Phyllis didn't appear to doubt for a moment since she was twenty-one. They all deal with the endings and beginnings that death brings. As she explained once she finished the manuscript, "for the dying has been with us for a long time now."[27]

She missed some poems, in the process. This one I found in her papers from 1975. It is as fine as any of her work, and speaks from the mystic heart that was comfortable with life's endings:

The dust of Eden lay
New and Dumb,
Beneath the hands
That shaped it into man.

Who sleeps in me
And dreams these dreams
I can not see;
The womb is set
Too deep in me.

But fallen and aware
I at least can know
Whose hands it is
Are working there.

There was also "To a Garden Companion," selected by Ted Kooser for his folksy 1980 collection, *The Windflower Almanac of Poetry*. She forgot to include it, too:

Primordial plaything
left over
from the childhood of God,
the grasshopper sits
on cantilever legs
considering what things
larger than himself
he can consume
without exciting evolution.

8

Her health was really failing in the final days of summer, and she knew it—not simply because of what physicians were telling her, but in how she felt. "I am feeling some rush on this now," she said, nervous about seeing the poems all the way to publication. "The neurology is failing—wheelchair, etc, skull now softening etc."[28] Indeed, just after getting the poetry manuscript off to its publisher, Phyllis began experiencing neurological problems, including optical migraines. She began taking opioids for the first time in her life. Her physicians had prescribed them months earlier, telling her she'd need them eventually, but Phyllis had been wary, fearful that they would dull her concentration. By the end of August she wanted them. An August 27 visit to her physician involved the logging or prescribing of twelve different medications intended to treat her thyroid, rashes on her skin, anxiety, mucus in the lungs, over-all lung function, infection in the eyes, vitamin D deficiency, cough, and serious pain. She also measured just 5'8½" tall and 157 pounds.

During the first days of September, medicated to levels that soothed her symptoms, she felt better and began talking about having one more book in her. It was wishful thinking—mind over body. On September 11, after a visit to her physicians, she started hospice, was hooked up with an oxygen concentrator, and began carrying a little box device around, wearing a cannula hose to pipe the air into her nose. The extra air seemed like a brief bit of revelation, for how much better it made her feel. A lack of oxygen was probably much of the reason for the misery she had been feeling over the previous weeks. That evening, cannula hose in place, she still gathered around the kitchen table for evening drinks with her grown children Rebecca and Sam Jr., who were there every day, as well as daughter Mary and her husband Emmett. For decades, each late afternoon, this was the family ritual, and Jack Daniels was always a guest.

9

In the middle of September, eldest daughter Nora noticed rapid debilitation. When her visit began one week earlier, her mother was walking with a cane and asking what she could eat. The final manuscript for *Hungry Spring and Ordinary Song* had been sent off three weeks earlier, but Nora had arrived passionately interested in the project, a longtime admirer of her mother's verse. She'd brought with her a folder of typewritten poems that Phyllis had overlooked (in some cases, completely forgotten), and encouraged her to add them. In a few cases, these had never been titled, even though they were published in journals in the 1970s. This is how "Perspective," "Morning Song," "Guiltless Ease," "Mary in Church," "The War," "As It Should Be," "Chet," "Manual Labor," "All Celibacy Laid Aside," and "To Sappho" made it into *Hungry Spring*. Phyllis also paused to consider a play, *Sappho of Lesbos*, that she'd begun decades earlier but never completed. Then, rather suddenly, ten days after Nora's arrival, Phyllis was in a wheelchair, awake only four hours a day, and forgetting whether or not she had eaten at all. It was heartbreaking to watch, but not surprising.

We can take Phyllis at her word that she was unafraid of what would come after death. She was confident to the end that death had no finality, that it was only a step along the way. However, she *was* afraid that she would experience the end of this life in the way that her father had died: in agony. He had died crying out for his mother, screaming in the ICU, a kind of terminal anxiety combined with intense physical pain.

By mid-afternoon on Monday, September 21, her pain had increased exponentially. She turned to Nora (an experienced hospice nurse), and asked if Nora would give her a large dose of morphine. Phyllis was face-to-face with the child of her youth, and yet, she also knew that

Nora was religiously devout. Nora said "no" to what she heard as a right-to-die request. Nevertheless, over the next sixteen hours, three of Phyllis's children together managed her symptoms so as to avoid undue pain, and, in Nora's words, "midwife her to Heaven."[29] In addition to the drugs, before going to sleep on Monday night, Phyllis asked for, and enjoyed, a hot toddy.

She died at about nine o'clock in the morning, in her sleep, on the morning of September 22. It was Erev Yom Kippur. Her old boss at *Publishers Weekly*, Daisy Maryles, wrote when she heard the news midday:

> Tonight begins the holiday of Yom Kippur and I will be spending this evening (for Kol Nidre) and a lot of time tomorrow in synagogue. I know I will be thinking of Phyllis—one of the more remarkable people I have known. Heaven—because that is where her soul is headed—is welcoming a true and unique angel. We lost ours but her impact on so many folks and on Religion in America is priceless.[30]

She left behind six of her seven children: Nora Katherine, Mary Gammon, Laura Lee, John Crockett, Samuel Milton, and Rebecca Rutledge. It was Year B in the Christian liturgical cycle, Tuesday in the twenty-fifth week of Ordinary Time. The heart of Phyllis's spiritual life was expressed in Ordinary Time, rather than in the festivals.

Unknown to those who looked to her as the creator of *The Divine Hours*, Phyllis most often used the fat, maroon, leather-bound *Benedictine Daily Prayer: A Short Breviary*, published by the monks in Collegeville, Minnesota, as her personal breviary when she was home. (It was too bulky to take on the road.) So taken was she with it that a few years after its publication, when Liturgical Press's publishing director asked if she would provide editorial counsel on a project, Phyllis asked to be paid not in dollars but in gratis copies. She gave them away to friends. In the weekday readings from her *Benedictine Daily Prayer*, she would have read this on Monday evening before going to sleep: "In days to come the mountain of the Lord's house shall be established as the highest of the mountains, and shall be raised up above the hills. People shall stream to it. . . ."[31] Such appropriate imagery for a girl from East Tennessee.

CHAPTER 20

Future Projects

There was much that Phyllis still wanted to do: books to write, audiences to convince, friends to enjoy, great-grandchildren to watch grow. Perhaps closest to her heart—a full circling of the storytelling of her father from childhood—she planned to write and video a project she was calling *Bible Stories Your Grandma Never Told You* (*because they were naughty, theologically*). In 2007–2008, she had mentioned the idea in an interview with *The Wittenberg Door* and written an article for *Sojourners* magazine with a similar title. She wanted to retell the tales of the Hebrew Bible that the last century of Sunday school lessons had sanitized (such as Tamar or Jephthah's daughter), and the ones that had become politically or theologically incorrect, such as Daniel in the Lions' Den or Noah and the Ark. She had always agreed with Dr. Johnson when he said: "If nothing but the bright side of characters should be shewn, we should sit down in despondency, and think it utterly impossible to imitate them in anything." After a long phone conversation with her editor at Baker, she knew they were interested.

But that project would go no further.

Then there was the already mentioned co-authored book for CPI's "In Conversation" series on the religious future of Emergence Christianity and Emergence Judaism. *One God: Judaism and Christianity 2,000 Years Later*, we began calling it when it was clear that it would not be another in the series after *The Great Emergence*. Our précis read:

> For centuries, Christianity has been pleased to teach that there was a mighty tree or root that was Judaism, that in time gave rise to the true branch, to the true purpose of its being, in the coming of Jesus as Messiah,

thereby obviating the old tradition from which it grew. This is known as the doctrine of Supersessionism. But Emergence, more and more, are having none of that, choosing instead to suggest a position for which the better metaphor is that of a tuning fork. The two arms of this fork arise from a common base, and the place of their separation from one another is 70 CE with the destruction of the Temple (thereby scattering everybody) and the coming, as a result, of rabbinic Judaism and Pauline Christianity. The two tracked side-by-side until 70, Jewish both, until they gradually separated. This separation, post-Shoah, is healing rapidly. The tuning fork that may emerge in the near future is one in which both tines vibrate, and the music happens only when they vibrate (once again) together.

Then there is the "Age of the Spirit" in which we live, whether as Christians or as Jews . . . and here is the truly heretical part of what we want to explore. Could it be that the last two thousand years have seen the expression of God, or at least our understanding of the Divine, in Christ-like terms, whereas now we are entering into a time when God the Spirit is what . . . even Who . . . we know and experience as normative? Ancient Judaism provided the vehicle and expression of God the Father; Christianity did the same for God the Son; and now the fully visible presence of the Spirit is rapidly becoming the God to Whom we turn. If so . . . if we are on to something . . . these will feel like challenging, dangerous, upsetting, times.

It was risky. "I have to do it after I get off the road [meaning, when she is fully retired from public life], because if it doesn't work, if it is wrong, then it will distract from everything else I have done and I can't afford to do that," she explained to a group of Canadians in January 2014.[1]

Then there was the book that she mentioned in the interview with David Gibson of Religion News Service that revealed her inoperable lung cancer to the world: a sort of last spiritual testament, a book about death and dying. The very subtitle of the Gibson piece, a quote from the interview, teased Phyllis's audience with the promise of this last book: "The dying is my next career." She may have been thinking of the lines from Emily Dickinson[2]:

'Tis not that Dying hurts us so—
'Tis Living—hurts us more—
But Dying—is a different way—
A Kind behind the Door—

There were other projects that were merely ideas, but ideas that tantalized her. One publisher asked her to consider a book about prayer and offered a title: *Praying for Mercy*. Her agent sent her that request on what turned out to be the very day that her cancer was confirmed for her by her physicians. It was a month before it would be made public. None of these projects would materialize. She responded to the last one by saying to her agent, "Actually, and you will croak on this one, what is happening right now is poetry, and we all know that that's a big money-maker. We will see. . . ."[3]

2

The impact of *The Divine Hours* was a lasting contribution to the way that Christians, particularly Protestants, mainline and evangelical, and Episcopalians, pray. People in mainline denominations were seeking a spiritual connection to the ancient church; Episcopalians needed a tool to open up what the Book of Common Prayer had already teased them with; and evangelicals were already, many of them, "on the Canterbury trail," as Robert E. Webber put it in his book with that title, discovering liturgical treasures often for the first time.[4] Her prayer manuals will continue to be used for decades to come.

One probably cannot say the same thing about her other books. The works on trends in religion were necessarily dated soon after she wrote them. Also, it was her midrashic, expansive ability to bring those books to life before audiences that sold them and made them succeed.

She christened Emergence Christianity, as Brian McLaren said, but since her absence from the scene to trumpet, track, and teach the zeitgeist, Emergence seems to be folding publicly into progressive Christianity, guided by the political statements of its leaders. Borne out of an expanded sensibility and theological possibility from evangelicalism, Emergence Christians have found their ideological kin, as well as their liturgical leaders (always essential to a spiritual movement), in already existent progressive traditions. This may mean that what was the emerging church circa 2005 has morphed into what late-nineteenth-century liberalism began, with postmodern tools added. This would mean that the sensibility of Emergence—for Phyllis it was always ultimately mystically understood, as something happening both outside of time, and within one of its every-five-hundred-year manifestations—has succumbed to the mostly political language (back to the head, instead of the heart) of progressivism. Bishop Spong would be more comfortable in this than would Phyllis, for whom the mystery of faith was always at least as important as faith's commitments.

However, another way to measure the size and impact of Emergence Christianity is to look at the spiritual practices that flourish in people's lives, often privately, today: the praying of the divine offices, the revival of fasting, the use of icons and home altars, for instance. As Phyllis often said, the energy or thrust of spirituality in Emergence is toward a return to the communal as it occurs in the home or family. Such things rarely involve leaders of any kind, or even church attendance. Again, Phyllis's subtle anti-establishment bent would be pleased—in fact, it *was* pleased. She remarked to an Emergence friend in 2015 who was talking of "wikifying church," "[That] has just got to be one of the most delightful images conceivable, and I can't help loving it. Part of my joie d vie is evil, of course; it springs from a strong desire to watch as whole herds of sacred cows are driven to market."[5]

Sales of *The Great Emergence* have dropped off substantially, but its effect on a generation of reformers is without question. It, and the work of Phyllis's midlife, the essays and the poetry, will stand with *The Divine Hours* and *Greed* as her written legacy. The poet, psychoanalyst, and author of *Women Who Run with the Wolves*, Clarissa Pinkola Estés, spoke for many when she told Phyllis: "[Y]our open-door intelligence in writing about religion and spirit has meant much to me. You have a warmth in your tone, a levity that is gently present also. It's a gift that you carry all these in your writing voice."[6] And then there is the impact of her life that remains intangible: she cared so extravagantly and for so many. Taken together, when one considers her life and work in every respect—from the early scholarship, to mentoring students, to encouraging the arts, teaching a generation of children to find their own poetry, curating and publishing important writers, writings of her own on liturgy and prayer and the spiritual life and the changes roiling the organizations of religion that she loved, and the indefatigable way that she taught hundreds of thousands of people from podiums for decades—Phyllis Tickle was surely one of the late twentieth century's most important advocates for the written word and the life of faith.

Afterword

My career in publishing began in 1993 when I left bookselling behind in Cambridge, Massachusetts, to become a publisher's sales representative. After a summer of calling on bookstores in Tennessee, Georgia, Virginia, Alabama, the Carolinas, and Florida (where one bookseller took one look at my camel hair jacket in July and said, "You aren't from around here, are you?"), I was off to the AAR/SBL in Washington, DC. It was also Phyllis's first AAR/SBL with *Publishers Weekly*. I sought her out in a café, where she sat with a colleague sipping something, probably intending to be away from scrutiny for a while, and asked her a question about the industry. I can't remember what the question was, but I stated an opinion and asked Phyllis what she thought of it. "I think you're right on, Mr. Sweeney!" she shot back at me. Buoyed, as she buoyed so many, I went my way believing that I was clever, and that the future was bright for all of us. I wasn't, and it was.

Julian Barnes, the British novelist, wrote not long ago: "The trawling net fills, then the biographer hauls it in, sorts, throws back, stores, fillets and sells. Yet consider what he doesn't catch: there is always far more of that. . . . [T]hink of everything that got away. . . ."[1] This is surely the case, here.

A poem of Phyllis's, to end:

The Cranes

Where along their migratory way
These cranes may also stop
I can not say.
The river's a dozen miles from here,
But twice, sometimes more,
Each year
They drop,
A fleet of sails

On a sea
Of grass,
Like manna and the quails
Come from some other land
To say,
"This way! This way!"

Acknowledgments

In the past, writing a book has always been a mostly solitary experience for me. Not so, this time. Sincere thanks go to the hundred or so people who have shared memories, resurrected their correspondence, and allowed me to quote from their personal writings. Some of your names appear in the notes of this book, but certainly not all. Thank you.

A few of those who are not mentioned in notes are Carol Brown, retired publishing executive, who reached out and shared illuminative material, and Memphis poet David Spicer who took the time to have an extensive email correspondence. Mike Leach also gave both material and immaterial help. Thanks also to those who made contributions to a research travel fund, enabling me to spend time in Rome, Georgia, at the Phyllis Tickle Archives housed at Shorter University. Thank you to Linda Floyd and Kristen Bailey, librarians and archivists at Shorter.

Many thanks to those who shared photographs that are included in the book, especially photographer Courtney Perry for permission to reproduce her famous shot of Phyllis and Nadia (photo 16). And thank you to F. Lynne Bachleda for sending the photo of two stanzas of a Natalie Bartlum poem at Tennessee Bicentennial Capitol Mall State Park's "Pathway of History" in Nashville, even though it didn't make the final cut.

Thank you to Paraclete Press, for permission to re-publish, in quite altered and expanded form, the essay that I originally wrote for the festschrift in honor of Phyllis, *Phyllis Tickle: Evangelist of the Future*. Thank you to Sr. Mercy Minor of Paraclete who transcribed a talk Phyllis gave to the staff of the press in 1998, and then shared that transcription with me. And thank you to Orbis Books, for permission to re-publish, with many amendments, the chronology that I first created for *Phyllis Tickle: Essential Spiritual Writings*. The first three paragraphs of chapter 7, here, also appeared in slightly different form in that earlier work.

Notes

Chronology

1. Phyllis Tickle, *The Shaping of a Life: A Spiritual Landscape* (New York: Doubleday, 2001), 84.

Author's Note

1. W. H. Auden, *The Complete Works of W. H. Auden: Prose*, vol. 5, *1963–1968*, ed. Edward Mendelson (Princeton: Princeton University Press, 2015), xiv.

Prologue

1. Terry Mattingly, "Hitting the 500 Year Wall," On Religion, Scripps Howard News Service, November 28, 2007.

2. From actual evaluation cards.

3. Kev Silva, "National Association of Evangelicals Seeks Common Ground with Mormonism," *Appraising Ministries* (blog), September 25, 2009, *http://apprising.org /2011/03/10/national-association-of-evangelicals-seeks-common-ground-with -mormonism/*. Another less-popular blogger headlined his May 27, 2009, post, "Rob Bell Invites Heretical Mystic Woman to Speak," *Truth in Grace* (blog), *https://truthingrace .com/2009/05/27/rob-bell-invites-heretical-mystic-woman-to-speak/* (see chapter 17.4).

4. Mark Oestreicher, "NYWC, Sunday Morning, "*whyismarko* (blog), November 18, 2007, *http://whyismarko.com/nywc-sunday-morning-2/*.

5. Tony Myles, "NYWC—Atlanta, Day 3, Part 1," *don't call me Veronica* (blog), November 17, 2007, *http://dontcallmeveronica.blogspot.com/2007/11/nywc-atlanta -day-three-part-1.html*.

6. Phyllis Tickle, *Embracing Emergence Christianity: Phyllis Tickle on the Church's Next Rummage Sale: A 6-Session Study*, with Tim Scorer (New York: Morehouse Education Resources, 2011), 35.

7. "No Nation Is Christian (and Phyllis Tickle Knows)," interview by Becky Garrison, *The Wittenberg Door*, November 28, 2007.

Chapter 1

1. See Phyllis Tickle, *What the Land Already Knows: Winter's Sacred Days (Stories from the Farm in Lucy)* (Chicago: Loyola Press, 2003), 63.

2. Phyllis inherited this book after her father's death. It was a treasured item in her library. Observed on July 14, 2015.

3. Interview with the author, email, July 28, 2015.

4. Phyllis Tickle, *The City Essays* (Memphis: The Dixie Flyer Press, 1982), 7.

5. Phyllis Tickle, *What the Heart Already Knows: Stories of Advent, Christmas, and Epiphany.* (Nashville: The Upper Room, 1985), 25.

6. Phyllis Tickle, *Hungry Spring and Ordinary Song: Collected Poems (An Autobiography of Sorts)* (Brewster, MA: Paraclete Press, 2015), 72.

7. Interview with the author, email, July 28, 2015.

8. *Hungry Spring*, 63. "Lucy at Dusk," just preceding, is at p. 50.

9. Interview with the author, email, August 6, 2015.

Chapter 2

1. See Phyllis Tickle, *My Father's Prayer: A Remembrance* (Nashville: The Upper Room, 1995), 22–23.

2. Phyllis Tickle, *Prayer Is a Place: America's Religious Landscape Observed* (New York: Doubleday, 2005), 102–3.

3. Interview with the author, June 10, 2015.

4. Fred W. Hoss, "Henry Johnson Realized His Dream," in *The Sunday Chronicle*, a weekly publication of Chronicle Publishing Co., Johnson City, TN, Sunday, May 21, 1922.

5. "How'd You Like to be the Policeman?" *Johnson City Staff News*, March, 15, 1926, Carroll E. King, editor.

6. This version of the essay is taken from Phyllis Tickle, *God-Talk in America* (New York: Crossroad Publishing, 1998). Much of the same appeared in *City Essays*, 31–2.

7. See William E. Diehl's *The Monday Connection: On Being an Authentic Christian in a Weekday World* (San Francisco: HarperSanFrancisco, 1991), in which he refers to Miller and quotes him, 18.

8. "Living with Selfhood: Books for the Dark Night," *The Christian Century*, April 14, 2015.

9. Tennessee Williams, *The Selected Letters of Tennessee Williams, Vol. 1: 1920–1945*, eds. Albert J. Devlin and Nancy M. Tischler (New York: New Directions, 2000), 359.

10. Interview with the author, June 10, 2015.

11. H. B. Teeter, "Zestful Betas, Full of Confidence, Sodas, Hamburgers, 'Take' Town in Spirit of Fun," *The Nashville Tennessean*, March 12, 1950.

12. "What Science Means to Me," *The Tennessee Teacher* XVIX, no. 1 (September 1951): 28–9.

13. Interview with the author, June 10, 2015.

14. Interview with the author, June 10, 2015.

15. "If I Could Change My High School Training," *Peabody Journal of Education* 29, no. 1 (1951): 37.

Chapter 3

1. *Shaping of a Life*, 55.

2. In her biography of Foster, *Sex Variant Woman: The Life of Jeannette Howard Foster* (Cambridge, MA: De Capo Press, 2008), 46, Joanne Passet writes that, as a college student in Rockford, Foster viewed Thompson as one of two "highly accomplished, homosexual women" on the faculty.

3. Joanne Passet, *Sex Variant Woman*, 81, 87.

4. *Shaping*, 91. There are other mistakes of fact in *Shaping*—for instance, referring to her paternal grandfather's birth year as 1890 instead of 1892.

5. *Shaping*, 36–7.

6. See *The Letters of T. S. Eliot, Volume 5: 1930–1931*, eds. Valerie Eliot and John Haffenden (New Haven: Yale University Press, 2015), 5, n. 3.
7. *Shaping*, 89, 90.

Chapter 4

1. Remembered by Phyllis to Ken Wilson, email, November 9, 2009.
2. Email exchange with Scot McKnight, February 19, 2014.
3. *Hungry Spring*, 17: from the commentary "below the line."
4. Interview with the author, June 11, 2015.
5. Nora Cannon, interview with the author, email, April 14, 2016. Also, *Shaping*, 283.
6. *Shaping*, 284.
7. Phyllis Tickle, *The Tickle Papers* (Nashville: Abingdon Press, 1989), 18.

Chapter 5

1. *Prayer Is a Place*, viii.
2. Interview with the author, email, February 5, 2016.
3. Dixie D. Johnson '66, "Scholar-Mentor Tribute," *Rhodes* (Summer 2014): 42–3.
4. Douglas W. Cupples, "The Memphis College of Art: Interview with Mrs. Phyllis Tickle, September 12, 1988," *https://archive.org/details/memphiscollegeof00cupp*.
5. Interview with Douglas W. Cupples, September 12, 1988.
6. *Prayer Is a Place*, 9; Nora Cannon, interview with the author, email, September 20, 2016.
7. Interview with Robert Scott, "Phyllis A. Tickle: Death and Divine Living," Trinity Television and New Media, Trinity Church Wall Street, New York, 2002, DVD.
8. *Shaping*, 254.
9. Nora Cannon, interview with the author, email, May 4, 2016.

Chapter 6

1. Nora Cannon, interview with the author, email, May 4, 2016.
2. Interview with the author, June 9, 2015.
3. This is stanza one of "The Laments." See *Hungry Spring*, 17. The quote that follows is from the same poem, stanza three (of four).
4. *City Essays*, 8.
5. Unpublished talk. "How Then Must We Live," The Trinity Institute, New York. April 5, 2002.
6. *Hungry Spring*, 17: stanza three of "The Laments."
7. Phyllis Tickle, ed., *Confessing Conscience: Churched Women on Abortion* (Nashville: Abingdon Press, 1990), 10.
8. Nora Cannon, interview with the author, email, September 25, 2016.
9. *Tickle Papers*, 110, 135.
10. *Confessing Conscience*, 10.
11. Nora Cannon, interviews with the author, email, September 25 and 28, 2016.
12. *365 Meditations for Women*, ed. Phyllis Tickle (Nashville: Abingdon Press, 1989), 12–13.

Chapter 7

1. Phyllis Tickle, *Figs and Fury* (Memphis: St. Luke's Press, 1976), 30.

2. Dorothy L. Sayers, *The Man Born to Be King* (London: Victor Gollancz Ltd, 1969), 4. May 1969 represented the twenty-fourth impression.

3. Dorothy L. Sayers, *The Man Born to Be King*, 23.

4. St. Michael's Parish, Memphis, produced *Puppeteers for Our Lady* in Advent 1982. Title was changed to *Tobias and the Angels* when St. Luke's Press published the drama in 1983.

5. Jeff Hardin, interview with the author, email, September 2, 2015.

6. Jeff Hardin, interview with the author, email, September 2, 2015.

7. Phyllis Tickle, *On Beyond Koch* (Memphis: St. Luke's Press, 1981), 116.

8. This classic remains popular and in print. See *Rose, Where Did You Get That Red? Teaching Great Poetry to Children*, by Kenneth Koch (New York: Vintage Books, 1990).

9. As remembered in a letter from Dr. Lorimer Pangilinan to Patty Bladen at The Brooks Museum, undated, ca. October 1983.

10. *Shaping*, 4.

11. Undated letter to Margaret Ingraham, ca. summer 1979.

12. Letter to Margaret Ingraham, October 17, 1979.

13. Shelby Foote, *September September* (New York: Random House, 1977), 302.

14. Letter to the Editor, *Seneca Review*, December 20, 1979.

15. Letter to Margaret Ingraham, undated, ca. December 1, 1979.

16. Letter from Margaret Ingraham to Phyllis Tickle, undated, ca. early 1980.

17. Telephone interview, Margaret Ingraham, July 8, 2016.

18. Letter to Margaret Ingraham, December 12, 1979.

19. Letter to Margaret Ingraham, undated, ca. January 3, 1980.

20. Margaret Ingraham, interview with the author, email, August 17, 2015.

21. Jeff Hardin, interview with the author, email, August 26, 2015. These events took place in 1983–4.

22. Phyllis Tickle, ed., *Homeworks: A Book of Tennessee Writers* (Knoxville: University of Tennessee Press, 1996), xx.

Chapter 8

1. Unpublished typescript of talk given in Atlanta, November 10, 1989.

2. *Old Hickory Review* 10: no. 2 (Fall–Winter 1978): 37. Published by The Jackson Writers Group, Jackson, TN.

3. Phyllis Tickle, *The Story of Two Johns* (Memphis: St. Luke's Press, 1976), 7.

4. Telephone interview with the author, July 17, 2015.

5. Telephone interview with the author, July 17, 2015.

6. *The Essential Etheridge Knight* (Pittsburgh: University of Pittsburgh Press, 1986), 115.

7. Phyllis Tickle email to Alice Faye Duncan (who was researching a biography of Etheridge Knight), July 23, 2015.

8. *The Good People of Gomorrah: A Memphis Miscellany*, ed. Gordon Osing (Memphis: St. Luke's Press, 1979), vi.

9. *The Good People of Gomorrah*, 3, 76. In her *Collected Poems*, Phyllis retitled the poem for her youngest child, "For Rebecca On a Sunday Morning."

10. *City Essays*, 44.

Chapter 9

1. On the sometimes "ferocity" of Southern writers, see Margaret Eby, *South Toward Home: Travels in Southern Literature* (New York: W.W. Norton, 2016), 11. "To My Pear Trees," first appeared in book form in *City Essays*, 45-6.

2. Email to Joy Jordan-Lake, January 7, 2004.

3. *Tickle Papers*, ch. 4.

4. *What the Land Already Knows*, 26.

5. Jose Ortega y Gasset, *The Dehuminization of Art and Notes on the Novel*, trans. Helene Weyl (Princeton: Princeton University Press, 1948), 30.

6. *Prayer Is a Place*, 7.

7. *Confessing Conscience*, 10.

8. Originally from *Wisdom in the Waiting*; included in *Phyllis Tickle: The Essential Writings* (Maryknoll: Orbis Books, 2015), 52.

9. From *Regula Tarnantensis*, quoted by Renie S. Choy in *Intercessory Prayer and the Monastic Ideal in the Time of the Carolingian Reforms* (New York: Oxford University Press, 2016), 84.

10. Rebecca Tickle, interview with the author, email, July 1, 2016.

11. Sam Tickle Jr., interview with the author, email, September 10, 2015. Many of the details that follow come from Sam Jr.'s memories.

12. Unpublished typescript of talk, The Society for the Study of Southern Literature at the Convention of the South Atlantic Modern Language Association, Atlanta, November 10, 1989.

13. Unpublished summary of her remarks sent to Dr. Price Caldwell, director of the festival. April 1986.

14. *Prayer Is a Place*, 15; for the story of her joining *PW*, see 17, 22.

15. Ken Wilson, interview with the author, email, September 8, 2016.

Chapter 10

1. Letter to George Baskin, March 14, 1986.

2. Michael Lawrence, interview with the author, email, October 5, 2016.

3. Phyllis Tickle, telephone interview with the author, July 14, 2015.

4. See *Religion and the Marketplace in the United States*, eds. Jan Stievermann, Philip Goff, and Detlef Junker (New York: Oxford University Press, 2015), 127–9.

5. Some of these details come from Lynn Garrett's, "A Tribute to Phyllis Tickle," *Publishers Weekly*, January 31, 2014.

6. "Tickle Named Religious Editor at 'Publishers Weekly,'" *Publishers Weekly*, December 14, 1992, 16.

7. *Prayer Is a Place*, 35.

8. *PW*, January 11, 1993, 24.

9. *PW*, April 12, 1993, 31; and *PW*, June 14, 1993, 38.

10. *PW*, August 16, 1993, 41.

11. First two instances: *PW*, September 13, 1993. The latter was a review of Larry Burkett's *Whatever Happened to the American Dream*. Then, *PW*, October 11, 1993, 40.

12. *PW*, November 8, 1993, 50 (review of *When the Bad Times Are Over for Good, by Gerald Mann*, published by McCracken).

13. *PW*, September 13, 1993, 41.

14. Mike Leach, fax, June 9, 1995.

15. Story told by Phyllis at Laity Lodge, Kerrville, TX, April 22, 2006.

16. Interview with the author, email, July 28, 2015.

17. Interview with the author, email, July 10, 2015.

18. Phyllis Tickle, *Ordinary Time: Stories of the Days between Ascensiontide and Advent* (Nashville: The Upper Room, 1987), 54.

19. First aired on February 4, 2000.

20. Kenneth L. Woodward, interview, "God Is Not My Buddy," homeliticsonline.com, 2002.

21. Bishop John S. Spong, card, November 22, 1999.

22. As relayed by Phyllis to third parties, Donna Kehoe and Ken Wilson, in email April 9, 2007.

Chapter 11

1. *Prayer Is a Place*, ix.

2. Paul Tillich, *The Irrelevance and Relevance of the Christian Message*, introduced by A. Durwood Foster (Cleveland: Pilgrim Press, 1996), 62.

3. See Appendix to Chapter 7, "On a Little-known Chapter of Mediterranean History," in Karl R. Popper, *In Search of a Better World: Lectures and Essays from Thirty Years* (New York: Routledge, 1996), 107–116.

4. *PW*, November 8, 1993, 50.

5. Phyllis Tickle, *Greed: The Seven Deadly Sins Series* (New York: Oxford University Press), 1.

6. Talk with Paraclete Press staff, Orleans, Massachusetts, January 13, 1998.

7. Phyllis Tickle, *The Great Emergence: How Christianity Is Changing and Why* (Grand Rapids, MI: Baker Books, 2008), 93.

8. *Prayer Is a Place*, 46.

9. Unpublished notes. This is how Phyllis herself described it in Chicago at BEA, May 2004, as the host of a panel discussing "Sacred Texts and Classic Titles."

10. *PW*, December 13, 1993, 32.

11. *Prayer Is a Place*, 116.

Chapter 12

1. Rebecca Tickle, interview with the author, email, August 7, 2015.

2. Previously unpublished, from the first draft book proposal (1998) that became *Shaping*.

3. Email to Ken Wilson, December 11, 2009.

4. As remembered and repeated by Phyllis to Ken Wilson, email, September 8, 2004.

5. Email to Ken Wilson, July 5, 2004.

6. First aired March 31, 2000.

7. Email to Ken Wilson, November 22, 2004.

8. Email to Ken Wilson, February 15, 2005.

9. Email to Ken Wilson, January 25, 2005.

10. *What the Heart Already Knows*, 10.

11. *A Reader's Companion to Crossing the Threshold of Hope: Sixteen Writers on the Pastoral Writings of Pope John Paul II*, ed. Charla H. Honea (Brewster, MA: Paraclete Press, 1996), 191. She refers to herself as Protestant three times in this essay.

12. First aired March 31, 2000.

13. Ken Wilson, *Jesus Brand Spirituality: He Wants His Religion Back* (Nashville: Thomas Nelson, 2008), viii.

14. *What the Heart Already Knows*, 10.

15. Email to Ken Wilson, May 15, 2004.

16. Beginning with the quote, "To his left . . ." see *Prayer Is a Place*, 185, 184, and 188. "Disgust" at the Dalai Lama, 72.

17. Part of "Life Is a Prayer," *Spirituality & Health*, Spring 2000.

18. Email to Ken Wilson, July 6, 2004.

19. Email to Ken Wilson, December 18, 2004.

20. Ken Wilson, written interview, September 1, 2016, and Megory Anderson, written interview, September 2, 2016. Also, emails from Phyllis Tickle to Ken Wilson, November 22, 2004 and December 28, 2004.

21. Email to Ken Wilson, November 22, 2004.

22. Thomas Hardy, *The Return of the Native*, ed. Tony Slade (New York: Penguin Books, 1999), 9, 11.

23. Email to Ken Wilson, January 10, 2005. Phyllis is remembering something she said to her friend and fellow Tennessee Episcopalian, Bill Craddock Jr.

24. The Shekinah was a shared experience with Lillian Miao. Lillian Miao, written interview, September 2, 2016. For hearing Jesus speak: email to Ken Wilson, December 6, 2004.

25. Email to Ken Wilson, November 22, 2004.

26. Email to Ken Wilson, December 7, 2004.

27. This quote, as well as the one immediately following it, come from an email to Ken Wilson, January 8, 2005.

28. *Prayer Is a Place*, 68.

29. Email to Ken Wilson, January 8, 2005.

30. *Greed*, 50–51.

31. Unpublished talk. "How Then Must We Live," The Trinity Institute, New York. April 5, 2002.

32. Accessed at *http://www.onbeing.org/program/spiritual-fallout-911/228*.

Chapter 13

1. *Shaping*, 153.

2. Email to Ken Wilson, July 19, 2004. The *Shaping* proposal was mailed to her agent, Joe Durepos, on December 7, 1998.

3. *Shaping*, 40.

4. *Confessing Conscience*, 9.

5. All from *Shaping*: bus ride, 111–15; shamanistic, 86; "not yet learned to pray," 75.

6. See *Shaping*, 205–11. Quotations from 208, 211, 210.

7. Letter to Mother Betty Pugsley, November 18, 2001.

8. *Prayer Is a Place*, 171.

9. Book proposal to Paraclete Press, September 1997.

10. First aired October 29, 1999, for their Halloween broadcast.

11. First aired May 7, 1999.

12. Email to Ryan Bolger, April 24, 2009.

Chapter 14

1. Interview with the author, June 10, 2015.

2. Sam Tickle, email to [private individual], November 4, 2009. A printout of this email was in a folder on Phyllis's desk when she died.

3. "Hymen Broken," *Hungry Spring*, 9.

4. *Shaping*, 85.

5. *Prayer Is a Place*, 302. Even as of July 2016 the only place listed in the directory under "Spirituality" on the website of the Memphis Gay and Lesbian Community Center was this church.

6. Email to Ken Wilson, January 9, 2005.

7. Timothy Meadows, interview with the author, email, July 21, 2016.

8. Interview with the author, email, July 29, 2015.

9. Interview with the author, email, July 30, 2015.

10. Interview with the author, email, July 30, 2015.

11. Interview with the author, email, July 30, 2015.

12. Interview with the author, email, July 30, 2015.

13. Jane Routh, interview with the author, email, July 19, 2016.

14. With reference to Rev. Andy MacBeth, interview with the author, email, July 26, 2016.

15. *Prayer Is a Place*, 124. Email to Ken Wilson, January 9, 2005.

16. Email to Tony Jones, November 9, 2008. She got the title correct for the book she was recommending, *Same-Sex Unions in Premodern Europe*, but the author is John (not James) Boswell.

17. Ken Wilson email to Phyllis Tickle, March 4, 2009.

18. Email to Ken Wilson, March 6, 2009.

19. Email to Ken Wilson, March 1, 2010.

20. Email to Ken Wilson, April 29, 2005. Also, from a February 1, 2005, email to Ken Wilson: "The reason I can move so blithely in and out of gay Christians and

congregations is not some kind of fancy theological argument that I can take and defend biblically; it's because I was told so . . ."

21. Timothy Meadows, interview with the author, email, July 21, 2016.

22. Bob Scott, interview with the author, email, August 10, 2016.

23. Draft proposal dated January 2008, submitted "by Phyllis Tickle, Michael Battle, Megory Anderson with Peter Schuller." Also with reference to the author's interview with Megory Anderson, August 1, 2016.

24. Ken Wilson, interview with the author, email, September 1, 2016.

Chapter 15

1. David Neff, foreword, *Common Roots: The Original Call to an Ancient-Future Faith*, Robert E. Webber (Grand Rapids: Zondervan, 2009), 20.

2. First aired May 17, 2002.

3. *The Hidden Ground of Love: The Letters of Thomas Merton on Religious Experience and Social Concerns*, ed. William H. Shannon (New York: Farrar, Straus, & Giroux, 1985), viii.

4. Unpublished talk, Trinity Institute Conference, Trinity Church Wall Street, September 28, 1999.

5. *Great Emergence*, 100, 101.

6. Talk at Rubicon 2011 conference, Holy Trinity Church, Dublin, Ireland.

7. Talk number one, "The Times in Which We Find Ourselves," Epiphany Explorations 2014 Conference, First Metropolitan United Church of Canada, January 18, 2014.

8. From "Phyllis Tickle: Like an Anthill," *Faith & Leadership*, August 30, 2010.

9. Lori Leibovich, "A look inside fundamentalism's answer to MTV: the postmodern church," *Mother Jones*, July/August 1998.

10. NetFax—A service of Leadership Network, No. 107, September 28, 1998.

11. *Prayer Is a Place*, 138.

12. Diana Butler Bass, *Christianity for the Rest of Us: How the Neighborhood Church Is Transforming the Faith* (New York: HarperOne, 2006), 209.

13. *Figs and Fury*, 22.

14. As remembered/quoted by Diana Butler Bass in *Christianity for the Rest of Us*, 22.

15. "Yes, No, or Maybe," Christian Wertenbaker, *Parabola* 31, no. 1 (Spring 2006): 128.

16. Brian McLaren, interview with the author, email, October 23, 2016.

17. Chad Allen, interview with the author, email, October 30, 2015.

18. Email to Chad Allen, November 13, 2007.

19. Email to Ken Wilson, September 8, 2004.

20. Bob Abernethy, letter to Phyllis, October 17, 2008.

21. In-person interview, Tripp Hudgins, July 11, 2015. In chapter 18 of *Emergence Christianity*, Phyllis wrote about the importance of "meta-narrative."

22. Review of *The Great Emergence*, June Sawyers, *Booklist*, October 1, 2008.

23. Video interview filmed at the Cornerstone Festival in Illinois, summer 2009.

24. Talk number one, "The Times in Which We Find Ourselves," Epiphany Explorations 2014 Conference, First Metropolitan United Church of Canada, January 18, 2014.

25. Sara Miles, private memo to Bishop Marc Andrus, December 8, 2008.

26. Robert E. Webber, *The Younger Evangelicals: Facing the Challenges of the New World* (Grand Rapids: Baker Books, 2002), 54. See also the table of contents.

27. Doug Pagitt, email to Phyllis, June 15, 2011.

28. Eric Elnes, blog post on Darkwoodbrew.org, originally posted in late July 2012.

29. Email to Eric Elnes, July 21, 2012.

30. Brian D. McLaren, *We Make the Road by Walking: A Year-long Quest for Spiritual Formation, Reorientation, and Activation* (Nashville: Jericho Books, 2015), xvii-xviii.

31. Unpublished speaking text, "Preaching at the Crossroads," Luther Seminary, Celebration of Biblical Preaching conference, October 7, 2013, 9.

32. Brian D. McLaren, *A New Kind of Christianity: Ten Questions that Are Transforming the Faith* (New York: HarperOne, 2010), 13.

Chapter 16

1. Letter to Margaret Ingraham, undated [postmarked January 15, 1980].

2. "Phyllis A. Tickle: Setting the Stage, A Culture Scan," Trinity Television and New Media, Spiritual Formation Conferences 2003, Trinity Church Wall Street, New York, 2003, DVD.

3. Antonio R. Damasio, *Descartes' Error: Emotion, Reason, and the Human Brain* (New York: Putnam, 1994), xii, xvii.

4. Antonio R. Damasio, *Descartes' Error*, xii, xvii.

5. Phyllis Tickle, "The Great Convergence: What's So Great? Part 5," video interview with Rev. Eric Elnes, *Darkwood Brew* (podcast), March 5, 2014, *https://darkwood brew.org/the-great-convergence-e5/*.

6. "Evodius of Uzalis to Augustine of Hippo," *The Penguin Book of the Undead: Fifteen Hundred Years of Supernatural Encounters*, ed. Scott G. Bruce (New York: Penguin Books, 2016), 45.

7. Phyllis Tickle, *Emergence Christianity: What It Is, Where It Is Going, and Why It Matters* (Grand Rapids, MI: Baker Books, 2012), 131.

8. Email exchange with Scot McKnight, February 19–20, 2014.

9. Kimberly Knight, "Sacred Space in Cyberspace," *Reflections: A Magazine of Theological and Ethical Inquiry from Yale Divinity School*, published at Yale Divinity School (Fall 2009): 44. This article was read and kept by Phyllis in a folder of Second Life materials.

10. *Emergence Christianity*, 152.

11. Email to Melissa McCarthy, July 2, 2007.

12. Mark Brown, *www.brownblog.info*, April 14, 2007, and January 16, 2008. Quoted from printed copies of these posts in Phyllis's files.

13. Email to unknown recipient ("Dearest T"), August 1, 2007.

14. This quote is from the narration of Tippett on the program, summarizing Phyllis's opinion after their interview. Quoted by Kimberly Knight in "Sacred Space in Cyberspace," *Reflections*.

15. *Emergence Christianity*, 153.

16. For example, see Koinonia Church, *http://secondlife.com/destination/koinonia -church*; and Qoheleth, *http://maps.secondlife.com/secondlife/Qoheleth/185/140/22*.

17. Kimberly Knight, interview with the author, email, February 8, 2017.

18. *Emergence Christianity*, 137.

19. Phyllis Tickle, *Re-Discovering the Sacred: Spirituality in America* (New York: Crossroad Publishing, 1995), 13.

20. "In the Beginning, Eden," *Holy Ground: A Gathering of Voices on Caring for Creation*, edited by Lyndsay Moseley and the Staff of Sierra Club Books (San Francisco: Sierra Club Books, 2008), 248.

21. Email to Lisa Crawford, December 26, 2006.

22. Interview with Becky Garrison at *The Wittenberg Door*, " 'No Nation Is Christian' (and Phyllis Tickle knows)," November 28, 2007.

23. Phyllis Tickle, *The Words of Jesus: A Gospel of the Sayings of Our Lord with Reflections by Phyllis Tickle* (San Francisco: Wiley/Jossey-Bass, 2008), 38.

24. *Words of Jesus*, 4, 5.

25. *http://www.westarinstitute.org/projects/christianity-seminar/fall-2014-meeting-report/*.

26. Interview with the author, email, July 21, 2005.

27. Email to [private individual], August 10, 2015.

Chapter 17

1. Email to Ken Wilson, May 26, 2009.

2. Email to Nancy Marshall, Episcopal bookseller in Seattle, February 21, 2001.

3. *Weavings: A Journal of the Christian Spiritual Life*, vol. XXV, no. 4 (Aug.–Oct. 2010), (Nashville: The Upper Room, 2010), 13.

4. Email to Peggy Ingraham, December 14, 2000.

5. Email to Lillian Miao, November 23, 2005.

6. Email to Lillian Miao, July 21, 2006.

7. Email to Andrew Miao, October 11, 2003.

8. Email to Donna Kehoe and Ken Wilson, May 18, 2007.

9. Email to Sybil MacBeth, March 26, 2004.

10. Jana Riess, interview with the author, email, September 14, 2016.

11. Email to Ken Wilson, September 2, 2004.

12. Email to Lynn Garrett, April 15, 2009.

13. For example, see Fighting for the Faith, podcast, Chris Rosebrough, May 14, 2009.

14. Interview with the author, email, Sr. Danielle Dwyer, December 6, 2016.

15. From "Phyllis Tickle: Like an Anthill," *Faith & Leadership*, August 30, 2010.

16. Interview with Becky Garrison at *The Wittenberg Door*, November 28, 2007.

17. Retrieved on July 11, 2015, at *http://julieclawson.com/2013/01/14/emergence-christianity-women-and-the-fall-of-christendom/*.

18. Phyllis first told this story in a short essay written for the alternative newspaper in Memphis, *The Dixie Flyer*. Republished in *City Essays*, 17–18.

19. From an essay by Albert Eide Parr, quoted by Richard B. Sewall, *The Life of Emily Dickinson*, single volume edition (Cambridge: Harvard University Press, 1994), 21, n. 4.

20. Email to Jerusalem Greer, November 15, 2014.

21. These two emails are from January 21 and 22, 2013, respectively.

22. Phyllis Tickle, *The Age of the Spirit: How the Ghost of an Ancient Controversy Is Shaping the Church*, with Jon M. Sweeney (Grand Rapids, MI: Baker Books, 2014), 147.

23. Karen Ward, *Listening to the Beliefs of Emerging Churches: Five Perspectives*, ed. Robert E. Webber (Grand Rapids, MI: Zondervan, 2007), 164.

24. Interview with the author, email, July 11, 2015.

25. Diana Butler Bass, *Christianity for the Rest of Us*, 242. In note 120 on p. 320 Butler Bass suggested then that Phyllis may not have realized that the typology came from Joachim.

26. John 14:9.

27. In January 2013, a young newspaper editor asked Phyllis if she would like to comment on the topic, "Is Atheism a Religion?" She wrote: "What atheism does not have is the architecture of mysteries. One might even argue that, to the extent that atheism lacks sacred story and narrative thrust, it also lacks transcendence and beauty, both of which are hallmarks of religion. Likewise, the perspective of atheism is caught within the created order, while that of religion, by definition, exceeds it." "Atheism Cannot Replace Religion," *New York Times*, January 22, 2013.

28. *Prayer Is a Place*, 69.

29. Email to Joanna Seibert, April 9, 2014.

30. Letter to Rabbi Dan Rosenberg, May 6, 2015.

31. Thomas Merton, in a letter to Rabbi Zalman Schachter, February 15, 1962. *The Hidden Ground of Love*, 535.

32. Commission for Religious Relations with the Jews, "The Gifts and the Calling of God Are Irrevocable: A Reflection on Theological Questions Pertaining to Catholic-Jewish Relations on the Occasion of the 50th Anniversary of 'Nostra Aetate.'"

33. *Shaping*, 253.

Chapter 18

1. Lori Leibovich, "A Look Inside Fundamentalism's Answer to MTV," *Mother Jones*, July/August 1998.

2. Mark Driscoll briefly provides this account in his book *Confessions of a Reformission Rev: Hard Lessons from an Emerging, Missional Church* (Grand Rapids, MI: Zondervan, 2006), 99–100. The account is undisputed by the others.

3. Email to Tony Jones, September 24, 2014.

4. Email to Brandan Robertson, February 21, 2015. Robertson's book would eventually be published by Darton, Longman & Todd in May 2016, dedicated to Phyllis.

5. See the 2015 poll at *www.prri.org* or *http://www.prri.org/research/beyond-same-sex-marriage-attitudes-on-lgbt-nondiscrimination-and-religious-exemptions-from-the-2015-american-values-atlas/*.

6. Email to Brian McLaren, September 9, 2014.

7. From "Marriage Is," in *I Like Being Married: Treasured Traditions, Rituals, and Stories*, eds. Michael Leach and Therese J. Borchard (New York: Doubleday, 2002), 11.

8. Opening segment, "Phyllis A. Tickle: Death and Divine Living," Trinity Television and New Media, DVD.

9. *Phyllis Tickle: Essential Spiritual Writings*, 27.

Chapter 19

1. Joanna Seibert, interview with the author, email, July 10, 2015.

2. John McQuistion II, interview with the author, email, September 14, 2016. The book, *Always We Begin Again: The Benedictine Way of Living* (Harrisburg, PA: Morehouse, 2011), is one that Phyllis helped shepherd toward its publisher in 1996.

3. Nadia Bolz-Weber email to Phyllis Tickle, September 2, 2006.

4. Email to Nathan Aaseng, July 17, 2014.

5. Kathleen Davis Niendorff, posted on "Phyllis Tickle Stories and Memories" Facebook page, August 12, 2015.

6. Michael Mott, *The Seven Mountains of Thomas Merton* (Boston: Houghton Mifflin, 1984), xxvi.

7. Email to Tony Jones, January 4, 2015.

8. Email exchange between Tony Jones and Phyllis, January 15, 2015.

9. Interview with the author, email, July 29, 2015.

10. *Wisdom in the Waiting*, xi.

11. Email to Jonathan Ryan, February 17, 2015.

12. "Phyllis A. Tickle: Death and Divine Living," Trinity Television and New Media, DVD.

13. "Treasures of Old and New," lecture one, February 12, 2005, Vineyard Church of Ann Arbor (Michigan), DVD.

14. Email to the author, April 23, 2015.

15. Email to Nora Cannon, Mary Ballard, Laura Palermo, etc., April 21, 2015.

16. Email to Nora Cannon, April 21, 2015.

17. Email to Ken Wilson, December 7, 2004.

18. Telephone interview with the author, July 14, 2015.

19. Letter from Bob Abernethy to Phyllis, June 20, 2015, and letter from Phyllis in response, July 1, 2015.

20. Email to Brian McLaren, July 2, 2015.

21. Email to Pamela Jordan, July 23, 2015.

22. Email to the author, August 4, 2015.

23. *Figs and Fury*, 40.

24. Email to Peggy Ingraham, March 7, 2002.

25. Email to Ken Wilson, July 6, 2004.

26. Robert Lowell, *Collected Poems*, eds. Frank Bidart and David Gewanter (New York: Farrar, Straus and Giroux, 2007), 992.

27. Email to the author, September 1, 2015.

28. Email to the author, August 29, 2015.

29. Interview with the author, email, Nora Cannon, October 11, 2015.

30. Interview with the author, email, Daisy Maryles, September 22, 2015.

31. See Micah 4:1–3 and *Benedictine Daily Prayer: A Short Breviary*, eds. Maxwell F. Johnson and the Monks of Saint John's Abbey (Collegeville, MN: Liturgical Press, 2005), 728–730.

Chapter 20

1. Talk three, "The Age of the Spirit," Epiphany Explorations 2014 Conference, First Metropolitan United Church of Canada, January 20, 2014.

2. Emily Dickinson, *Final Harvest: Emily Dickinson's Poems*, selection and introduction by Thomas H. Johnson (Boston: Little, Brown and Company, 1961), 71.

3. Email to Joe Durepos, April 20, 2015.

4. Robert E. Webber, *Evangelicals on the Canterbury Trail: Why Evangelicals Are Attracted to the Liturgical Church* (Waco, TX: Word, 1985).

5. Email to [private individual], July 4, 2015. Recipient intentionally withheld.

6. Hand-written card sent to Phyllis Tickle, undated, ca. 2010.

Afterword

1. Julian Barnes, *Flaubert's Parrot* (New York: Vintage, 1990), 38.

Index